Christopher & ...

QUICK
LIBRARY

VNR'S OS/2 SERIES

OS/2®

QUICK REFERENCE LIBRARY

VOLUME 3

WORKPLACE SHELL FUNCTIONS

NORA SCHOLIN

VAN NOSTRAND REINHOLD

I(T)P™ A Division of International Thomson Publishing Inc.

New York • Albany • Bonn • Boston • Detroit • London • Madrid • Melbourne
Mexico City • Paris • San Francisco • Singapore • Tokyo • Toronto

Copyright © 1995 by Van Nostrand Reinhold

I(T)P A Division of International Thomson Publishing Company.
ITP logo is a trademark under license.

ISBN 0-442-01899-1

Printed in the United States of America.
For more information contact:

Van Nostrand Reinhold
115 Fifth Avenue
New York, NY 10003

International Thomson Publishing GmbH
Königswinterer Strasse 418
53227 Bonn
Germany

International Thomson Publishing
Berkshire House
168-173 High Holborn
London WC1V 7AA
England

International Thomson Publishing Asia
221 Henderson Road
#05 10 Henderson Building
Singapore 0315

Thomas Nelson Australia
102 Dodds Street
South Melbourne, Victoria 3205
Australia

International Thomson Publishing Japan
Hirakawacho Kyowa Building, 3F
2-2-1 Hirakawa-cho, Chiyoda-ku
Tokyo 102
Japan

Nelson Canada
1120 Birchmount Road
Scarborough, Ontario
M1K 5G4, Canada

1 2 3 4 5 6 7 8 9 10 RADCV 01 00 99 98 97 96 95 94

OS/2 Accredited logo is a trademark of IBM Corp. and is used by Van Nostrand Reinhold under licence. "OS/2 Quick Reference Library, Volume 3, Workplace Shell Functions," is independently published by Van Nostrand Reinhold. IBM Corp. is not responsible in any way for the contents of this publication.

Van Nostrand Reinhold is an accredited member of the IBM Independent Vendor League.

Library of Congress Cataloging in Publication Data

[Available on request.]

Notices

The author and publishers of this book make no warranty of any kind, expressed or implied, with regard to the documentation contained in this book. You are responsible for selecting all your configurations and applications of hardware and software. The author and publishers shall not be liable in any event for any loss or damages in connection with, or arising out of, use of this book.

Information is this book is subject to change without notice.

Trademarks

The following terms are trademarks of the IBM Corporation:

IBM
OS/2
Presentation Manager
Workplace Shell

Special Thanks

To **Marcia Muench**, for her excellent typing; **Warren Muench**, for his advice and support; **Sandra Kipp**, for checking the methods against the code; and **Dr. Sheila A. Harnett**, for reviewing each class and method.

OS/2 Quick Reference Library

Volume 1
WIN Functions

Volume 2
Message Functions

Volume 3
Workplace Shell Functions

Volume 4
GPI Functions

Volume 5
DOS Functions

Volume 6
Miscellaneous Functions

Contents

Chapter 3
Workplace Instance Methods 81

Chapter 4
Workplace Class Methods 491

Appendix A
Data Type Structures

Appendix B
WIN Functions for WPS

Chapter 1
How to Use This Book

This book is Volume 3 of the *OS/2 Quick Reference Library*. This library is designed for OS/2 programmers who need concise and current information at their fingertips.

Each volume contains a major category of OS/2 functions. Volume 3 contains the OS/2 Workplace Shell methods and classes.

This chapter briefly explains how the classes and methods are structured and provides general information about the Workplace Shell methods. Chapter 2 contains all the workplace object classes. Chapter 3 contains all the instance methods. Chapter 4 contains all the class methods.

> **Note:** Each class and method has been checked against the actual code to ensure accuracy.

Appendix A contains the data type structures for the methods. Appendix B contains the WIN functions that use the workplace objects.

Conventions Used in This Book

To provide a consistent format for easy reading and understanding, the following conventions are used throughout this book:

- New terms are *italicized* the first time they are defined. Italics are also used for special emphasis of words or phrases.

- Except where otherwise noted, data types, error codes, and file names are capitalized (for example: ULONG, PMERR_INVALID_PARAMETER, CONFIG.SYS file).

Class Structure Used in This Book

Each workplace object class is structured as follows:

Class name: Each class name is immediately followed by a brief description of what the class is used for.

Class definition file: Name of the class definition file.

Class hierarchy: Shows where the class fits into the overall class hierarchy.

Instance methods: Lists the instance methods (by category) that apply to this object class. Page numbers are included for easy cross-referencing.

Class methods: Lists the class methods (by category) that apply to this object class. Page numbers are included for easy cross-referencing.

Method Structure Used in This Book

Each instance and class method is structured as follows:

Method name: Each method name is immediately followed by a brief description of what the method does.

Include identifier: Indicates the #define directive that contains the most commonly used INCL_ identifier. Global include identifiers and the # include directive are listed below.

Method prototypes: Shows an example of the correct placement of the method's data types and parameters. (Data type structures are described in Appendix A.)

Parameters: Lists and briefly describes all the parameters belonging to the method, including any important values.

Returns: Lists any return values and their descriptions for the method's return data type.

Remarks: Describes information that could impact the use of the method.

Method usage: Describes when the method can be called and how it is used.

Method override: Describes if and why the method should be overridden.

Related methods: Lists any methods that can be used in connection with the method. Page numbers are included for easy cross-referencing.

General Information About Methods

The information here applies to all instance and class methods.

Global Include Identifiers:

#define INCL_PM

Include Directive:

#include <os2.h>

Error Code Functions to Be Called if Error Occurs:

WinGetLastError
WinGetErrorInfo

Additional Information:

For workplace object classes: Instances of most WP classes can be created as a workplace objects. Except where stated otherwise, these instances are initially created by the system.

Chapter 2
Workplace Object Classes

This chapter contains important and commonly referenced function information in a condensed format. For more detailed information on WP classes, see the online OS/2 Toolkit.

WPAbstract

This is the abstract object storage class. The storage medium for objects that are descendants of this class is the INI file (any object class derived from WPAbstract will have persistent storage for its instance variables in the INI file). An abstract object does not have a file name, just a numeric handle that can be used to identify it. However, it can be optionally assigned an object id to uniquely identify it. No instances of this class are initially created by the system.

Note: WPAbstract, WPFileSystem, and WPTransient are base storage classes.

CLASS DEFINITION FILE:

```
wpabs.idl
```

CLASS HIERARCHY:

```
SOMObject
  WPObject
    WPAbstract
```

OVERRIDDEN WPObject INSTANCE METHODS:

wpCopyObject	Page 170
wpDragOver	Page 191
wpMoveObject	Page 245
wpQueryHandle	Page 314
wpQueryIcon	Page 316
wpQueryIconData	Page 317
wpQueryNameClashOptions	Page 328
wpRestoreState	Page 377

WPAbstract CLASS METHODS:

OVERRIDDEN WPObject CLASS METHODS:

WPBitmap

This is the bit-map object class. Instances of this class is created initially by the system for each bit map in the system.

CLASS DEFINITION FILE:

wpbitmap.idl

CLASS HIERARCHY:

```
SOMObject
  WPObject
    WPFileSystem
      WPDataFile
        WPBitmap
```

OVERRIDDEN WPObject INSTANCE METHODS:

wpSetupOnce   Page 477

OVERRIDDEN WPFileSystem CLASS METHODS:

wpclsQueryInstanceFilter   Page 534
wpclsQueryInstanceType   Page 535

OVERRIDDEN WPObject CLASS METHODS:

wpclsInitData   Page 501
wpclsQueryDefaultHelp   Page 513
wpclsQueryTitle   Page 549

WPClock

This is the system clock object class. An instance of this class has the title "System Clock" and resides in the System Setup folder.

CLASS DEFINITION FILE:

wpclock.idl

CLASS HIERARCHY:

```
SOMObject
  WPObject
    WPAbstract
      WPClock
```

WPClock INSTANCE METHODS:

wpAddClockAlarmPage	Page 81
wpAddClockDateTimePage	Page 83
wpAddClockView1Page	Page 84
wpAddClockView2Page	Page 85

OVERRIDDEN WPObject INSTANCE METHODS:

wpAddObjectWindowPage	Page 124
wpAddSettingsPages	Page 139
wpFilterPopupMenu	Page 199
wpMenuItemHelpSelected	Page 232
wpMenuItemSelected	Page 235
wpModifyPopupMenu	Page 240
wpOpen	Page 248
wpRestoreState	Page 377
wpSaveState	Page 390

OVERRIDDEN WPObject CLASS METHODS:

wpclsQueryDefaultHelp	Page 513
wpclsQueryDefaultView	Page 515
wpclsQueryIconData	Page 528
wpclsQueryStyle	Page 547
wpclsQueryTitle	Page 549

WPColorPalette

This is the color palette object class. Two instances of this class are created and placed in the System Setup folder with the titles "Mixed Color Palette" and "Solid Color Palette".

CLASS DEFINITION FILE:

wpclrpal.idl

CLASS HIERARCHY:

```
SOMObject
  WPObject
    WPAbstract
      WPPalette
        WPColorPalette
```

OVERRIDDEN WPPalette INSTANCE METHODS:

wpDragCell	Page 188
wpEditCell	Page 196
wpPaintCell	Page 250
wpQueryPaletteHelp	Page 335

OVERRIDDEN WPObject INSTANCE METHODS:

wpInitData	Page 214
wpMenuItemHelpSelected	Page 232
wpSetup	Page 474

OVERRIDDEN WPPalette CLASS METHODS:

wpclsQueryEditString	Page 520

OVERRIDDEN WPObject CLASS METHODS:

wpclsCreateDefaultTemplates	Page 491
wpclsQueryDefaultHelp	Page 513
wpclsQueryIconData	Page 528
wpclsQueryStyle	Page 547
wpclsQueryTitle	Page 549

WPCommandFile

This is the command file object class. All DOS and OS/2 commands and batch files are instances of this class.

An instance of this class is created initially by the system for each command file in the system. Each instance has a title corresponding to the file name of the command file it represents and resides in a folder corresponding to the physical directory in which the program file resides.

CLASS DEFINITION FILE:

wpcmdf.idl

CLASS HIERARCHY:

```
SOMObject
  WPObject
    WPFileSystem
      WPDataFile
        WPProgramFile
          WPCommandFile
```

OVERRIDDEN WPObject INSTANCE METHODS:

wpPrintObject   Page 256

OVERRIDDEN WPFileSystem CLASS METHODS:

wpclsQueryInstanceFilter   Page 534
wpclsQueryInstanceType   Page 535

OVERRIDDEN WPObject CLASS METHODS:

wpclsQueryStyle   Page 547
wpclsQueryTitle   Page 549

WPCountry

This is the country object class. An instance of this class has the title "Country" and resides in the System Setup folder.

CLASS DEFINITION FILE:

wpctry.idl

CLASS HIERARCHY:

```
SOMObject
  WPObject
    WPAbstract
      WPCountry
```

WPCountry INSTANCE METHODS:

wpAddCountryDatePage	Page 86
wpAddCountryNumbersPage	Page 87
wpAddCountryPage	Page 88
wpAddCountryTimePage	Page 89

OVERRIDDEN WPObject INSTANCE METHODS:

wpAddObjectWindowPage	Page 124
wpAddSettingsPages	Page 139
wpFilterPopupMenu	Page 199
wpInitData	Page 214

OVERRIDDEN WPObject CLASS METHODS:

wpclsQueryDefaultHelp	Page 513
wpclsQueryDefaultView	Page 515
wpclsQueryIconData	Page 528
wpclsQueryStyle	Page 547
wpclsQueryTitle	Page 549

WPDataFile

This is the data-file object class. An instance of this class in template form has the title "Data file" and resides in the Templates folder.

CLASS DEFINITION FILE:

wpdataf.idl

CLASS HIERARCHY:

```
SOMObject
  WPObject
    WPFileSystem
      WPDataFile
```

WPDataFile INSTANCE METHODS:

OVERRIDDEN WPFileSystem INSTANCE METHODS:

OVERRIDDEN WPObject INSTANCE METHODS:

OVERRIDDEN WPObject CLASS METHODS:

WPDesktop

This is the workplace desktop object class. An instance of this class
has the title "Desktop" and initially resides in the root directory of
the drive containing the user profile.

CLASS DEFINITION FILE:

wpdesk.idl

CLASS HIERARCHY:

```
SOMObject
  WPObject
    WPFileSystem
      WPFolder
        WPDesktop
```

WPDesktop INSTANCE METHODS:

OVERRIDDEN WPObject INSTANCE METHODS:

OVERRIDDEN WPDesktop CLASS METHODS:

OVERRIDDEN WPObject CLASS METHODS:

WPDisk

This is the file-system device object class. It is used to represent all types of file-system devices, including:

- CD-ROM drives
- Fixed disk drives
- Floppy diskette drives
- Magnetic tape drives
- Network drives
- RAM drives
- PCMCIA devices

Instances of this class are created initially by the system for each file system device available. Each instance has a title corresponding to a file-system device and resides in the Drives folder.

If a local, file-system device (such as a floppy drive) exists, an instance of this class also will be created on the Desktop and represent this device. These instances appear as WPShadow objects, which are shadows of WPDisk objects.

CLASS DEFINITION FILE:

wpdisk.idl

CLASS HIERARCHY:

```
SOMObject
  WPObject
    WPAbstract
      WPDisk
```

WPDisk INSTANCE METHODS:

wpAddDiskDetailsPage	Page 96
wpEjectDisk	Page 197
wpLockDrive	Page 230
wpQueryDriveLockStatus	Page 300
wpQueryLogicalDrive	Page 326
wpQueryRootFolder	Page 352
wpSetCorrectDiskIcon	Page 414

OVERRIDDEN WPObject INSTANCE METHODS:

OVERRIDDEN WPObject CLASS METHODS:

WPDrives

This is the file-system device-folder object class. An instance of this class has the title "Drives" and resides in the OS/2 System folder.

CLASS DEFINITION FILE:

```
wpdrives.idl
```

CLASS HIERARCHY:

```
SOMObject
  WPObject
    WPFileSystem
      WPFolder
        WPDrives
```

OVERRIDDEN WPFolder METHODS:

wpPopulate	Page 252

OVERRIDDEN WPObject METHODS:

wpFilterPopupMenu	Page 199
wpMenuItemHelpSelected	Page 232
wpMenuItemSelected	Page 235
wpModifyPopupMenu	Page 240

OVERRIDDEN WPObject CLASS METHODS:

wpclsQueryDefaultHelp	Page 513
wpclsQueryIconData	Page 528
wpclsQueryStyle	Page 547
wpclsQueryTitle	Page 549

WPFileSystem

This is the file-system object storage class that represents all file system objects including directory (folder), data file, executable file, and root directory (drive) objects. This class also provides persistent storage of instance variables for all classes derived from it. Persistent data for instances of WPFileSystem subclasses are stored in the extended attributes (EAs) of the file or directory.

Note: WPAbstract, WPFileSystem, and WPTransient are base storage classes.

It is not intended that instances of WPFileSystem be created.

CLASS DEFINITION FILE:

wpfsys.idl

CLASS HIERARCHY:

```
SOMObject
  WPObject
    WPFileSystem
```

WPFileSystem INSTANCE METHODS:

wpAddFileMenuPage	Page 98
wpAddFile1Page	Page 100
wpAddFile2Page	Page 101
wpAddFile3Page	Page 102
wpConfirmKeepAssoc	Page 165
wpConfimRenameFileWithExt	Page 167
wpIsDiskSwapped	Page 223
wpPrintPlainTextFile	Page 258
wpQueryAttr	Page 274
wpQueryCreation	Page 284
wpQueryDateInfo	Page 285
wpQueryDisk	Page 294
wpQueryEASize	Page 301
wpQueryFilename	Page 304
wpQueryFileSize	Page 305
wpQueryLastAccess	Page 322
wpQueryLastWrite	Page 323
wpQueryRealName	Page 348
wpQueryType	Page 359
wpRefresh	Page 361

OVERRIDDEN WPObject INSTANCE METHODS:

WPFileSystem CLASS METHODS:

OVERRIDDEN WPObject CLASS METHODS:

WPFolder

This is the folder object class. An instance of this class in template form has the title "Folder" and resides in the Templates folder. Every directory in the system is represented by a WPFolder object.

CLASS DEFINITION FILE:

```
wpfolder.idl
```

CLASS HIERARCHY:

```
SOMObject
  WPObject
    WPFileSystem
      WPFolder
```

WPFolder INSTANCE METHODS:

```
WPFolder instance methods are grouped by the function
categories that follow.
```

FOLDER ATTRIBUTES METHODS:

FOLDER CONTENT METHODS:

FOLDER STATE METHODS:

OBJECT POSITION METHODS:

SETTINGS NOTEBOOK METHODS:

OVERRIDDEN WPFileSystem INSTANCE METHODS:

OVERRIDDEN WPObject INSTANCE METHODS:

WPFolder CLASS METHODS:

OVERRIDDEN WPObject CLASS METHODS:

WPFontPalette

This is the font-palette object class. An instance of this class has the title "Font Palette" and resides in the System Setup folder.

CLASS DEFINITION FILE:

```
wpfntpal.idl
```

CLASS HIERARCHY:

```
SOMObject
  WPObject
    WPAbstract
      WPPalette
        WPFontPalette
```

WPFontPalette INSTANCE METHODS:

wpGetFattrsFromPSZ   Page 208

OVERRIDDEN WPPalette INSTANCE METHODS:

wpDragCell	Page 188
wpEditCell	Page 196
wpPaintCell	Page 250
wpQueryPaletteHelp	Page 335
wpSetupCell	Page 476

OVERRIDDEN WPObject INSTANCE METHODS:

wpMenuItemHelpSelected	Page 232
wpSetup	Page 474

OVERRIDDEN WPPalette CLASS METHODS:

wpclsQueryEditString   Page 520

OVERRIDDEN WPObject CLASS METHODS:

wpclsQueryDefaultHelp	Page 513
wpclsQueryIconData	Page 528
wpclsQueryStyle	Page 547
wpclsQueryTitle	Page 549

WPIcon

This is the icon object class. All .ICO files are represented by instances of this class. An instance of this class is created initially by the system for each icon file in the system.

CLASS DEFINITION FILE:

wpicon.idl

CLASS HIERARCHY:

```
SOMObject
  WPObject
    WPFileSystem
      WPDataFile
        WPIcon
```

OVERRIDDEN WPObject INSTANCE METHODS:

wpSetupOnce   Page 477

OVERRIDDEN WPFileSystem CLASS METHODS:

wpclsQueryInstanceFilter   Page 534
wpclsQueryInstanceType   Page 535

OVERRIDDEN WPObject CLASS METHODS:

wpclsInitData   Page 527
wpclsQueryDefaultHelp   Page 513
wpclsQueryTitle   Page 549

WPJob

This is the job object class. An instance of this class is created by a printer object in its icon or detail view.

CLASS DEFINITION FILE:

wpjob.idl

CLASS HIERARCHY:

```
SOMObject
  WPObject
    WPTransient
      WPJob
```

WPJob INSTANCE METHODS:

wpDeleteJob	Page 183
wpHoldJob	Page 211
wpPrintJobNext	Page 254
wpQueryJobFile	Page 319
wpQueryJobId	Page 320
wpQueryJobType	Page 321
wpQueryPrintObject	Page 341
wpReleaseJob	Page 364
wpStartJobAgain	Page 481

OVERRIDDEN WPObject INSTANCE METHODS:

wpAddObjectGeneralPage	Page 123
wpAddSettingsPages	Page 139
wpDragOver	Page 191
wpDrop	Page 192
wpFilterPopupMenu	Page 199
wpFree	Page 206
wpInitData	Page 214
wpMenuItemHelpSelected	Page 232
wpMenuItemSelected	Page 235
wpModifyPopupMenu	Page 240
wpOpen	Page 248
wpQueryDetailsData	Page 292
wpQueryIcon	Page 316
wpQueryTitle	Page 358
wpSetTitle	Page 470
wpUnInitData	Page 484

OVERRIDDEN WPObject CLASS METHODS:

WPKeyboard

This is the keyboard object class. An instance of this class has the title "Keyboard" and resides in the System Setup folder.

CLASS DEFINITION FILE:

wpkeybd.idl

CLASS HIERARCHY:

```
SOMObject
  WPObject
    WPAbstract
      WPKeyboard
```

WPKeyboard INSTANCE METHODS:

OVERRIDDEN WPObject INSTANCE METHODS:

OVERRIDDEN WPAbstract CLASS METHODS:

OVERRIDDEN WPObject CLASS METHODS:

WPLaunchPad

This is the front-panel object class. An instance of this class is created initially by the system. It has the title "LaunchPad" and resides in the System Startup folder.

CLASS DEFINITION FILE:

```
wplnchpd.idl
```

CLASS HIERARCHY:

```
SOMObject
  WPObject
    WPAbstract
      WPLaunchPad
```

WPLaunchPad INSTANCE METHODS:

OVERRIDDEN WPObject INSTANCE METHODS:

OVERRIDDEN WPObject CLASS METHODS:

WPMet

This is the metafile object class. All .MET files are of this class. An instance of this class is created initially by the system for each metafile in the system.

CLASS DEFINITION FILE:

```
wpmet.idl
```

CLASS HIERARCHY:

```
SOMObject
  WPObject
    WPFileSystem
      WPDataFile
        WPMet
```

OVERRIDDEN WPObject INSTANCE METHODS:

wpSetupOnce   Page 477

OVERRIDDEN WPFileSystem CLASS METHODS:

wpclsQueryInstanceFilter   Page 534
wpclsQueryInstanceType   Page 535

OVERRIDDEN WPObject CLASS METHODS:

wpclsInitData   Page 527
wpclsQueryDefaultHelp   Page 513
wpclsQueryTitle   Page 549

WPMinWinViewer

This is the minimized window-viewer object class. This is a special folder that contains only minimized window objects. An instance of this class is created by the system during initialization.

CLASS DEFINITION FILE:

wpmwv.idl

CLASS HIERARCHY:

```
SOMObject
  WPObject
    WPFileSystem
      WPFolder
        WPMinWinViewer
```

WPMinWinViewer INSTANCE METHODS:

wpFindMinWindow   Page 203

OVERRIDDEN WPFolder INSTANCE METHODS:

wpAddFolderIncludePage   Page 105
wpAddFolderView2Page   Page 109
wpAddFolderView3Page   Page 110

OVERRIDDEN WPFileSystem INSTANCE METHODS:

wpAddFileMenuPage   Page 98

OVERRIDDEN WPObject INSTANCE METHODS:

wpAddObjectWindowPage   Page 124
wpDragOver   Page 191
wpFilterPopupMenu   Page 199
wpMenuItemSelected   Page 235
wpModifyPopupMenu   Page 240
wpOpen   Page 248

OVERRIDDEN WPObject CLASS METHODS:

WPMouse

This is the mouse object class. An instance of this class has the title "Mouse" and resides in the System Setup folder.

CLASS DEFINITION FILE:

wpmouse.idl

CLASS HIERARCHY:

```
SOMObject
  WPObject
    WPAbstract
      WPMouse
```

WPMouse INSTANCE METHODS:

OVERRIDDEN WPObject INSTANCE METHODS:

OVERRIDDEN WPAbstract CLASS METHODS:

OVERRIDDEN WPObject CLASS METHODS:

WPNetgrp

This is the network group object class. Instances of this class are created for every LAN system in a WPNetwork.

CLASS DEFINITION FILE:

wpnetgrp.ild

CLASS HIERARCHY:

```
SOMObject
  WPObject
    WPFileSystem
      WPFolder
        WPNetgrp
```

WPNetgrp INSTANCE METHODS:

OVERRIDDEN WPFolder INSTANCE METHODS:

OVERRIDDEN WPFileSystem INSTANCE METHODS:

OVERRIDDEN WPObject INSTANCE METHODS:

OVERRIDDEN WPObject CLASS METHODS:

WPNetLink

This is the network-link object class. This object handles saving and restoring of data for the shared-directory object by providing a persistent link or reference to that shared directory. The purpose of this link is to locally store all the instance data of the shared directory that this object is linked to and then reroute all requests for help, context menus, open views, etc. to this object.

CLASS DEFINITION FILE:

wpnetlnk,idl

CLASS HIERARCHY:

```
SOMObject
  WPObject
    WPAbstract
      WPShadow
        WPNetLink
```

WPNetLink INSTANCE METHODS:

wpQueryObjectNetId	Page 334
wpSetObjectNetId	Page 452

OVERRIDDEN WPObject INSTANCE METHODS:

wpCreateShadowObject	Page 174
wpFilterPopupMenu	Page 199
wpInitData	Page 214
wpMenuItemHelpSelected	Page 232
wpModifyPopupMenu	Page 240
wpQueryStyle	Page 356
wpRestoreState	Page 377
wpSaveState	Page 390
wpUnInitData	Page 484

OVERRIDDEN WPObject CLASS METHODS:

wpclsQueryStyle	Page 547
wpclsQueryTitle	Page 549

WPNetwork

This is the network object class. This is the Network folder created on the Desktop and visible if LAN is attached to the machine used.

CLASS DEFINITION FILE:

wpnetwrk.idl

CLASS HIERARCHY:

```
SOMObject
  WPObject
    WPFileSystem
      WPFolder
        WPNetwork
```

OVERRIDDEN WPFolder INSTANCE METHODS:

OVERRIDDEN WPFileSystem INSTANCE METHODS:

OVERRIDDEN WPObject INSTANCE METHODS:

OVERRIDDEN WPObject CLASS METHODS:

WPObject

This is the root workplace object class. This is the fundamental class from which all workplace objects are derived, irrespective of where they are actually stored. Immediate descendant classes of WPObject are called *storage classes* because they take responsibility for storing the object information, typically in a persistent form.

A workplace object of this class cannot be created. Predefined workplace object storage classes are:

- WPAbstract
- WPFileSystem
- WPTransient

CLASS DEFINITION FILE:

wpobject.idl

CLASS HIERARCHY:

SOMObject
  WPObject

OVERRIDDEN WPObject INSTANCE METHODS:

WPObject instance methods can be grouped by the function categories that follow.

DIRECT MANIPULATION METHODS:

ERROR HANDLING METHODS:

MEMORY MANAGEMENT METHODS:

MISCELLANEOUS METHODS:

OBJECT USAGE METHODS:

POP-UP MENU METHODS:

QUERY AND SET OBJECT INFORMATION METHODS:

SAVE/RESTORE STATE METHODS:

SETTINGS NOTEBOOK METHODS:

SETUP/CLEANUP METHODS:

SOMObject INSTANCE METHODS:

The following methods are overridden to modify the behavior defined by an ancestor class:

- somDefaultInit
- somInit
- somUnInit

OVERRIDDEN WPObject CLASS METHODS:

OVERRIDDEN SOMObject CLASS METHODS:

The *somUnInit* method is overridden to modify the behavior defined by an ancestor class.

OVERRIDDEN SOMClass METHODS:

The following methods are overridden to modify the behavior defined by an ancestor class:

- somClassReady
- somNew
- somRenew

WPPalette

This is the palette object class. There are no instances of this class initially created by the system.

CLASS DEFINITION FILE:

wppalet.idl

CLASS HIERARCHY:

```
SOMObject
  WPObject
    WPAbstract
      WPPalette
```

WPPalette INSTANCE METHODS:

wpDragCell	Page 188
wpEditCell	Page 196
wpInitCellStructs	Page 213
wpPaintCell	Page 250
wpPaintPalette	Page 251
wpQueryPaletteHelp	Page 335
wpQueryPaletteInfo	Page 337
wpRedrawCell	Page 360
wpRestoreCellData	Page 371
wpSaveCellData	Page 381
wpSelectCell	Page 396
wpSetPaletteInfo	Page 453
wpSetupCell	Page 476
wpShowPalettePointer	Page 479

OVERRIDDEN WPObject INSTANCE METHODS:

wpFilterPopupMenu	Page 199
wpInitData	Page 214
wpMenuItemHelpSelected	Page 232
wpMenuItemSelected	Page 235
wpModifyPopupMenu	Page 240
wpOpen	Page 248
wpRestoreState	Page 377
wpSaveState	Page 390
wpSetup	Page 474
wpUnInitData	Page 484

WPPalette CLASS METHODS:

OVERRIDDEN WPObject CLASS METHODS:

WPPdr

This is the printer-driver object class. An instance of this class is created by the printer object in its settings view.

CLASS DEFINITION FILE:

wppdr.idl

CLASS HIERARCHY:

```
SOMObject
  WPObject
    WPTransient
      WPPdr
```

OVERRIDDEN WPObject INSTANCE METHODS:

OVERRIDDEN WPObject CLASS METHODS:

WPPif

This is the PIF (Picture Interchange Format) object class. All PIF
files are instances of this class. An instance of this class is created
initially by the system for each PIF file in the system.

CLASS DEFINITION FILE:

```
wppif.idl
```

CLASS HIERARCHY:

```
SOMObject
  WPObject
    WPFileSystem
      WPDataFile
        WPPif
```

OVERRIDDEN WPObject INSTANCE METHODS:

wpSetupOnce   Page 477

OVERRIDDEN WPFileSystem CLASS METHODS:

wpclsQueryInstanceFilter   Page 534
wpclsQueryInstanceType   Page 535

OVERRIDDEN WPObject CLASS METHODS:

wpclsInitData   Page 501
wpclsQueryDefaultHelp   Page 513
wpclsQueryTitle   Page 549

WPPointer

This is the pointer object class. All pointers are of this class and can be templated. An instance of this class is created initially by the system for each pointer in the system.

CLASS DEFINITION FILE:

wpptr.idl

CLASS HIERARCHY:

```
SOMObject
  WPObject
   WPFileSystem
     WPDataFile
       WPPointer
```

OVERRIDDEN WPObject INSTANCE METHODS:

wpSetupOnce   Page 477

OVERRIDDEN WPFileSystem CLASS METHODS:

wpclsQueryInstanceFilter   Page 534
wpclsQueryInstanceType   Page 535

OVERRIDDEN WPObject CLASS METHODS:

wpclsInitData   Page 501
wpclsQueryDefaultHelp   Page 513
wpclsQueryTitle   Page 549

WPPort

This is the port object class. An instance of this class is created by the printer object in its settings view.

CLASS DEFINITION FILE:

wpport.idl

CLASS HIERARCHY:

```
SOMObject
  WPObject
    WPTransient
      WPPort
```

OVERRIDDEN WPObject INSTANCE METHODS:

OVERRIDDEN WPObject CLASS METHODS:

WPPower

This is the power object class, which represents Power Management support. An instance of this class is created initially by systems that support Power Management and cannot be deleted. It has the title "Power" and resides in the System Setup folder.

CLASS DEFINITION FILE:

```
wppower.idl
```

CLASS HIERARCHY:

```
SOMObject
  WPObject
    WPAbstract
      WPPower
```

WPPower INSTANCE METHODS:

OVERRIDDEN WPObject INSTANCE METHODS:

OVERRIDDEN WPObject CLASS METHODS:

WPPrinter

This is the printer object class. An instance of this class is created initially by the system in its template form. It has the title "Printer" and resides in the Templates folder.

Instances of this class also are created initially by the system for each printer configured. Each instance has a title corresponding to the description of the configured queue and printer and resides on the Desktop.

CLASS DEFINITION FILE:

```
wpprint.idl
```

CLASS HIERARCHY:

```
SOMObject
  WPObject
    WPAbstract
      WPPrinter
```

WPPrinter INSTANCE METHODS:

wpDeleteAllJobs	Page 178
wpJobAdded	Page 227
wpJobChanged	Page 228
wpJobDeleted	Page 229
wpHoldPrinter	Page 212
wpQueryComputerName	Page 278
wpQueryPrinterName	Page 340
wpQueryQueueOptions	Page 346
wpQueryRemoteOptions	Page 351
wpReleasePrinter	Page 365
wpSetComputerName	Page 412
wpSetDefaultPrinter	Page 418
wpSetPrinterName	Page 456
wpSetQueueOptions	Page 463
wpSetRemoteOptions	Page 466

OVERRIDDEN WPObject INSTANCE METHODS:

wpAddSettingsPages	Page 139
wpCopiedFromTemplate	Page 169
wpCopyObject	Page 170
wpCreateAnother	Page 171

OVERRIDDEN WPObject CLASS METHODS:

WPProgram

This is the program object class. This class provides an object that represents an executable program and allows the user to run that program by simply double-clicking on the program object. The program can also contain a variety of useful additional parameters, such as the environment for the program and the parameters that are passed to it.

An instance of this class is initially created by the system in its template form with the title "Program". It resides in the Templates folder.

Other instances of this class initially created by the system include:

- "DOS Window" in the Command Prompts folder
- "OS/2 Window" in the Command Prompts folder
- "DOS Full Screen" in the Command Prompts folder
- "OS/2 Full Screen" in the Command Prompts folder
- Every object in the Games folder
- Some objects in the Information folder
- Every object in the Productivity folder

CLASS DEFINITION FILE:

`wppgm.idl`

CLASS HIERARCHY:

```
SOMObject
  WPObject
    WPAbstract
      WPProgram
```

WPProgram INSTANCE METHODS:

OVERRIDDEN WPObject INSTANCE METHODS:

OVERRIDDEN WPObject CLASS METHODS:

WPProgramFile

This is the program-file object class. All executable files are of this class. From the Settings notebook pages for object of this class, it is possible to set up associations to various data file types (such as .TYPE EAs). It also is possible to set up a default working directory and specify parameters to the executable to be used when it is opened from the Workplace Shell.

Instances of this class are created initially by the system for each program file in the system. Each instance has a title corresponding to the file name of the program file it represents and resides in a folder corresponding to the physical directory in which the program file resides.

CLASS DEFINITION FILE:

```
wppgmf.idl
```

CLASS HIERARCHY:

```
SOMObject
  WPObject
    WPFileSystem
      WPProgramFile
```

WPProgramFile INSTANCE METHODS:

wpAddProgramAssociationPage	Page 127
wpAddProgramPage	Page 129
wpAddProgramSessionPage	Page 131
wpQueryAssociationFilter	Page 266
wpQueryAssociationType	Page 270
wpQueryProgramAssociations	Page 345
wpQueryProgDetails	Page 342
wpSetAssociationFilter	Page 400
wpSetAssociationType	Page 404
wpSetProgDetails	Page 457
wpSetProgIcon	Page 460
wpSetProgramAssociations	Page 462

OVERRIDDEN WPFileSystem INSTANCE METHODS:

wpSetAssociatedFileIcon	Page 398

OVERRIDDEN WPObject INSTANCE METHODS:

OVERRIDDEN WPObject CLASS METHODS:

WPQdr

This is the queue-driver object class. An instance of this class is created by the printer object in its settings view.

CLASS DEFINITION FILE:

wpqdr.idl

CLASS HIERARCHY:

```
SOMObject
  WPObject
    WPTransient
      WPQdr
```

OVERRIDDEN WPObject INSTANCE METHODS:

wpAddSettingsPage	Page 139
wpDragOver	Page 191
wpDrop	Page 192
wpFilterPopupMenu	Page 199
wpFree	Page 206
wpInitData	Page 214
wpMenuItemHelpSelected	Page 232
wpMenuItemSelected	Page 235
wpModifyPopupMenu	Page 240
wpOpen	Page 248
wpQueryIcon	Page 316
wpQueryTitle	Page 358
wpUnInitData	Page 484

OVERRIDDEN WPObject CLASS METHODS:

wpclsQueryDefaultHelp	Page 513
wpclsQueryDefaultView	Page 515
wpclsQueryIcon	Page 527
wpclsQueryStyle	Page 547
wpclsQueryTitle	Page 549

WPRootFolder

This class represents the root folder (or directory) of a file system device. Instances of this class exist for every file-system device available. Each instance is paired with a WPDisk object, which represents a particular device.

CLASS DEFINITION FILE:

wprootf.idl

CLASS HIERARCHY:

```
SOMObject
  WPObject
    WPFileSystem
      WPFolder
        WPRootFolder
```

OVERRIDDEN WPFileSystem INSTANCE METHODS:

wpAddFile1Page	Page 100
wpAddFile2Page	Page 101
wpAddFile3Page	Page 102

OVERRIDDEN WPObject INSTANCE METHODS:

wpFilterPopupMenu	Page 199
wpOpen	Page 248
wpRefresh	Page 361
wpRestoreState	Page 377
wpSaveState	Page 390
wpSetDefaultView	Page 419
wpSetTitle	Page 470

OVERRIDDEN WPObject CLASS METHODS:

wpclsIsInitData	Page 501
wpclsQueryDefaultView	Page 515
wpclsQueryStyle	Page 547
wpclsUnInitData	Page 558

WPRPrinter

This is the remote (network) printer object class. An instance of this class represents a printer resource on another computer or server. For proper behavior, a network must be installed. Each instance has a title corresponding to the remote resource and resides on the Desktop.

CLASS DEFINITION FILE:

wprprint.idl

CLASS HIERARCHY:

```
SOMObject
  WPObject
    WPAbstract
      WPPrinter
        WPRPrinter
```

WPRPrinter INSTANCE METHODS:

OVERRIDDEN WPObject INSTANCE METHODS:

OVERRIDDEN WPObject CLASS METHODS:

WPSchemePalette

This is the scheme-palette object class. An instance of this class has the title "Scheme Palette" and resides in the System Setup folder. There are currently no methods defined for the WPSchemePalette workplace object class.

CLASS DEFINITION FILE:

```
wpscheme.idl
```

CLASS HIERARCHY:

```
SOMObject
  WPObject
    WPAbstract
      WPPalette
        WPSchemePalette
```

OVERRIDDEN WPPalette INSTANCE METHODS:

wpDragCell	Page 188
wpEditCell	Page 196
wpPaintCell	Page 250
wpQueryPaletteHelp	Page 335
wpSetupCell	Page 476

OVERRIDDEN WPObject INSTANCE METHODS:

wpMenuItemHelpSelected	Page 232
wpSetup	Page 474

OVERRIDDEN WPPalette CLASS METHODS:

wpclsQueryEditString	Page 520

OVERRIDDEN WPObject CLASS METHODS:

wpclsQueryDefaultHelp	Page 513
wpclsQueryIconData	Page 528
wpclsQueryStyle	Page 547
wpclsQueryTitle	Page 549

WPServer

This is the server object class. Instances of this class are created for every server in a WPNetgrp folder that is accessible to the user.

CLASS DEFINITION FILE:

wpserver.idl

CLASS HIERARCHY:

```
SOMObject
  WPObject
    WPFileSystem
      WPFolder
        WPServer
```

WPServer INSTANCE METHODS:

wpAddServerPage	Page 134
wpQuerySrvIdentity	Page 355

OVERRIDDEN WPFolder INSTANCE METHODS:

wpAddFolderIncludePage	Page 105
wpDeleteContents	Page 179
wpPopulate	Page 252

OVERRIDDEN WPFileSystem INSTANCE METHODS:

wpAddFile1Page	Page 100
wpAddFile2Page	Page 101
wpAddFile3Page	Page 102

OVERRIDDEN WPObject INSTANCE METHODS:

wpAddObjectGeneralPage	Page 123
wpAddSettingsPages	Page 139
wpFilterPopupMenu	Page 199
wpInitData	Page 214
wpMenuItemHelpSelected	Page 232
wpMenuItemSelected	Page 235
wpModifyPopupMenu	Page 240
wpOpen	Page 248
wpRestoreState	Page 377
wpSaveState	Page 390

OVERRIDDEN WPObject CLASS METHODS:

WPShadow

This is the shadow object class. An instance of this class provides a persistent link or reference to another object by storing the location and identity of the object that it is linked to and then rerouting all requests for help, context menus, and open views to the object to which it is linked.

CLASS DEFINITION FILE:

wpshadow.idl

CLASS HIERARCHY:

```
SOMObject
  WPObject
    WPAbstract
      WPShadow
```

WPShadow INSTANCE METHODS:

OVERRIDDEN WPObject INSTANCE METHODS:

OVERRIDDEN WPObject CLASS METHODS:

WPSharedDir

This is the shared-directory object class. Instances of this class are created for every shared directory in a WPServer folder that is accessible to the user.

CLASS DEFINITION FILE:

wpshdir.idl

CLASS HIERARCHY:

```
SOMObject
  WPObject
    WPFileSystem
      WPFolder
        WPShareDir
```

WPSharedDir INSTANCE METHODS:

wpAddResourcePage	Page 133

OVERRIDDEN WPFolder INSTANCE METHODS:

wpAddFolderIncludePage	Page 105
wpPopulate	Page 252

OVERRIDDEN WPFileSystemINSTANCE METHODS:

wpAddFile1Page	Page 100
wpAddFile2Page	Page 101
wpAddFile3Page	Page 102

OVERRIDDEN WPObject INSTANCE METHODS:

wpAddObjectGeneralPage	Page 123
wpAddSettingsPages	Page 139
wpFilterPopupMenu	Page 199
wpInitData	Page 214
wpMenuItemHelpSelected	Page 232
wpMenuItemSelected	Page 235
wpModifyPopupMenu	Page 240
wpOpen	Page 248
wpRestoreState	Page 377
wpSaveState	Page 390

OVERRIDDEN WPObject CLASS METHODS:

WPShredder

This is the shredder-device object class. An instance of this class has the title "Shredder" and resides on the LaunchPad.

There are currently no methods defined for the WPShredder workplace object class.

CLASS DEFINITION FILE:

wpshred.idl

CLASS HIERARCHY:

```
SOMObject
  WPObject
    WPAbstract
      WPShredder
```

OVERRIDDEN WPObject INSTANCE METHODS:

wpAddObjectWindowPage	Page 124
wpDragOver	Page 191
wpDrop	Page 192
wpFilterPopupMenu	Page 199

OVERRIDDEN WPObject CLASS METHODS:

wpclsQueryDefaultHelp	Page 513
wpclsQueryDefaultView	Page 515
wpclsQueryIconData	Page 528
wpclsQueryStyle	Page 547
wpclsQueryTitle	Page 549

WPSound

This is the sound object class. An instance of this class has the title "Sound" and resides in the System Setup folder.

CLASS DEFINITION FILE:

```
wpsound.idl
```

CLASS HIERARCHY:

```
SOMObject
  WPObject
    WPAbstract
      WPSound
```

WPSound INSTANCE METHODS:

wpAddSoundWarningBeepPage   Page 140

OVERRIDDEN WPObject INSTANCE METHODS:

wpAddObjectWindowPage	Page 124
wpAddSettingsPages	Page 139
wpFilterPopupMenu	Page 199

OVERRIDDEN WPObject CLASS METHODS:

wpclsQueryDefaultHelp	Page 513
wpclsQueryDefaultView	Page 515
wpclsQueryIconData	Page 528
wpclsQueryStyle	Page 547
wpclsQueryTitle	Page 549

WPSpecialNeeds

This is the special-needs object class. An instance of this class is created initially by the system when the keyboard special-needs mode is activated via the keyboard object settings. It has the title "Special Needs" and resides on the Desktop.

CLASS DEFINITION FILE:

wpspneed.idl

CLASS HIERARCHY:

```
SOMObject
  WPObject
    WPAbstract
      WPSpecialNeeds
```

OVERRIDDEN WPObject INSTANCE METHODS:

wpFilterPopupMenu   Page 199

OVERRIDDEN WPObject CLASS METHODS:

wpclsQueryDefaultHelp   Page 513
wpclsQueryIconData   Page 528
wpclsQueryTitle   Page 549

WPSpool

This is the spooler object class. An instance of this class has the title "Spooler" and resides in the System Setup folder.

CLASS DEFINITION FILE:

wpspool.idl

CLASS HIERARCHY:

```
SOMObject
  WPObject
    WPAbstract
      WPSpool
```

OVERRIDDEN WPSpool INSTANCE METHODS:

OVERRIDDEN WPObject INSTANCE METHODS:

OVERRIDDEN WPObject CLASS METHODS:

WPStartup

This is the Startup folder object class. Any object in this folder is automatically opened every time the system is restarted.

The startup folder is used to automatically open objects that are not necessarily running when the system is shutdown. This includes items such as a batch file that initializes the network and then terminates.

An instance of this class has the title "Startup" and resides in the OS/2 System folder.

CLASS DEFINITION FILE:

```
wpstart.idl
```

CLASS HIERARCHY:

```
SOMObject
  WPObject
    WPFileSystem
      WPFolder
        WPStartup
```

OVERRIDDEN WPObject INSTANCE METHODS:

wpFree	Page 206
wpRestoreState	Page 377
wpSetupOnce	Page 477

OVERRIDDEN WPObject CLASS METHODS:

wpclsQueryDefaultHelp	Page 513
wpclsQueryIconData	Page 528
wpclsQueryStyle	Page 547
wpclsQueryTitle	Page 549

WPSystem

This is the system object class. An instance of this class has the title "System" and resides in the System Setup folder.

CLASS DEFINITION FILE:

wpsystem.idl

CLASS HIERARCHY:

```
SOMObject
  WPObject
    WPAbstract
      WPSystem
```

WPSystem INSTANCE METHODS:

OVERRIDDEN WPObject INSTANCE METHODS:

WPAbstract CLASS METHODS:

OVERRIDDEN WPObject CLASS METHODS:

WPTemplates

This is the Templates folder object class. This class of folder always contains a template instance of every class of object the user can create that supports the "Create another" action.

A WPTemplates object is a normal folder in all respects except that:

- It always contains a template for every class that supports them.
- The last template for each object class can not be deleted from the folder.

An instance of this class has the title "Templates" and resides in the OS/2 System folder. A template instance is also created for each data type defined in an application's ASSOCTABLE resource.

CLASS DEFINITION FILE:

```
wptemps.idl
```

CLASS HIERARCHY:

```
SOMObject
  WPObject
    WPFileSystem
      WPFolder
        WPTemplates
```

OVERRIDDEN WPFolder INSTANCE METHODS:

wpPopulate   Page 252

OVERRIDDEN WPObject INSTANCE METHODS:

wpSetup   Page 474

OVERRIDDEN WPObject CLASS METHODS:

WPTransient

This is the non-persistent object-storage class; it has no storage medium. This means that instances of object classes derived from WPTransient do not persist across reboots.

This class is available for applications that must utilize a large amount of workplace functionality (such as context menus and Settings notebooks) in their object class without being a file, directory, or record in the INI file.

There are no instances of this class initially created by the system.

Note: WPAbstract, WPFileSystem, and WPTransient are base storage classes.

CLASS DEFINITION FILE:

```
wptrans.idl
```

CLASS HIERARCHY:

```
SOMObject
  WPObject
    WPTransient
```

OVERRIDDEN WPObject INSTANCE METHODS:

wpCopyObject	Page 170
wpQueryHandle	Page 314
wpSaveDeferred	Page 384

OVERRIDDEN WPObject CLASS METHODS:

wpclsQueryStyle	Page 547
wpclsQueryTitle	Page 549

WPWinConfig

This is the WIN-OS/2 configuration object class. This object stores and allows the user to modify the default settings for WIN-OS/2 applications. It initially resides in the System Setup folder. An instance of this class can be created as a workplace object.

CLASS DEFINITION FILE:

`wincfg.idl`

CLASS HIERARCHY:

```
SOMObject
  WPObject
    WPAbstract
      WPWinConfig
```

WPWinConfig INSTANCE METHODS:

OVERRIDDEN WPObject INSTANCE METHODS:

OVERRIDDEN WPObject CLASS METHODS:

Chapter 3
Workplace Instance Methods

This chapter contains an alphabetical listing of the workplace instance methods. These methods are valid for a specific object.

wpAddClockAlarmPage

This instance method adds the *Alarm* page to the Settings notebook of an object.

INCLUDE IDENTIFIER:

```
#define INCL_WINWORKPLACE
```

FUNCTION PROTOTYPE:

```
ULONG wpAddClockAlarmPage(WPClock *somSelf,
                          HWND hwndNotebook);
```

PARAMETERS:

```
somSelf      - Pointer to the object on which the
               method is invoked
hwndNotebook - Settings notebook handle
```

RETURNS:

```
0        - Error occurred
PageId   - Identifier for inserted page
```

METHOD USAGE:

```
The method must be called only from within an override
of wpAddSettingsPages.
```

METHOD OVERRIDE:

```
This method should be overridden to replace or remove
the Alarm page from the object's Settings notebook. To
remove the page, the override method should return
SETTINGS_PAGE_REMOVED without calling the parent
```

method. To replace the page with another page, the override method should call wpInsertSettingsPage without calling the parent method.

RELATED METHODS:

wpAddClockDateTimePage

This instance method adds the *Date/Time* page to the Settings notebook of the WPClock object.

INCLUDE IDENTIFIER:

```
#define INCL_WINWORKPLACE
```

FUNCTION PROTOTYPE:

```
ULONG wpAddClockDateTimePage(WPClock *somSelf,
                             HWND hwndNotebook);
```

PARAMETERS:

```
somSelf        - Pointer to the object on which the
                 method is invoked
hwndNotebook   - Settings notebook handle
```

RETURNS:

```
0        - Error occurred
PageId   - Identifier for inserted page
```

METHOD USAGE:

This method must be called only from within an override of wpAddSettingsPages.

METHOD OVERRIDE:

This method should be overridden to replace or remove the *Date/Time* page from the object's Settings notebook. To remove the page, the override method should return SETTINGS_PAGE_REMOVED without calling the parent method. To replace the page with another page, the override method should call wpInsertSettingsPage without calling the parent method.

RELATED METHODS:

wpAddClockView1Page

This instance method adds the *View 1* page to the Settings notebook of the Country object.

INCLUDE IDENTIFIER:

```
#define INCL_WINWORKPLACE
```

FUNCTION PROTOTYPE:

```
ULONG wpAddClockView1Page(WPClock *somSelf,
                          HWND hwndNotebook);
```

PARAMETERS:

```
somSelf       - Pointer to the object on which the
                method is invoked
hwndNotebook  - Settings notebook handle
```

RETURNS:

```
0       - Error occurred
PageId  - Identifier for inserted page
```

METHOD USAGE:

This method must be called only from within an override of wpAddSettingsPages.

METHOD OVERRIDE:

This method should be overridden to replace or remove the *View 1* page from the object's Settings notebook. To remove the page, the override method should return SETTINGS_PAGE_REMOVED without calling the parent method. To replace the page with another page, the override method should call wpInsertSettingsPage without calling the parent method.

RELATED METHODS:

wpAddClockView2Page

This instance method adds the *View 2* page to the Settings note-book of an object.

INCLUDE IDENTIFIER:

```
#define INCL_WINWORKPLACE
```

FUNCTION PROTOTYPE:

```
ULONG wpAddClockView2Page(WPClock *somSelf,
                          HWND hwndNotebook);
```

PARAMETERS:

somSelf   - Pointer to the object on which the
                  method is invoked
hwndNotebook   - Settings notebook handle

RETURNS:

0   - Error occurred
PageId   - Identifier for inserted page

METHOD USAGE:

This method must be called only from within an override
of wpAddSettingsPages.

METHOD OVERRIDE:

This method should be overridden to replace or remove
the *View 2* page from the object's Settings notebook. To
remove the page, the override method should return
SETTINGS_PAGE_REMOVED without calling the parent
method. To replace the page with another page, the
override method should call wpInsertSettingsPage without calling the parent method.

RELATED METHODS:

wpAddCountryDatePage

This instance method adds the *Date* page to the Settings notebook of an object.

INCLUDE IDENTIFIER:

```
#define INCL_WINWORKPLACE
```

FUNCTION PROTOTYPE:

```
ULONG wpAddCountryDatePage(WPCountry *somSelf,
                            HWND hwndNotebook);
```

PARAMETERS:

somSelf   - Pointer to the object on which the
               method is invoked
hwndNotebook - Settings notebook handle

RETURNS:

0   - Error occurred
PageId   - Identifier for inserted page

METHOD USAGE:

This method must be called only from within an override of wpAddSettingsPages.

METHOD OVERRIDE:

This method should be overridden to replace or remove the *Date* page from the object's Settings notebook. To remove the page, the override method should return SETTINGS_PAGE_REMOVED without calling the parent method. To replace the page with another page, the override method should call wpInsertSettingsPage without calling the parent method.

RELATED METHODS:

wpAddCountryNumbersPage

This instance method adds the *Numbers* page to the Settings notebook of an object.

INCLUDE IDENTIFIER:

```
#define INCL_WINWORKPLACE
```

FUNCTION PROTOTYPE:

```
ULONG wpAddCountryNumbersPage(WPCountry *somSelf,
                             HWND hwndNotebook);
```

PARAMETERS:

somSelf	- Pointer to the object on which the method is invoked
hwndNotebook	- Settings notebook handle

RETURNS:

0	- Error occurred
PageId	- Identifier for inserted page

METHOD USAGE:

This method must be called only from within an override of wpAddSettingsPages.

METHOD OVERRIDE:

This method should be overridden to replace or remove the *Numbers* page from the object's Settings notebook. To remove the page, the override method should return SETTINGS_PAGE_REMOVED without calling the parent method. To replace the page with another page, the override method should call wpInsertSettingsPage without calling the parent method.

RELATED METHODS:

wpAddCountryPage

This instance method adds the *Country* page to the Settings notebook of an object.

INCLUDE IDENTIFIER:

```
#define INCL_WINWORKPLACE
```

FUNCTION PROTOTYPE:

```
ULONG wpAddCountryPage(WPCountry *somSelf,
                       HWND hwndNotebook);
```

PARAMETERS:

```
somSelf        - Pointer to the object on which the
                 method is invoked
hwndNotebook   - Settings notebook handle
```

RETURNS:

```
0        - Error occurred
PageId   - Identifier for inserted page
```

METHOD USAGE:

This method must be called only from within an override of wpAddSettingsPages.

METHOD OVERRIDE:

This method should be overridden to replace or remove the *Country* page from the object's Settings notebook. To remove the page, the override method should return SETTINGS_PAGE_REMOVED without calling the parent method. To replace the page with another page, the override method should call wpInsertSettingsPage without calling the parent method.

RELATED METHODS:

wpAddCountryTimePage

This instance method adds the *Time* page to the Settings notebook of an object.

INCLUDE IDENTIFIER:

```
#define INCL_WINWORKPLACE
```

FUNCTION PROTOTYPE:

```
ULONG wpAddCountryTimePage(WPCountry *somSelf,
                           HWND hwndNotebook);
```

PARAMETERS:

somSelf	- Pointer to the object on which the method is invoked
hwndNotebook	- Settings notebook handle

RETURNS:

0	- Error occurred
PageId	- Identifier for inserted page

METHOD USAGE:

This method must be called only from within an override of wpAddSettingsPages.

METHOD OVERRIDE:

This method should be overridden to replace or remove the *Time* page from the object's Settings notebook. To remove the page, the override method should return SETTINGS_PAGE_REMOVED without calling the parent method. To replace the page with another page, the override method should call wpInsertSettingsPage without calling the parent method.

RELATED METHODS:

wpAddSettingsPages	Page 139
wpInsertSettingsPage	Page 219

wpAddDDEPage

This instance method adds the DDE Details page to the Settings notebook of an object.

INCLUDE IDENTIFIER:

```
#define INCL_WINWORKPLACE
```

FUNCTION PROTOTYPE:

```
ULONG wpAddDDEPage(WPWinConfig *somSelf,
                HWND hwndNotebook);
```

PARAMETERS:

```
somSelf        - Pointer to the object on which the
                 method is invoked
hwndNotebook   - Handle to Settings notebook
```

RETURNS:

```
Return value of 0 indicates that the DDE details page
was not added to the Settings notebook.
```

METHOD USAGE:

```
This method can be called at any time.
```

METHOD OVERRIDE:

```
This method should always be overridden to replace or
remove the Dynamic Data Exchange (DDE) details page from
an object that is a descendent of WPWinConfig. An
override of this method does not call the parent.
```

RELATED METHODS:

wpAddDesktopArcRest1Page

This instance method adds the *Archive* page to the Settings notebook of an object.

INCLUDE IDENTIFIER:

```
#define INCL_WINWORKPLACE
```

FUNCTION PROTOTYPE:

```
ULONG wpAddDesktopArcRest1Page(WPDesktop *somSelf,
                              HWND hwndNotebook);
```

PARAMETERS:

```
somSelf        - Pointer to the object on which the
                 method is invoked
hwndNotebook   - Settings notebook handle
```

RETURNS:

```
0          - Error occurred
PageId     - Identifier for the inserted page
```

METHOD USAGE:

```
This method must be called only from within an override
of the wpAddSettingsPages method.
```

METHOD OVERRIDE:

```
This method should always be overridden to replace or
remove the Archive page from the object's Settings
notebook. To remove the page, the override method must
return SETTINGS_PAGE_REMOVED without calling the parent
method. To replace the page with another page, the
override method must call wpInsertSettingsPage without
calling the parent method.
```

RELATED METHODS:

```
wpAddSettingsPages              Page 139
wpInsertSettingsPage            Page 219
```

wpAddDesktopDefDT1Page

This instance method adds the *Desktop* page to the Settings notebook of an object.

INCLUDE IDENTIFIER:

```
#define INCL_WINWORKPLACE
```

FUNCTION PROTOTYPE:

```
ULONG wpAddDesktopDefDT1Page(WPDesktop *somSelf,
                            HWND hwndNotebook);
```

PARAMETERS:

```
somSelf        - Pointer to the object on which the
                 method is invoked
hwndNotebook   - Settings notebook handle
```

RETURNS:

```
0        - Error occurred
PageId   - Identifier for inserted page
```

METHOD USAGE:

This method must be called only from within an override of the wpAddSettingsPages method.

METHOD OVERRIDE:

This method should always be overridden to replace or remove the *Desktop* page from the object's Settings notebook. To remove the page, the override method should return SETTINGS_PAGE_REMOVED without calling the parent method. To replace the page with another page, the override method should call wpInsertSettingsPage without calling the parent method.

RELATED METHODS:

wpAddSettingsPages   Page 139
wpInsertSettingsPage   Page 219

wpAddDesktopLockup1Page

This instance method adds the *Lockup 1* page to the Settings notebook of an object.

INCLUDE IDENTIFIER:

```
#define INCL_WINWORKPLACE
```

FUNCTION PROTOTYPE:

```
ULONG wpAddDesktopLockup1Page(WPDesktop *somSelf,
                             HWND hwndNotebook);
```

PARAMETERS:

```
somSelf        - Pointer to the object on which the
                 method is invoked
hwndNotebook - Settings notebook handle
```

RETURNS:

```
0            - Error occurred
PageId    - Identifier for inserted page
```

METHOD USAGE:

This method must be called only from within an override of wpAddSettingsPages.

METHOD OVERRIDE:

This method should be overridden to replace or remove the *Lockup 1* page from the object's Settings notebook. To remove the page, the override method should return SETTINGS_PAGE_REMOVED without calling the parent method. To replace the page with another page, the override method should call wpInsertSettingsPage without calling the parent method.

RELATED METHODS:

wpAddDesktopLockup2Page

This instance method adds the *Lockup 2* page to the Settings notebook of an object.

INCLUDE IDENTIFIER:

```
#define INCL_WINWORKPLACE
```

FUNCTION PROTOTYPE:

```
ULONG wpAddDesktopLockup2Page(WPDesktop *somSelf,
                             HWND hwndNotebook);
```

PARAMETERS:

```
somSelf        - Pointer to the object on which the
                 method is invoked
hwndNotebook   - Settings notebook handle
```

RETURNS:

```
0         - Error occurred
PageId    - Identifier for inserted page
```

METHOD USAGE:

```
This method must be called only from within an override
of wpAddSettingsPages.
```

METHOD OVERRIDE:

```
This method should be overridden to replace or remove
the Lockup 2 page from the object's Settings notebook.
To remove the page, the override method should return
SETTINGS_PAGE_REMOVED without calling the parent
method. To replace the page with another page, the
override method should call wpInsertSettingsPage with-
out calling the parent method.
```

RELATED METHODS:

```
wpAddSettingsPages              Page 139
wpInsertSettingsPage            Page 219
```

wpAddDesktopLockup3Page

This instance method adds the *Lockup 3* page to the Settings notebook of an object.

INCLUDE IDENTIFIER:

```
#define INCL_WINWORKPLACE
```

FUNCTION PROTOTYPE:

```
ULONG wpAddDesktopLockup3Page(WPDesktop *somSelf,
                              HWND hwndNotebook);
```

PARAMETERS:

somSelf   - Pointer to the object on which the
                 method is invoked
hwndNotebook   - Settings notebook handle

RETURNS:

0   - Error occurred
PageId   - Identifier for inserted page

METHOD USAGE:

This method must be called only from within an override of wpAddSettingsPages.

METHOD OVERRIDE:

This method should be overridden to replace or remove the *Lockup 3* page from the object's Settings notebook. To remove the page, the override method should return SETTINGS_PAGE_REMOVED without calling the parent method. To replace the page with another page, the override method should call wpInsertSettingsPage without calling the parent method.

RELATED METHODS:

wpAddSettingsPages   Page 139
wpInsertSettingsPage   Page 219

wpAddDiskDetailsPage

This instance method adds the *Details* page to the Settings notebook of an object.

INCLUDE IDENTIFIER:

```
#define INCL_WINWORKPLACE
```

FUNCTION PROTOTYPE:

```
ULONG wpAddDiskDetailsPage(WPDisk *somSelf,
                           HWND hwndNotebook);
```

PARAMETERS:

```
somSelf       - Pointer to the object on which the
                method is invoked
hwndNotebook  - Settings notebook handle
```

RETURNS:

```
0        - Error occurred
PageId   - Identifier for inserted page
```

METHOD USAGE:

This method must be called only from within an override of wpAddSettingsPages.

METHOD OVERRIDE:

This method should be overridden to replace or remove the *Details* page from the object's Settings notebook. To remove the page, the override method should return SETTINGS_PAGE_REMOVED without calling the parent method. To replace the page with another page, the override method should call wpInsertSettingsPage without calling the parent method.

RELATED METHODS:

wpAddDMSQDisplayTypePage

This instance method adds the DMSQ Display Type page to the Settings notebook of an object.

INCLUDE IDENTIFIER:

```
#define INCL_WINWORKPLACE
```

FUNCTION PROTOTYPE:

```
ULONG wpAddDMSQDisplayTypePage(WPSystem *somSelf,
                                HWND hwndNotebook);
```

PARAMETERS:

```
somSelf        - Pointer to the object on which the
                 method is invoked
hwndNotebook   - Window handle to Settings notebook
```

RETURNS:

```
A return value of 0 indicates that the DMSQ Display Type
page was not added to the Settings notebook.
```

METHOD OVERRIDE:

```
This method should always be overridden to replace or
remove the DMSQ Display Type page from an object that
is a descendent of WPSystem. An override of this method
does not call the parent.
```

RELATED METHODS:

```
wpAddSettingsPages           Page 139
wpInsertSettingsPage         Page 219
```

wpAddFileMenuPage

This instance method adds the *Menu* page to the Settings notebook of an object.

INCLUDE IDENTIFIER:

```
#define INCL_WINWORKPLACE
```

FUNCTION PROTOTYPE:

```
ULONG wpAddFileMenuPage(WPFileSystem *somSelf,
                        HWND hwndNotebook);
```

PARAMETERS:

```
somSelf        - Pointer to the object on which the
                 method is invoked
hwndNotebook - Settings notebook handle
```

RETURNS:

```
0       - Error occurred
PageId  - Identifier for inserted page
```

METHOD USAGE:

This method must be called only from within an override of wpAddSettingsPages.

METHOD OVERRIDE:

This method should be overridden to replace or remove the *Menu* page from the object's Settings notebook. To remove the page, the override method should return SETTINGS_PAGE_REMOVED without calling the parent method. To replace the page with another page, the override method should call wpInsertSettingsPage without calling the parent method.

RELATED METHODS:

wpAddFileTypePage

This instance method adds the *Type* page to the Settings notebook of an object.

INCLUDE IDENTIFIER:

```
#define INCL_WINWORKPLACE
```

FUNCTION PROTOTYPE:

```
ULONG wpAddFileTypePage(WPDataFile *somSelf,
                        HWND hwndNotebook);
```

PARAMETERS:

```
somSelf       - Pointer to the object on which the
                method is invoked
hwndNotebook  - Settings notebook handle
```

RETURNS:

```
0         - Error occurred
PageId    - Identifier for inserted page
```

METHOD USAGE:

This method must be called only from within an override of wpAddSettingsPages.

METHOD OVERRIDE:

This method should be overridden to replace or remove the *Type* page from the object's Settings notebook. To remove the page, the override method should return SETTINGS_PAGE_REMOVED without calling the parent method. To replace the page with another page, the override method should call wpInsertSettingsPage without calling the parent method.

RELATED METHODS:

```
wpAddSettingsPages          Page 139
wpQueryType                 Page 359
wpSetTitle                  Page 470
```

wpAddFile1Page

This instance method adds the *File 1* page to the Settings notebook of an object.

INCLUDE IDENTIFIER:

```
#define INCL_WINWORKPLACE
```

FUNCTION PROTOTYPE:

```
ULONG wpAddFile1Page(WPFileSystem *somSelf,
                 HWND hwndNotebook);
```

PARAMETERS:

```
somSelf       - Pointer to the object on which the
                method is invoked
hwndNotebook - Settings notebook handle
```

RETURNS:

```
0        - Error occurred
PageId  - Identifier for inserted page
```

METHOD USAGE:

```
This method must be called only from within an override
of wpAddSettingsPages.
```

METHOD OVERRIDE:

```
This method should be overridden to replace or remove
the File 1 page from the object's Settings notebook. To
remove the page, the override method should return
SETTINGS_PAGE_REMOVED without calling the parent
method. To replace the page with another page, the
override method should call wpInsertSettingsPage with-
out calling the parent method.
```

RELATED METHODS:

```
wpAddSettingsPages              Page 139
wpInsertSettingsPage            Page 219
```

wpAddFile2Page

This instance method adds the *File 2* page to the Settings notebook of an object.

INCLUDE IDENTIFIER:

```
#define INCL_WINWORKPLACE
```

FUNCTION PROTOTYPE:

```
ULONG wpAddFile2Page(WPFileSystem *somSelf,
                     HWND hwndNotebook);
```

PARAMETERS:

```
somSelf         - Pointer to the object on which the
                  method is invoked
hwndNotebook    - Settings notebook handle
```

RETURNS:

```
0        - Error occurred
PageId   - Identifier for inserted page
```

METHOD USAGE:

This method must be called only from within an override of wpAddSettingsPages.

METHOD OVERRIDE:

This method should be overridden to replace or remove the *File 2* page from the object's Settings notebook. To remove the page, the override method should return SETTINGS_PAGE_REMOVED without calling the parent method. To replace the page with another page, the override method should call wpInsertSettingsPage without calling the parent method.

RELATED METHODS:

wpAddFile3Page

This instance method adds the *File 3* page to the Settings notebook of an object.

INCLUDE IDENTIFIER:

```
#define INCL_WINWORKPLACE
```

FUNCTION PROTOTYPE:

```
ULONG wpAddFile3Page(WPFileSystem *somSelf,
                     HWND hwndNotebook);
```

PARAMETERS:

```
somSelf        - Pointer to the object on which the
                 method is invoked
hwndNotebook   - Settings notebook handle
```

RETURNS:

```
0         - Error occurred
PageId    - Identifier for inserted page
```

METHOD USAGE:

This method must be called only from within an override of wpAddSettingsPages.

METHOD OVERRIDE:

This method should be overridden to replace or remove the *File 3* page from the object's Settings notebook. To remove the page, the override method should return SETTINGS_PAGE_REMOVED without calling the parent method. To replace the page with another page, the override method should call wpInsertSettingsPage without calling the parent method.

RELATED METHODS:

wpAddSettingsPages   Page 139
wpInsertSettingsPage   Page 219

wpAddFirstChild

This instant method adds one child to a folder.

INCLUDE IDENTIFIER:

#define INCL_WINWORKPLACE

FUNCTION PROTOTYPE:

WPObject *wpAddFirstChild(WPFolder *somSelf);

PARAMETERS:

somSelf   - Pointer to the object on which the method
            is invoked

RETURNS:

Pointer to the instantiated child object.

REMARKS:

This method is called when a folder appears in a tree
view. wpAddFirstChild adds only one child to the folder;
therefore, when the folder appears in the tree view, it
has the correct expansion emphasis. When the folder is
expanded, it will be fully populated.

METHOD OVERRIDE:

This method should be overridden only if another way of
adding the first child folder subclass is required.

wpAddFolderBackgroundPage

This instance method adds the *Background* page to the Settings notebook of an object.

INCLUDE IDENTIFIER:

```
#define INCL_WINWORKPLACE
```

FUNCTION PROTOTYPE:

```
ULONG wpAddFolderBackgroundPage(WPFolder *somSelf,
                                HWND hwndNotebook);
```

PARAMETERS:

```
somSelf        - Pointer to the object on which the
                 method is invoked
hwndNotebook   - Settings notebook handle
```

RETURNS:

```
0         - Error occurred
PageId    - Identifier for inserted page
```

METHOD USAGE:

```
This method must be called only from within an override
of wpAddSettingsPages.
```

METHOD OVERRIDE:

```
This method should be overridden to replace or remove
the Background page from the object's Settings notebook.
To remove the page, the override method should return
SETTINGS_PAGE_REMOVED without calling the parent
method. To replace the page with another page, the
override method should call wpInsertSettingsPage with-
out calling the parent method.
```

RELATED METHODS:

wpAddFolderIncludePage

This instance method adds the *Include* page to the Settings notebook of an object.

INCLUDE IDENTIFIER:

```
#define INCL_WINWORKPLACE
```

FUNCTION PROTOTYPE:

```
ULONG wpAddFolderIncludePage(WPFolder *somSelf,
                             HWND hwndNotebook);
```

PARAMETERS:

somSelf   - Pointer to the object on which the
                method is invoked
hwndNotebook - Settings notebook handle

RETURNS:

0   - Error occurred
PageId   - Identifier for inserted page

METHOD USAGE:

This method must be called only from within an override of wpAddSettingsPages.

METHOD OVERRIDE:

This method should be overridden to replace or remove the *Include* page from the object's Settings notebook. To remove the page, the override method should return SETTINGS_PAGE_REMOVED without calling the parent method. To replace the page with another page, the override method should call wpInsertSettingsPage without calling the parent method.

RELATED METHODS:

wpAddFolderSelfClosePage

This instance method adds the *Folder Automatic Close* page to the
Settings notebook of an object.

INCLUDE IDENTIFIER:

```
#define INCL_WINWORKPLACE
```

FUNCTION PROTOTYPE:

```
ULONG wpAddFolderSelfClosePage(WPFolder *somSelf,
                               HWND hwndNotebook);
```

PARAMETERS:

```
somSelf        - Pointer to the object on which the
                 method is invoked
hwndNotebook   - Handle of Settings notebook
```

RETURNS:

A return value of 0 indicates that the *Folder Automatic
Close* page was not added to the Settings notebook.

METHOD USAGE:

This method is called only during wpAddSettingsPages
processing.

METHOD OVERRIDE:

This method is always overridden to replace or remove
the *Folder Automatic Close* page from an object that is
a descendant of WPFolder. An override of this method
does not call the parent.

RELATED METHODS:

wpAddFolderSortPage

This instance method adds the *Sort* page to the Settings notebook of an object.

INCLUDE IDENTIFIER:

```
#define INCL_WINWORKPLACE
```

FUNCTION PROTOTYPE:

```
ULONG wpAddFolderSortPage(WPFolder *somSelf,
                          HWND hwndNotebook);
```

PARAMETERS:

```
somSelf        - Pointer to the object on which the
                 method is invoked
hwndNotebook   - Settings notebook handle
```

RETURNS:

```
0        - Error occurred
PageId   - Identifier for inserted page
```

METHOD USAGE:

This method must be called only from within an override of wpAddSettingsPages.

METHOD OVERRIDE:

This method should be overridden to replace or remove the *Sort* page from the object's Settings notebook. To remove the page, the override method should return SETTINGS_PAGE_REMOVED without calling the parent method. To replace the page with another page, the override method should call wpInsertSettingsPage without calling the parent method.

RELATED METHODS:

```
wpAddSettingsPages            Page 139
wpInsertSettingsPage          Page 219
```

wpAddFolderView1Page

This instance method adds the *View 1* page to the Settings notebook of an object.

INCLUDE IDENTIFIER:

```
#define INCL_WINWORKPLACE
```

FUNCTION PROTOTYPE:

```
ULONG wpAddFolderView1Page(WPFolder *somSelf,
                           HWND hwndNotebook);
```

PARAMETERS:

```
somSelf        - Pointer to the object on which the
                 method is invoked
hwndNotebook   - Settings notebook handle
```

RETURNS:

```
0        - Error occurred
PageId   - Identifier for inserted page
```

METHOD USAGE:

```
This method must be called only from within an override
of wpAddSettingsPages.
```

METHOD OVERRIDE:

```
This method should be overridden to replace or remove
the View 1 page from the object's Settings notebook. To
remove the page, the override method should return
SETTINGS_PAGE_REMOVED without calling the parent
method. To replace the page with another page, the
override method should call wpInsertSettingsPage with-
out calling the parent method.
```

RELATED METHODS:

wpAddFolderView2Page

This instance method adds the *View 2* page to the Settings notebook of an object.

INCLUDE IDENTIFIER:

```
#define INCL_WINWORKPLACE
```

FUNCTION PROTOTYPE:

```
ULONG wpAddFolderView2Page(WPFolder *somSelf,
                           HWND hwndNotebook);
```

PARAMETERS:

```
somSelf        - Pointer to the object on which the
                 method is invoked
hwndNotebook   - Settings notebook handle
```

RETURNS:

```
0        - Error occurred
PageId   - Identifier for inserted page
```

METHOD USAGE:

```
This method must be called only from within an override
of wpAddSettingsPages.
```

METHOD OVERRIDE:

```
This method should be overridden to replace or remove
the View 2 page from the object's Settings notebook. To
remove the page, the override method should return
SETTINGS_PAGE_REMOVED without calling the parent
method. To replace the page with another page, the
override method should call wpInsertSettingsPage with-
out calling the parent method.
```

RELATED METHODS:

wpAddFolderView3Page

This instance method adds the *View 3* page to the Settings notebook of an object.

INCLUDE IDENTIFIER:

```
#define INCL_WINWORKPLACE
```

FUNCTION PROTOTYPE:

```
ULONG wpAddFolderView3Page(WPFolder *somSelf,
                           HWND hwndNotebook);
```

PARAMETERS:

```
somSelf        - Pointer to the object on which the
                 method is invoked
hwndNotebook   - Settings notebook handle
```

RETURNS:

```
0       - Error occurred
PageId  - Identifier for inserted page
```

METHOD USAGE:

```
This method must be called only from within an override
of wpAddSettingsPages.
```

METHOD OVERRIDE:

```
This method should be overridden to replace or remove
the View 3 page from the object's Settings notebook. To
remove the page, the override method should return
SETTINGS_PAGE_REMOVED without calling the parent
method. To replace the page with another page, the
override method should call wpInsertSettingsPage with-
out calling the parent method.
```

RELATED METHODS:

```
wpAddSettingsPages            Page 139
wpInsertSettingsPage          Page 219
```

wpAddKeyboardMappingsPage

This instance method adds the *Mappings* page to the Settings notebook of an object.

INCLUDE IDENTIFIER:

```
#define INCL_WINWORKPLACE
```

FUNCTION PROTOTYPE:

```
ULONG wpAddKeyboardMappingsPage(WPKeyboard *somSelf,
                                HWND hwndNotebook);
```

PARAMETERS:

```
somSelf        - Pointer to the object on which the
                 method is invoked
hwndNotebook   - Settings notebook handle
```

RETURNS:

```
0        - Error occurred
PageId   - Identifier for inserted page
```

METHOD USAGE:

This method must be called only from within an override of wpAddSettingsPages.

METHOD OVERRIDE:

This method should be overridden to replace or remove the *Mappings* page from the object's Settings notebook. To remove the page, the override method should return SETTINGS_PAGE_REMOVED without calling the parent method. To replace the page with another page, the override method should call wpInsertSettingsPage without calling the parent method.

RELATED METHODS:

wpAddKeyboardSpecialNeeds-Page

This instance method adds the *Special Needs* page to the Settings notebook of an object.

INCLUDE IDENTIFIER:

```
#define INCL_WINWORKPLACE
```

FUNCTION PROTOTYPE:

```
ULONG wpAddKeyboardSpecialNeedsPage
                            (WPKeyboard *somSelf,
                             HWND hwndNotebook);
```

PARAMETERS:

somSelf	- Pointer to the object on which the method is invoked
hwndNotebook	- Settings notebook handle

RETURNS:

0	- Error occurred
PageId	- Identifier for inserted page

METHOD USAGE:

This method must be called only from within an override of wpAddSettingsPages.

METHOD OVERRIDE:

This method should be overridden to replace or remove the *Special Needs* page from the object's Settings notebook. To remove the page, the override method should return SETTINGS_PAGE_REMOVED without calling the parent method. To replace the page, the override method should call wpInsertSettingsPage without calling the parent.

RELATED METHODS:

wpAddSettingsPages	Page 139
wpInsertSettingsPage	Page 219

wpAddKeyboardTimingPage

This instance method adds the *Timing* page to the Settings notebook of an object.

INCLUDE IDENTIFIER:

```
#define INCL_WINWORKPLACE
```

FUNCTION PROTOTYPE:

```
ULONG wpAddKeyboardTimingPage(WPKeyboard *somSelf,
                             HWND hwndNotebook);
```

PARAMETERS:

```
somSelf          - Pointer to the object on which the
                   method is invoked
hwndNotebook     - Settings notebook handle
```

RETURNS:

```
0        - Error occurred
PageId   - Identifier for inserted page
```

METHOD USAGE:

This method must be called only from within an override of wpAddSettingsPages.

METHOD OVERRIDE:

This method should be overridden to replace or remove the *Timing* page from the object's Settings notebook. To remove the page, the override method should return SETTINGS_PAGE_REMOVED without calling the parent method. To replace the page with another page, the override method should call wpInsertSettingsPage without calling the parent method.

RELATED METHODS:

wpAddLaunchPadPage1

This instance method adds the *LaunchPad* page to the Settings notebook of an object.

INCLUDE IDENTIFIER:

```
#define INCL_WINWORKPLACE
```

FUNCTION PROTOTYPE:

```
ULONG wpAddLaunchPadPage1(WPLaunchPad *somSelf,
                          HWND hwndNotebook);
```

PARAMETERS:

```
somSelf        - Pointer to the object on which the
                 method is invoked
hwndNotebook   - Handle to Settings notebook
```

RETURNS:

A return value of 0 indicates that the *LaunchPad* page was not added to the Settings notebook.

METHOD OVERRIDE:

This method should always be overridden to replace or remove the *LaunchPad* page from the Settings notebook of an object that is a descendant of WPLaunchPad. An override of this method does not call the parent.

RELATED METHODS:

wpAddLaunchPadPage2

This instance method adds the *LaunchPad* page 2 to the Settings notebook of an object.

INCLUDE IDENTIFIER:

#define INCL_WINWORKPLACE

FUNCTION PROTOTYPE:

```
ULONG wpAddLaunchPadPage2(WPLaunchPad *somSelf,
                          HWND hwndNotebook);
```

PARAMETERS:

somSelf   - Pointer to the object on which the
                   method is invoked
hwndNotebook   - Handle to Settings notebook

RETURNS:

A return value of 0 indicates that the *LaunchPad* page 2 was not added to the Settings notebook.

METHOD OVERRIDE:

This method should always be overridden to replace or remove the *LaunchPad* page 2 from the Settings notebook of an object that is a descendent of WPLaunchPad. An override of this method does not call the parent.

RELATED METHODS:

wpAddMouseCometPage

This instance method adds the Comet Cursor page to the Settings notebook of an object.

INCLUDE IDENTIFIER:

```
#define INCL_WINWORKPLACE
```

FUNCTION PROTOTYPE:

```
ULONG wpAddMouseCometPage(WPMouse *somSelf,
                          HWND hwndNotebook);
```

PARAMETERS:

```
somSelf       - Pointer to the object on which the
                method is invoked
hwndNotebook  - Handle of Settings notebook
```

RETURNS:

```
A return value of 0 indicates that the Comet Cursor page
was not added to the Settings notebook.
```

METHOD USAGE:

```
This method is called only during wpAddSettingsPages
processing.
```

METHOD OVERRIDE:

```
This method is always overridden to replace or remove
the Comet Cursor page from an object that is a descendant
of WPMouse. An override of this method does not call the
parent.
```

RELATED METHODS:

```
wpAddSettingsPages          Page 139
wpInsertSettingsPage        Page 219
```

wpAddMouseMappingsPage

This instance method adds the *Mappings* page to the Settings notebook of an object.

INCLUDE IDENTIFIER:

```
#define INCL_WINWORKPLACE
```

FUNCTION PROTOTYPE:

```
ULONG wpAddMouseMappingsPage(WPMouse *somSelf,
                             HWND hwndNotebook);
```

PARAMETERS:

```
somSelf        - Pointer to the object on which the
                 method is invoked
hwndNotebook   - Settings notebook handle
```

RETURNS:

```
0        - Error occurred
PageId   - Identifier for inserted page
```

METHOD USAGE:

This method must be called only from within an override of wpAddSettingsPages.

METHOD OVERRIDE:

This method should be overridden to replace or remove the *Mappings* page from the object's Settings notebook. To remove the page, the override method should return SETTINGS_PAGE_REMOVED without calling the parent method. To replace the page with another page, the override method should call wpInsertSettingsPage without calling the parent method.

RELATED METHODS:

wpAddMousePtrPage

This instance method adds the *Mouse Pointer Customization* page to the Settings notebook of an object.

INCLUDE IDENTIFIER:

```
#define INCL_WINWORKPLACE
```

FUNCTION PROTOTYPE:

```
ULONG wpAddMousePtrPage(WPMouse *somSelf,
                        HWND hwndNotebook);
```

PARAMETERS:

```
somSelf       - Pointer to the object on which the
                method is invoked
hwndNotebook  - Handle of Settings notebook
```

RETURNS:

A return value of 0 indicates that the *Mouse Pointer Customization* page was not added to the Settings notebook.

METHOD USAGE:

This method is called only during wpAddSettingsPages processing.

METHOD OVERRIDE:

This method is always overridden to replace or remove the *Mouse Pointer Customization* page from an object that is a descendant of WPMouse. An override of this method does not call the parent.

RELATED METHODS:

wpAddMouseTimingPage

This instance method adds the *Timing* page to the Settings notebook of an object.

INCLUDE IDENTIFIER:

```
#define INCL_WINWORKPLACE
```

FUNCTION PROTOTYPE:

```
ULONG wpAddMouseTimingPage(WPMouse *somSelf,
                           HWND hwndNotebook);
```

PARAMETERS:

somSelf   - Pointer to the object on which the
                method is invoked
hwndNotebook - Settings notebook handle

RETURNS:

0   - Error occurred
PageId   - Identifier for inserted page

METHOD USAGE:

This method must be called only from within an override of wpAddSettingsPages.

METHOD OVERRIDE:

This method should be overridden to replace or remove the *Timing* page from the object's Settings notebook. To remove the page, the override method should return SETTINGS_PAGE_REMOVED without calling the parent method. To replace the page with another page, the override method should call wpInsertSettingsPage without calling the parent method.

RELATED METHODS:

wpAddMouseTypePage

This instance method adds the *Type* page to the Settings notebook of an object.

INCLUDE IDENTIFIER:

```
#define INCL_WINWORKPLACE
```

FUNCTION PROTOTYPE:

```
ULONG wpAddMouseTypePage(WPMouse *somSelf,
                         HWND hwndNotebook);
```

PARAMETERS:

```
somSelf        - Pointer to the object on which the
                 method is invoked
hwndNotebook   - Settings notebook handle
```

RETURNS:

```
0         - Error occurred
PageId    - Identifier for inserted page
```

METHOD USAGE:

This method must be called only from within an override of wpAddSettingsPages.

METHOD OVERRIDE:

This method should be overridden to replace or remove the *Type* page from the object's Settings notebook. To remove the page, the override method should return SETTINGS_PAGE_REMOVED without calling the parent method. To replace the page with another page, the override method should call wpInsertSettingsPage without calling the parent method.

RELATED METHODS:

wpAddNetworkPage

This instance method adds the *Network* page to the Settings notebook of a remote printer object.

INCLUDE IDENTIFIER:

```
#define INCL_WINWORKPLACE
```

FUNCTION PROTOTYPE:

```
ULONG wpAddNetworkPage(WPRPrinter *somSelf,
                       HWND hwndNotebook);
```

PARAMETERS:

```
somSelf        - Pointer to the object on which the
                 method is invoked
hwndNotebook   - Settings notebook handle
```

RETURNS:

```
0        - Error occurred
PageId   - Identifier for the inserted page
```

METHOD USAGE:

This method can be called only from within an override of wpAddSettingsPages.

METHOD OVERRIDE:

This method can be overridden to replace or remove the *Network* page from the object's Settings notebook.

RELATED METHODS:

```
wpAddSettingsPages              Page 139
wpInsertSettingsPage            Page 219
```

wpAddNetworkPage

This instance method adds the *Network* details page to the Settings notebook of a remote printer object.

INCLUDE IDENTIFIER:

```
#define INCL_WINWORKPLACE
```

FUNCTION PROTOTYPE:

```
ULONG wpAddNetworkPage(WPNetgrp *somSelf,
                       HWND hwndNotebook);
```

PARAMETERS:

```
somSelf       - Pointer to the object on which the
                method is invoked
hwndNotebook  - Settings notebook handle
```

RETURNS:

```
0        - Network details page not added
ulPageId - Identifier for the inserted page
```

METHOD OVERRIDE:

This method should always be overridden to replace or remove the *Network* details page from the Settings notebook of an object that is a descendent of WPNetgrp. An override of this method does not call the parent method.

RELATED METHODS:

wpAddSettingsPages   Page 139
wpInsertSettingsPage   Page 219

wpAddObjectGeneralPage

This instance method adds the *General* page to the Settings notebook of an object.

INCLUDE IDENTIFIER:

```
#define INCL_WINWORKPLACE
```

FUNCTION PROTOTYPE:

```
ULONG wpAddObjectGeneralPage(WPObject *somSelf,
                             HWND hwndNotebook);
```

PARAMETERS:

somSelf	- Pointer to the object on which the method is invoked
hwndNotebook	- Settings notebook handle

RETURNS:

0	- Error occurred
PageId	- Identifier for inserted page

METHOD USAGE:

This method must be called only from within an override of wpAddSettingsPages.

METHOD OVERRIDE:

This method should be overridden to replace or remove the *General* page from the object's Settings notebook. To remove the page, the override method should return SETTINGS_PAGE_REMOVED without calling the parent method. To replace the page with another page, the override method should call wpInsertSettingsPage without calling the parent method.

RELATED METHODS:

wpAddSettingsPages	Page 139
wpInsertSettingsPage	Page 219

wpAddObjectWindowPage

This instance method adds the *Standard Options* page to the Settings notebook of an object.

INCLUDE IDENTIFIER:

```
#define INCL_WINWORKPLACE
```

FUNCTION PROTOTYPE:

```
ULONG wpAddObjectWindowPage(WPObject *somSelf,
                            HWND hwndNotebook);
```

PARAMETERS:

```
somSelf       - Pointer to the object on which the
                method is invoked
hwndNotebook  - Handle of Settings notebook
```

RETURNS:

```
Return value of 0 indicates that the Standard Options
page was not added to the Settings notebook.
```

METHOD USAGE:

```
This method is called only during wpAddSettingsPages
processing.
```

METHOD OVERRIDE:

```
This method is always overridden to replace or remove
the Standard Options page from an object that is a
descendant of WPObject. An override of this method does
not call the parent.
```

RELATED METHODS:

```
wpAddSettingsPages              Page 139
wpInsertSettingsPage            Page 219
```

wpAddPowerPage

This instance method adds the standard *Power* page to the Settings
notebook of the Power object.

INCLUDE IDENTIFIER:

```
#define INCL_WINWORKPLACE
```

FUNCTION PROTOTYPE:

```
ULONG wpAddPowerPage(WPPower *somSelf,
                     HWND hwndNotebook);
```

PARAMETERS:

```
somSelf        - Pointer to the object on which the
                 method is invoked
hwndNotebook   - Settings notebook handle
```

RETURNS:

```
0        - Error occurred
PageId   - Identifier for inserted page
```

RELATED METHODS:

wpAddPowerViewPage	Page 126
wpChangePowerState	Page 154
wpQueryAutoRefresh	Page 275
wpQueryPowerConfirmation	Page 338
wpQueryPowerManagement	Page 339
wpQueryRefreshRate	Page 350
wpSetAutoRefresh	Page 409
wpSetPowerConfirmation	Page 454
wpSetPowerManagement	Page 455
wpSetRefreshRate	Page 465

wpAddPowerViewPage

This instance method adds the standard *Power View* page to the Settings notebook of the Power object.

INCLUDE IDENTIFIER:

```
#define INCL_WINWORKPLACE
```

FUNCTION PROTOTYPE:

```
ULONG wpAddPowerViewPage(WPPower *somSelf,
                         HWND hwndNotebook);
```

PARAMETERS:

```
somSelf       - Pointer to the object on which the
                method is invoked
hwndNotebook  - Settings notebook handle
```

RETURNS:

```
0        - Error occurred
PageId   - Identifier for inserted page
```

RELATED METHODS:

wpAddProgramAssociationPage

This WPProgram instance method adds the *Association* page to the Settings notebook of an object.

INCLUDE IDENTIFIER:

```
#define INCL_WINWORKPLACE
```

FUNCTION PROTOTYPE:

```
ULONG wpAddProgramAssociationPage(WPProgram *somSelf,
                                  HWND hwndNotebook);
```

PARAMETERS:

somSelf   - Pointer to the object on which the
                method is invoked
hwndNotebook - Settings notebook handle

RETURNS:

0   - Error occurred
PageId - Identifier for inserted page

METHOD USAGE:

This method must be called only from within an override of wpAddSettingsPages.

METHOD OVERRIDE:

This method should be overridden to replace or remove the *Association* page from the object's Settings notebook. To remove the page, the override method should return SETTINGS_PAGE_REMOVED without calling the parent method. To replace the page with another page, the override method should call wpInsertSettingsPage without calling the parent method.

RELATED METHODS:

wpAddProgramAssociationPage

This WPProgramFile instance method adds the *Association* page to the Settings notebook of an object.

INCLUDE IDENTIFIER:

```
#define INCL_WINWORKPLACE
```

FUNCTION PROTOTYPE:

```
ULONG wpAddProgramAssociationPage
                        (WPProgramFile *somSelf,
                         HWND hwndNotebook);
```

PARAMETERS:

somSelf   - Pointer to the object on which the
               method is invoked
hwndNotebook - Settings notebook handle

RETURNS:

0   - Error occurred
PageId   - Identifier for inserted page

METHOD USAGE:

This method must be called only from within an override of wpAddSettingsPages.

METHOD OVERRIDE:

This method should be overridden to replace or remove the *Association* page from the object's Settings notebook. To remove the page, the override method should return SETTINGS_PAGE_REMOVED without calling the parent method. To replace the page with another page, the override method should call wpInsertSettingsPage without calling the parent method.

RELATED METHODS:

wpAddProgramPage

This WPProgram instance method adds the *Program* page to the Settings notebook of an object.

INCLUDE IDENTIFIER:

```
#define INCL_WINWORKPLACE
```

FUNCTION PROTOTYPE:

```
ULONG wpAddProgramPage(WPProgram *somSelf,
                       HWND hwndNotebook);
```

PARAMETERS:

```
somSelf        - Pointer to the object on which the
                 method is invoked
hwndNotebook   - Settings notebook handle
```

RETURNS:

```
0        - Error occurred
PageId   - Identifier for inserted page
```

METHOD USAGE:

This method must be called only from within an override of wpAddSettingsPages.

METHOD OVERRIDE:

This method should be overridden to replace or remove the *Program* page from the object's Settings notebook. To remove the page, the override method should return SETTINGS_PAGE_REMOVED without calling the parent method. To replace the page with another page, the override method should call wpInsertSettingsPage without calling the parent method.

RELATED METHODS:

wpAddProgramPage

This WPProgramFile instance method adds the *Program* page to the Settings notebook of an object.

INCLUDE IDENTIFIER:

```
#define INCL_WINWORKPLACE
```

FUNCTION PROTOTYPE:

```
ULONG wpAddProgramPage(WPProgramFile *somSelf,
                       HWND hwndNotebook);
```

PARAMETERS:

```
somSelf        - Pointer to the object on which the
                 method is invoked
hwndNotebook   - Settings notebook handle
```

RETURNS:

```
0        - Error occurred
PageId   - Identifier for inserted page
```

METHOD USAGE:

```
This method must be called only from within an override
of wpAddSettingsPages.
```

METHOD OVERRIDE:

```
This method should be overridden to replace or remove
the Program page from the object's Settings notebook.
To remove the page, the override method should return
SETTINGS_PAGE_REMOVED without calling the parent
method. To replace the page with another page, the
override method should call wpInsertSettingsPage with-
out calling the parent method.
```

RELATED METHODS:

wpAddProgramSessionPage

This WPProgram instance method adds the *Session* page to the Settings notebook of an object.

INCLUDE IDENTIFIER:

```
#define INCL_WINWORKPLACE
```

FUNCTION PROTOTYPE:

```
ULONG wpAddProgramSessionPage(WPProgram *somSelf,
                              HWND hwndNotebook);
```

PARAMETERS:

```
somSelf        - Pointer to the object on which the
                 method is invoked
hwndNotebook   - Settings notebook handle
```

RETURNS:

```
0         - Error occurred
PageId    - Identifier for inserted page
```

METHOD USAGE:

This method must be called only from within an override of wpAddSettingsPages.

METHOD OVERRIDE:

This method should be overridden to replace or remove the *Session* page from the object's Settings notebook. To remove the page, the override method should return SETTINGS_PAGE_REMOVED without calling the parent method. To replace the page with another page, the override method should call wpInsertSettingsPage without calling the parent method.

RELATED METHODS:

wpAddProgramSessionPage

This WPProgramFile instance method adds the *Session* page to the Settings notebook of an object.

INCLUDE IDENTIFIER:

```
#define INCL_WINWORKPLACE
```

FUNCTION PROTOTYPE:

```
ULONG wpAddProgramSessionPage(WPProgramFile *somSelf,
                             HWND hwndNotebook);
```

PARAMETERS:

```
somSelf        - Pointer to the object on which the
                 method is invoked
hwndNotebook   - Settings notebook handle
```

RETURNS:

```
0        - Error occurred
PageId   - Identifier for inserted page
```

METHOD USAGE:

This method must be called only from within an override of wpAddSettingsPages.

METHOD OVERRIDE:

This method should be overridden to replace or remove the *Session* page from the object's Settings notebook. To remove the page, the override method should return SETTINGS_PAGE_REMOVED without calling the parent method. To replace the page with another page, the override method should call wpInsertSettingsPage without calling the parent method.

RELATED METHODS:

wpAddResourcePage

This instance method adds the *Resource* details page to the Settings notebook of an object.

INCLUDE IDENTIFIER:

```
#define INCL_WINWORKPLACE
```

FUNCTION PROTOTYPE:

```
ULONG wpAddResourcePage(WPSharedDir *somSelf,
                        HWND hwndNotebook);
```

PARAMETERS:

somSelf   - Pointer to the object on which the
                 method is invoked
hwndNotebook   - Handle to the Settings notebook

RETURNS:

A return value of 0 indicates that the *Resource* details page was not added to the Settings notebook.

METHOD OVERRIDE:

This method should always be overridden to replace or remove the *Resource* details page from an object that is a descendant of WPSharedDir. An override of this method does not call the parent.

RELATED METHODS:

wpAddSettingsPages   Page 139
wpInsertSettingsPage   Page 219

wpAddServerPage

This instance method adds the *Server* details page to the Settings notebook of an object.

INCLUDE IDENTIFIER:

```
#define INCL_WINWORKPLACE
```

FUNCTION PROTOTYPE:

```
ULONG wpAddServerPage(WPServer *somSelf,
                 HWND hwndNotebook);
```

PARAMETERS:

somSelf	- Pointer to the object on which the method is invoked
hwndNotebook	- Handle to the Settings notebook

RETURNS:

A return value of 0 indicates that the *Server* details page was not added to the Settings notebook.

METHOD OVERRIDE:

This method should always be overridden to replace or remove the *Server* details page from an object that is a descendant of WPServer. An override of this method does not call the parent.

RELATED METHODS:

wpAddSettingsPages   Page 139
wpInsertSettingsPage   Page 219

wpAddSessionPage

This instance method adds the *3.0 Session* details page to the Settings notebook of an object.

INCLUDE IDENTIFIER:

`#define INCL_WINWORKPLACE`

FUNCTION PROTOTYPE:

```
ULONG wpAddSessionPage(WPWinConfig *somSelf,
                       HWND hwndNotebook);
```

PARAMETERS:

somSelf   - Pointer to the object on which the
                   method is invoked
hwndNotebook - Handle to Settings notebook

RETURNS:

A return value of 0 indicates that the *3.0 Session* details pages was not added to the Settings notebook.

RELATED METHODS:

wpAddSession31Page

This instance method adds the *3.1 Session* details page to the Settings notebook of an object.

INCLUDE IDENTIFIER:

```
#define INCL_WINWORKPLACE
```

FUNCTION PROTOTYPE:

```
ULONG wpAddSession31Page(WPWinConfig *somSelf,
                         HWND hwndNotebook);
```

PARAMETERS:

```
somSelf        - Pointer to the object on which the
                 method is invoked
hwndNotebook   - Handle to Settings notebook
```

RETURNS:

```
A return value of 0 indicates that the 3.1 Session
details page was not added to the Settings notebook.
```

METHOD OVERRIDE:

```
This method should always be overridden to replace or
remove the 3.1 Session details page from an object that
is a descendant of WPWinConfig. An override of this
method does not call the parent.
```

RELATED METHODS:

wpAddSetPathPage

This instance method adds the *Set Path* page to the Settings notebook of an object.

INCLUDE IDENTIFIER:

```
#define INCL_WINWORKPLACE
```

FUNCTION PROTOTYPE:

```
ULONG wpAddSetPathPage(WPSpool *somSelf,
                       HWND hwndNotebook);
```

PARAMETERS:

somSelf   - Pointer to the object on which the
                  method is invoked
hwndNotebook   - Settings notebook handle

RETURNS:

0   - Error occurred
PageId   - Identifier for the inserted page

METHOD USAGE:

This method must be called only from within an override of wpAddSettingsPages.

METHOD OVERRIDE:

This method can be overridden to replace or remove the *Set Path* page from the object's Settings notebook.

RELATED METHODS:

wpAddSetPriorityPage

This instance method adds the *Set Priority* page to the Settings notebook of an object.

INCLUDE IDENTIFIER:

```
#define INCL_WINWORKPLACE
```

FUNCTION PROTOTYPE:

```
ULONG wpAddSetPriorityPage(WPSpool *somSelf,
                           HWND hwndNotebook);
```

PARAMETERS:

somSelf   - Pointer to the object on which the
                 method is invoked
hwndNotebook   - Settings notebook handle

RETURNS:

0   - Error occurred
PageId   - Identifier for the inserted page

METHOD USAGE:

This method must be called only from within an override of wpAddSettingsPages.

METHOD OVERRIDE:

This method can be overridden to replace or remove the *Set Priority* page from the object's Settings notebook.

RELATED METHODS:

wpAddSettingsPages   Page 139
wpInsertSettingsPage   Page 219

wpAddSettingsPages

This instance method adds all of its settings pages to the Settings notebook of an object.

INCLUDE IDENTIFIER:

```
#define INCL_WINWORKPLACE
```

FUNCTION PROTOTYPE:

```
BOOL wpAddSettingsPages(WPObject *somSelf,
                        HWND hwndNotebook);
```

PARAMETERS:

```
somSelf        - Pointer to the object on which the
                 method is invoked
hwndNotebook   - Settings notebook handle
```

RETURNS:

```
TRUE   - Successful completion
FALSE  - Error occurred
```

METHOD USAGE:

```
This method usually is called only by the system.
```

METHOD OVERRIDE:

```
This method should be overridden to add or remove pages
from the Settings notebook. To add a page, you must call
wpInsertSettingsPage. To remove a page, the method that
adds the page should be overridden and return SET-
TINGS_PAGE_REMOVED without calling its parent method.
Usually, the parent method should be called first. This
puts pages added by this method at the top of the
Settings notebook, above the pages added by ancestor
classes. Calling the parent last puts pages added by
this method at the bottom of the Settings notebook, below
the pages added by ancestor classes.
```

RELATED METHODS:

```
wpInsertSettingsPage            Page 219
```

wpAddSoundWarningBeepPage

This instance method adds the *Warning Beep* page to the Settings notebook of an object.

INCLUDE IDENTIFIER:

```
#define INCL_WINWORKPLACE
```

FUNCTION PROTOTYPE:

```
ULONG wpAddSoundWarningBeepPage(WPSound *somSelf,
                                HWND hwndNotebook);
```

PARAMETERS:

somSelf   – Pointer to the object on which the
                  method is invoked
hwndNotebook   – Settings notebook handle

RETURNS:

0   – Error occurred
PageId   – Identifier for inserted page

METHOD USAGE:

This method must be called only from within an override of wpAddSettingsPages.

METHOD OVERRIDE:

This method should be overridden to replace or remove the *Warning Beep* page from the object's Settings notebook. To remove the page, the override method should return SETTINGS_PAGE_REMOVED without calling the parent method. To replace the page with another page, the override method should call wpInsertSettingsPage without calling the parent method.

RELATED METHODS:

wpAddSettingsPages   Page 139
wpInsertSettingsPage   Page 219

wpAddSysFdrDefViewPage

This instance method adds the *Default Folder View* page to the Settings notebook of an object.

INCLUDE IDENTIFIER:

```
#define INCL_WINWORKPLACE
```

FUNCTION PROTOTYPE:

```
ULONG wpAddSysFdrDefViewPage(WPSystem *somSelf,
                            HWND hwndNotebook);
```

PARAMETERS:

```
somSelf        - Pointer to the object on which the
                 method is invoked
hwndNotebook   - Handle to Settings notebook
```

RETURNS:

A return value of 0 indicates that the *Default Folder View* page was not added to the Settings notebook.

METHOD USAGE:

This method can be called at any time.

METHOD OVERRIDE:

this method should always be overridden to replace or remove the *Default Folder View* page from an object that is a descendant of WPSystem. An override of this method does not call the parent.

RELATED METHODS:

wpAddSysFdrSelfClosePage

This instance method adds the *Folder Automatic Close* page to the Settings notebook of an object.

INCLUDE IDENTIFIER:

```
#define INCL_WINWORKPLACE
```

FUNCTION PROTOTYPE:

```
ULONG wpAddSysFdrSelfClosePage(WPSystem *somSelf,
                               HWND hwndNotebook);
```

PARAMETERS:

```
somSelf       - Pointer to the object on which the
                method is invoked
hwndNotebook  - Handle to Settings notebook
```

RETURNS:

A return value of 0 indicates that the *Folder Automatic Close* page was not added to the Settings notebook.

METHOD USAGE:

This method can be called at any time.

METHOD OVERRIDE:

This method should always be overridden to replace or remove the *Folder Automatic Close* page from an object that is a descendant of WPSystem. An override of this method does not call the parent.

RELATED METHODS:

```
wpAddSettingsPages          Page 139
wpInsertSettingsPage        Page 219
```

wpAddSystemConfirmationPage

This instance method adds the *Confirmation* page to the Settings notebook of an object.

INCLUDE IDENTIFIER:

```
#define INCL_WINWORKPLACE
```

FUNCTION PROTOTYPE:

```
ULONG wpAddSystemConfirmationPage(WPSystem *somSelf,
                                  HWND hwndNotebook);
```

PARAMETERS:

somSelf   - Pointer to the object on which the
                   method is invoked
hwndNotebook   - Settings notebook handle

RETURNS:

0   - Error occurred
PageId   - Identifier for inserted page

METHOD USAGE:

This method must be called only from within an override of wpAddSettingsPages.

METHOD OVERRIDE:

This method should be overridden to replace or remove the *Confirmation* page from the object's Settings notebook. To remove the page, the override method should return SETTINGS_PAGE_REMOVED without calling the parent method. To replace the page with another page, the override method should call wpInsertSettingsPage without calling the parent method.

RELATED METHODS:

wpAddSettingsPages   Page 139
wpInsertSettingsPage   Page 219

wpAddSystemInputPage

This instance method adds the *Input* page to the Settings notebook of an object.

INCLUDE IDENTIFIER:

```
#define INCL_WINWORKPLACE
```

FUNCTION PROTOTYPE:

```
ULONG wpAddSystemInputPage(WPSystem *somSelf,
                           HWND hwndNotebook);
```

PARAMETERS:

```
somSelf        - Pointer to the object on which the
                 method is invoked
hwndNotebook   - Handle to Settings notebook
```

RETURNS:

```
A return value of 0 indicates that the Input page was
not added to the Settings notebook.
```

METHOD USAGE:

```
This method can be called at any time.
```

METHOD OVERRIDE:

```
This method should always be overridden to replace or
remove the Input page from an object that is a descendant
of WPSystem. An override of this method does not call
the parent.
```

RELATED METHODS:

```
wpAddSettingsPages          Page 139
wpInsertSettingsPage        Page 219
```

wpAddSystemLogoPage

This instance method adds the *Logo* page to the Settings notebook of an object.

INCLUDE IDENTIFIER:

```
#define INCL_WINWORKPLACE
```

FUNCTION PROTOTYPE:

```
ULONG wpAddSystemLogoPage(WPSystem *somSelf,
                          HWND hwndNotebook);
```

PARAMETERS:

somSelf   - Pointer to the object on which the
                 method is invoked
hwndNotebook   - Settings notebook handle

RETURNS:

0   - Error occurred
PageId   - Identifier for inserted page

METHOD USAGE:

This method must be called only from within an override of wpAddSettingsPages.

METHOD OVERRIDE:

This method should be overridden to replace or remove the *Logo* page from the object's Settings notebook. To remove the page, the override method should return SETTINGS_PAGE_REMOVED without calling the parent method. To replace the page with another page, the override method should call wpInsertSettingsPage without calling the parent method.

RELATED METHODS:

wpAddSettingsPages   Page 139
wpInsertSettingsPage   Page 219

wpAddSystemPrintScreenPage

This instance method adds the *Print Screen* page to the Settings notebook of an object.

INCLUDE IDENTIFIER:

```
#define INCL_WINWORKPLACE
```

FUNCTION PROTOTYPE:

```
ULONG wpAddSystemPrintScreenPage(WPSystem *somSelf,
                                 HWND hwndNotebook);
```

PARAMETERS:

```
somSelf        - Pointer to the object on which the
                 method is invoked
hwndNotebook   - Settings notebook handle
```

RETURNS:

```
0        - Error occurred
PageId   - Identifier for inserted page
```

METHOD USAGE:

```
This method must be called only from within an override
of wpAddSettingsPages.
```

METHOD OVERRIDE:

```
This method should be overridden to replace or remove
the  Print  Screen  page  from  the  object's  Settings
notebook. To remove the page, the override method should
return SETTINGS_PAGE_REMOVED without calling the parent
method.  To  replace  the  page  with  another  page,  the
override method should call wpInsertSettingsPage with-
out calling the parent method.
```

RELATED METHODS:

wpAddSystemScreenPage

This instance method adds the *Screen* page to the Settings notebook of an object.

INCLUDE IDENTIFIER:

```
#define INCL_WINWORKPLACE
```

FUNCTION PROTOTYPE:

```
ULONG wpAddSystemScreenPage(WPSystem *somSelf,
                            HWND hwndNotebook);
```

PARAMETERS:

```
somSelf        - Pointer to the object on which the
                 method is invoked
hwndNotebook   - Window handle to Settings notebook
```

RETURNS:

```
A return value of 0 indicates that the Screen page was
not added to the Settings notebook.
```

METHOD OVERRIDE:

```
This method should always be overridden to replace or
remove the Screen page from an object that is a
descendant of WPSystem. An override of this method does
not call the parent.
```

RELATED METHODS:

```
wpAddSettingsPages              Page 139
wpInsertSettingsPage            Page 219
```

wpAddSystemWindowPage

This instance method adds the *Window* page to the Settings notebook of an object.

INCLUDE IDENTIFIER:

```
#define INCL_WINWORKPLACE
```

FUNCTION PROTOTYPE:

```
ULONG wpAddSystemWindowPage(WPSystem *somSelf,
                            HWND hwndNotebook);
```

PARAMETERS:

```
somSelf       - Pointer to the object on which the
                method is invoked
hwndNotebook  - Settings notebook handle
```

RETURNS:

```
0         - Error occurred
PageId    - Identifier for inserted page
```

METHOD USAGE:

```
This method must be called only from within an override
of wpAddSettingsPages.
```

METHOD OVERRIDE:

```
This method should be overridden to replace or remove
the Window page from the object's Settings notebook. To
remove the page, the override method should return
SETTINGS_PAGE_REMOVED without calling the parent
method. To replace the page with another page, the
override method should call wpInsertSettingsPage with-
out calling the parent method.
```

RELATED METHODS:

```
wpAddSettingsPages        Page 139
wpInsertSettingsPage      Page 219
```

wpAddTitleConfirmationPage

This instance method adds the *Title Confirmation* page to the Settings notebook of an object.

INCLUDE IDENTIFIER:

```
#define INCL_WINWORKPLACE
```

FUNCTION PROTOTYPE:

```
ULONG wpAddTitleConfirmationPage(WPSystem *somSelf,
                                 HWND hwndNotebook);
```

PARAMETERS:

```
somSelf        - Pointer to the object on which the
                 method is invoked
hwndNotebook   - Window handle for Settings notebook
```

RETURNS:

```
A return value of 0 indicates that the Title Confirmation
page was not added to the Settings notebook.
```

METHOD OVERRIDE:

```
This method should always be overridden to replace or
remove the Title Confirmation page form an object that
is a descendant of WPSystem. An override of this method
does not call the parent.
```

RELATED METHODS:

```
wpAddSettingsPages             Page 139
wpInsertSettingsPage           Page 219
```

wpAddToContent

This instance method adds an object to a folder's *content lis*t.

INCLUDE IDENTIFIER:

```
#define INCL_WINWORKPLACE
```

FUNCTION PROTOTYPE:

```
BOOL wpAddToContent(WPFolder *somSelf,
                    WPObject *Object);
```

PARAMETERS:

```
somSelf - Pointer to the object on which the method
          is invoked
Object  - Pointer to the object to be added to the
          folder's content list
```

RETURNS:

```
TRUE    - Successful completion
FALSE   - Error occurred
```

METHOD OVERRIDE:

This method should be overridden to intercept the notification of the "added an object to a folder" event for subclasses that define their own folder view. The parent must always be called.

RELATED METHODS:

```
wpDeleteFromContent              Page 180
```

wpAddToObjUseList

This instance method adds an item type to an object's in-use list.

INCLUDE IDENTIFIER:

#define INCL_WINWORKPLACE

FUNCTION PROTOTYPE:

```
BOOL wpAddToObjUseList(WPObject *somSelf,
                       PUSEITEM pUseItem);
```

PARAMETERS:

somSelf - Pointer to the object on which the method
           is invoked
pUseItem - Pointer to a USEITEM structure

RETURNS:

TRUE   - Successful completion
FALSE - Error occurred

REMARKS:

This method adds a specified *use-item* type to an object's
in-use (USEITEM) list. Every workplace object in the
system has an in-use list, which is a linked list of
USEITEM structures that provide the object with important information such as the number of container
(WC_CONTAINER) windows into which it has been inserted,
the number of open views of itself that already exist,
the number of shadows that exist of this object, and how
much memory it has allocated.

The USEITEM structure consists of an item type and a
pointer to the next USEITEM structure; it is immediately
followed by an item type-specific structure.

METHOD USAGE:

The following item types can be added to the use list:

- **USAGE_MEMORY** - This item specifies a block of memory allocated for this object using wpAllocMem.

Items of this type add a MEMORYITEM structure to the end of the USEITEM structure.

- **USAGE_OPENVIEW** - When a view of an object is opened, one of these items is added to the in-use list. If multiple concurrent views are not enabled for this object, USAGE_OPENVIEW items are used to automatically switch to the open view when the user chooses to open the same view again. This behavior is controlled by the application by calling wpOpen or wpSwitchTo.

  This item is also used to update the title-bar text and switch-entry text when the user changes the object title. If this type is specified, the in-use emphasis bit is turned on for all inserted records for this object.

  Items of this type concatenate a VIEWITEM structure to the end of the USEITEM structure.

- **USAGE_RECORD** - For every view (WC_CONTAINER) window that the object is inserted into, there is one of these items on its in-use list. This enables an object to refresh its appearance in all views at the same time. Items of this type add a RECORDITEM structure to the end of the USEITEM structure.

- **USAGE_LINK** - For every shadow of the object that is "awake", there is one of these items on its in-use list.

METHOD OVERRIDE:

This method can be overridden to receive notification of changes in the use of an object.

RELATED METHODS:

wpAllocMem

This instance method allocates memory for use by an object.

INCLUDE IDENTIFIER:

#define INCL_WINWORKPLACE

FUNCTION PROTOTYPE:

```
PBYTE wpAllocMem(WPObject *somSelf, ULONG cbBytes
                 PULONG prc);
```

PARAMETERS:

```
somSelf  - Pointer to the object on which the method
           is invoked.
cbBytes  - Specifies the size of memory required.
prc      - Pointer to error. Values:  NULL, prc
```

RETURNS:

```
NULL   - Not enough memory available
Other  - Pointer to the newly allocated memory
```

REMARKS:

Memory allocated by wpAllocMem should be deallocated
when no longer needed by calling wpFreeMem. Allocated
memory not cleaned up by an object is deallocated
automatically when the object is no longer in use.

METHOD USAGE:

This method can be called at any time to allocate memory
to be used only for this object.

METHOD OVERRIDE:

This method should be overridden if a substitute memory
allocation facility is to be used. Object classes
overriding this method should also override wpFreeMem.

RELATED METHODS:

wpFreeMem   Page 207

wpChangePowerState

This instance method performs the power management state-change requests to the OS/2 Power Management subsystem.

INCLUDE IDENTIFIER:

```
#define INCL_WINWORKPLACE
```

FUNCTION PROTOTYPE:

```
BOOL wpChangePowerState(WPPower *somSelf,
                        ULONG ulParm1,
                        ULONG ulParm2);
```

PARAMETERS:

```
somSelf  - Pointer to the object on which the method
           is invoked
ulParm1  - Contains a complex value composed of the
           following USHORT values:
               SubId - Requested power state id. Value:
                       0006H
               0      - Reserved
ulParm2  - Contains a complex value composed of the
           following USHORT values:
               DevId     - Requested device id. Value:
                           0001H
               PwrState - Power state to which device
                          specified by DevId is set.
                          Values:
                          0001H - Standby
                          0002H - Suspend
```

RETURNS:

```
TRUE   - Successful
FALSE  - Unsuccessful
```

RELATED METHODS:

wpClose

This instance method closes all open views of an object.

INCLUDE IDENTIFIER:

```
#define INCL_WINWORKPLACE
```

FUNCTION PROTOTYPE:

```
BOOL wpClose(WPObject *somSelf);
```

PARAMETERS:

```
somSelf  - Pointer to the object on which the method
           is invoked
```

RETURNS:

```
TRUE   - Successful completion
FALSE  - Error occurred
```

REMARKS:

This method cycles through the object's in-use list that was created by calls to wpAddToObjUseList. All open windows specified by USAGE_OPENVIEW items are sent a WM_CLOSE message. Running executables specified by USAGE_OPENVIEW items will be terminated.

METHOD USAGE:

This method should be called to close all open views of the object and to free all allocated resources.

METHOD OVERRIDE:

If overridden, this method should call the parent last to ensure allocated resources are properly deallocated.

RELATED METHODS:

wpCnrDeleteUseItem

This instance method deletes the USAGE_OPENVIEW of the container associated with the given object's in-use list.

INCLUDE PARAMETERS:

```
#define INCL_WINWORKPLACE
```

FUNCTION PROTOTYPE:

```
BOOL wpCnrDeleteUseItem(WPObject *somSelf,
                        HWND hwndCnr);
```

PARAMETERS:

```
somSelf  - Pointer to the object on which the method
           is invoked
hwndCnr  - Container handle
```

RETURNS:

```
TRUE   - Successful completion
FALSE  - Error occurred
```

RELATED METHODS:

wpCnrInsertObject

This instance method inserts a record into a container-control window.

INCLUDE IDENTIFIER:

#define INCL_WINWORKPLACE

FUNCTION PROTOTYPE:

```
PMINIRECORDCORE wpCnrInsertObject(WPObject *somSelf,
                                  HWND hwndCnr,
                                  PPOINTL pIcon,
                                  PMINIRECORDCORE
                                  pParent,
                                  PRECORDINSERT
                                  pRecInsert);
```

PARAMETERS:

somSelf   - Pointer to the object on which the
              method is invoked.
hwndCnr   - Handle of the container-control window.
pIcon   - Initial icon position in the container-
              control window.
pParent   - Pointer to parent record; specifies the
              record of the immediate parent of the
              record specified by pIcon. pParent
              should be set to NULL if the record has
              no parent or tree view is not supported.
pRecInsert - Record position. Values:
                  NULL
                  Other

RETURNS:

NULL   - Error occurred
Other - Pointer to the inserted record

REMARKS:

This method places an object into a container-control
window (WC_CONTAINER). These container windows can be
created by the application or by the system.

A record inserted by this method is added to the in-use list (see wpAddToObjUseList for more information on an object's in-use list).

METHOD USAGE:

This method is used to give workplace object behavior (such as context menu support) to records inserted directly into a WC_CONTAINER container-control window. To remove the record from the container, a call to wpCnrRemoveObject should be made.

METHOD OVERRIDE:

This method is not usually overridden.

RELATED METHODS:

wpCnrRefreshDetails

This instance method causes all currently visible RECORDCORE structures to be refreshed with the current object details.

INCLUDE IDENTIFIER:

```
#define INCL_WINWORKPLACE
```

FUNCTION PROTOTYPE:

```
VOID wpCnrRefreshDetails(WPObject *somSelf);
```

PARAMETERS:

```
somSelf  - Pointer to the object on which the method
           is invoked
```

RETURNS:

None.

METHOD USAGE:

This method can be called at any time to update current object details.

METHOD OVERRIDE:

This method is generally not overridden.

wpCnrRemoveObject

This instance method removes a record from a container-control window.

INCLUDE IDENTIFIER:

```
#define INCL_WINWORKPLACE
```

FUNCTION PROTOTYPE:

```
BOOL wpCnrRemoveObject(WPObject *somSelf,
                       HWND hwndCnr);
```

PARAMETERS:

```
somSelf  - Pointer to the object on which the method
           is invoked
hwndCnr  - Handle of the container-control
           (WC_CONTAINER) window
```

RETURNS:

```
TRUE   - Successful completion
FALSE  - Error occurred
```

REMARKS:

This method causes the item to be removed from the in-use list.

METHOD USAGE:

This method should be called to remove records inserted by a call to wpCnrInsertObject.

METHOD OVERRIDE:

This method is not usually overridden.

RELATED METHODS:

wpCnrSetEmphasis

This instance method changes an object's visual emphasis.

INCLUDE IDENTIFIER:

```
#define INCL_WINWORKPLACE
```

FUNCTION PROTOTYPE:

```
BOOL wpCnrSetEmphasis(WPObject *somSelf,
                      ULONG ulEmphasisAttr);
```

PARAMETERS:

```
somSelf          - Pointer to the object on which the
                   method is invoked
ulEmphasisAttr   - CRA_* flags
```

RETURNS:

```
TRUE    - Successful completion
FALSE   - Error occurred
```

REMARKS:

```
This method changes all visual references to this object
to show it with the specified emphasis attributes. This
method is called automatically to set and reset
CRA_INUSE emphasis state during the processing of
wpAddToObjUseList and wpDeleteFromObjUseList, respec-
tively. This method is only valid for objects inserted
into a container control using wpCnrInsertObject.
```

METHOD USAGE:

```
This method can be called at any time to set the emphasis
for an object in an open folder. Some restrictions apply
as to which CRA_* flags can be used.
```

METHOD OVERRIDE:

```
This method is not usually overridden.
```

RELATED METHODS:

wpConfirmDelete

This instance method prompts the user to confirm the deletion of an object.

INCLUDE IDENTIFIER:

```
#define INCL_WINWORKPLACE
```

FUNCTION PROTOTYPE:

```
ULONG wpConfirmDelete(WPObject *somSelf,
                      ULONG fConfirmations);
```

PARAMETERS:

```
somSelf         - Points to object where method invoked
fConfirmations - Confirmation flags. Values:
                    CONFIRM_DELETE
                    CONFIRM_DELETEFOLDER
```

RETURNS:

```
OK_DELETE       - Delete of this object is confirmed
NO_DELETE       - Delete of this object is canceled
CANCEL_DELETE   - Deletion from here on is canceled
```

REMARKS:

This method is called during the processing of wpDelete only if the system confirm on delete flag is set.

METHOD USAGE:

This method usually is called only by the system.

METHOD OVERRIDE:

This method should be overridden to remove or replace the user prompt to confirm the delete operation.

RELATED METHODS:

wpDelete	Page 177
wpFree	Page 206

wpConfirmKeepAssoc

This instance method determines whether to rename the given file with different extensions and warns that associations might need to be fixed.

INCLUDE IDENTIFIER:

```
#define INCL_WINWORKPLACE
```

FUNCTION PROTOTYPE:

```
ULONG wpConfirmKeepAssoc(WPFileSystem *somSelf);
```

PARAMETERS:

```
somSelf  - Pointer to the object on which the method
           is invoked
```

RETURNS:

```
KEEP_RENAMEFILESWITHEXT      - File is renamed; any
                               associations are added
                               to the Menu page
DISCARD_RENAMEFILESWITHEXT - File is renamed; old
                               associations are
                               discarded (not added to
                               Menu page)
CANCEL_RENAMEFILESWITHEXT  - File is not renamed;
                               title is not changed
```

METHOD USAGE:

This method can be called only when confirmations are on and the extensions are different. It may be called by any class that wants to handle the prompting or overriding of return values.

RELATED METHODS:

```
wpConfirmRenameFileWithExt      Page 167
wpSetTitleAndRenameFile         Page 471
```

wpConfirmObjectTitle

This instance method displays the Object Title Confirmation dialog.

INCLUDE IDENTIFIER:

```
#define INCL_WINWORKPLACE
```

FUNCTION PROTOTYPE:

```
ULONG wpConfirmObjectTitle(WPObject *somSelf,
                           WPFolder *Folder,
                           WPObject **ppDuplicate,
                           PSZ pszTitle,
                           ULONG cbTitle,
                           ULONG menuId);
```

PARAMETERS:

somSelf	— Pointer to the object on which the method is invoked
Folder	— Pointer to the folder involved in operation
ppDuplicate	— Pointer to address of object with same title in folder
pszTitle	— Initial or returned name
cbTitle	— Length of name's buffer (pszTitle)
menuId	— Id of the operation being performed

RETURNS:

One of the following flags, indicating the action taken when two objects have the same title:

```
NAMECLASH_RENAME
NAMECLASH_APPEND
NAMECLASH_REPLACE
NAMECLASH_NONE
NAMECLASH_RENAME_KEEPASSOC
NAMECLASH_NONE_KEEPASSOC
```

METHOD OVERRIDE:

This method should not be overridden; all return codes and menu ids are reserved values.

wpConfirmRenameFileWithExt

This instance method prompts the user whether to rename this file
with possibly a different extension.

INCLUDE IDENTIFIER:

```
#define INCL_WINWORKPLACE
```

FUNCTION PROTOTYPE:

```
ULONG wpConfirmRenameFileWithExt
                                (WPFileSystem *somSelf);
```

PARAMETERS:

```
somSelf  - Pointer to the object on which the method
           is invoked
```

RETURNS:

```
CANCEL_RENAMEFILESWITHEXT   - File is not renamed;
                              title is not changed
DISCARD_RENAMEFILESWITHEXT - File is renamed; old
                              extension is discarded
KEEP_RENAMEFILESWITHEXT     - File is renamed; old
                              extension is kept
```

REMARKS:

This method is called when confirmations are set for
wpSetTitleAndRenameFile and extensions are different.

METHOD USAGE:

This method can be called any time by a class that wants
to handle the prompting or override the return value.

METHOD OVERRIDE:

This method is generally not overridden.

RELATED METHODS:

wpSetTitleAndRenameFile   Page 471

wpContainsFolders

This instance method determines whether the folder contains any subfolders.

INCLUDE IDENTIFIER:

```
#define INCL_WINWORKPLACE
```

FUNCTION PROTOTYPE:

```
BOOL wpContainsFolders(WPFolder *somSelf,
                       BOOL *pfSubFolders);
```

PARAMETERS:

```
somSelf        - Pointer to the object on which the
                 method is invoked.
pfSubFolders   - Flag indicating whether folder
                 contains subfolders. Values:
                     TRUE
                     FALSE
```

RETURNS:

```
TRUE    - Successful completion
FALSE   - Error occurred
```

METHOD OVERRIDE:

```
This method is generally not overridden.
```

RELATED METHODS:

```
wpclsQueryOpenFolders          Page 541
```

wpCopiedFromTemplate

This instance method allows an object to perform class-specific processing when a new object is created from a template.

INCLUDE IDENTIFIER:

```
#define INCL_WINWORKPLACE
```

FUNCTION PROTOTYPE:

```
VOID wpCopiedFromTemplate(WPObject *somSelf);
```

PARAMETERS:

```
somSelf  - Pointer to the object on which the method
           is invoked
```

RETURNS:

```
The return value is VOID.
```

REMARKS:

This method is called immediately after a new object is created from a template. The system does not do any default processing for this method. wpCopiedFromTemplate is typically overridden to perform class-specific initialization on a created object. For example, a customer-order-form class would prefill the date, time, and order number in an instance of itself that was created from a template.

METHOD USAGE:

This method usually is called only by the system.

METHOD OVERRIDE:

This method should be overridden by object classes that need to initialize the new object after it is created from a template.

wpCopyObject

This instance method creates a new copy of the object.

INCLUDE IDENTIFIER:

```
#define INCL_WINWORKPLACE
```

FUNCTION PROTOTYPE:

```
WPObject *wpCopyObject(WPObject *somSelf,
                       WPFolder *Folder, BOOL fLock);
```

PARAMETERS:

```
somSelf - Pointer to the object on which the method
          is invoked.
Folder  - Pointer to a Folder object in which to place
          this new object; pointer can be determined
          by issuing a call to wpclsQueryFolder.
fLock   - Lock object flag. If FALSE, the newly
          created object is made dormant whenever the
          object and folder containing the object are
          closed. If TRUE, the new object remains
          active until caller issues wpUnlockObject.
```

RETURNS:

```
NULL  - Error occurred
Other - Pointer to the new object created
```

REMARKS:

```
Copies of an object can always be deleted and moved by
default, even if the original has the OBJSTYLE_NODELETE
or OBJSTYLE_NOMOVE style set.
```

METHOD USAGE:

```
This method can be called any time to create a copy of
an existing object.
```

METHOD OVERRIDE:

```
This method can be overridden by classes that need to
keep track of where instances are generated.
```

wpCreateAnother

This instance method creates another object.

INCLUDE IDENTIFIER:

```
#define INCL_WINWORKPLACE
```

FUNCTION PROTOTYPE:

```
WPObject *wpCreateAnother(WPObject *somSelf,
                          PSZ pszTitle,
                          PSZ pszSetupEnv,
                          WPFolder *Folder);
```

PARAMETERS:

```
somSelf      - Pointer to the object on which the
               method is invoked.
pszTitle     - String containing the title of object.
pszSetupEnv  - Environment setup string. This
               parameter is a super-string containing
               parameters to the new object that are
               extracted when wpSetup method is
               called on that object.
Folder       - Pointer to container.
```

RETURNS:

```
Object  - Pointer to the new object
```

REMARKS:

This instance method gives a subclass the opportunity to return an object of its own choosing; for example, WPProgramFile returns an instance of WPProgram.

METHOD OVERRIDE:

This method can be overridden only in a subclass.

RELATED METHODS:

```
wpCreateFromTemplate        Page 172
wpCreateShadowObject        Page 174
```

wpCreateFromTemplate

This instance method creates an object from a template.

INCLUDE IDENTIFIER:

```
#define INCL_WINWORKPLACE
```

FUNCTION PROTOTYPE:

```
WPObject *wpCreateFromTemplate(WPObject *somSelf,
                               WPFolder *Folder,
                               BOOL fLock);
```

PARAMETERS:

```
somSelf - Pointer to the object on which the method
          is invoked.
Folder  - Pointer to a Folder object in which to place
          this new object; pointer can be determined
          by issuing a call to wpclsQueryFolder.
fLock   - Lock object flag. If FALSE, the newly
          created object is made dormant whenever the
          object and folder containing the object are
          closed. If TRUE, the new object remains
          active until caller issues wpUnlockObject.
```

RETURNS:

```
NULL   - Error occurred
Other  - Pointer to the new object
```

REMARKS:

The new object is an identical copy of the template object except that the OBJSTYLE_TEMPLATE object style is taken out. The wpCopiedFromTemplate method is called on the new object.

METHOD USAGE:

This method can be called at any time to create a new object from a template object.

METHOD OVERRIDE:

This method is not usually overridden.

RELATED METHODS:

wpCopyObject   Page 170
wpclsNew   Page 506

wpCreateShadowObject

This instance method creates a shadow of an object.

INCLUDE IDENTIFIER:

```
#define INCL_WINWORKPLACE
```

FUNCTION PROTOTYPE:

```
WPObject *wpCreateShadowObject(WPObject *somSelf,
                              WPFolder *Folder,
                              BOOL fLock);
```

PARAMETERS:

```
somSelf - Pointer to the object on which the method
          is invoked.
Folder  - Pointer to a Folder object in which to place
          this new object; pointer can be determined
          by issuing a call to wpclsQueryFolder.
fLock   - Lock object flag. If FALSE, the newly
          created object is made dormant whenever the
          object and folder containing the object are
          closed. If TRUE, the new object remains
          active until caller issues wpUnlockObject.
```

RETURNS:

```
NULL   - Error occurred
Other  - Pointer to the new shadow object
```

REMARKS:

```
The new object is created as an instance of WPShadow.
```

METHOD USAGE:

```
This method can be called at any time to create a shadow
object for this object.
```

METHOD OVERRIDE:

```
This method is not usually overridden.
```

wpCreateShadowObjectExt

This instance method creates a shadow of an object.

INCLUDE IDENTIFIER:

#define INCL_WINWORKPLACE

FUNCTION PROTOTYPE:

```
WPObject *wpCreateShadowObjectExt(WPObject *somSelf,
                                  WPFolder *Folder,
                                  BOOL fLock,
                                  PSZ pszSetup,
                                  M_WPObject
                                  shadowClass);
```

PARAMETERS:

somSelf
  - Pointer to the object on which the method is invoked.

Folder
  - Pointer to Folder object in which to place new shadow object. This pointer can be determined by issuing a call to wpclsQueryFolder.

fLock
  - Lock object flag. If this flag is FALSE, new shadow object will be made dormant whenever the object and the folder containing the object are closed. If this flag is TRUE, new object will remain awake until caller issues wpUnlockObject on it.

pszSetup
  - Pointer to setup string.

shadowClass
  - Class of new shadow object.

RETURNS:

Object
  - Pointer to new shadow object

NULL
  - Error occurred

REMARKS:

This method is used instead of wpCreateShadowObject when setup string needs to be passed to the new shadow object or when the shadow is to be created as a subclass of a shadow.

METHOD USAGE:

This method can be called at any time in order to create a shadow object for this object.

METHOD OVERRIDE:

This method is generally not overridden.

wpDelete

This instance method deletes an object and prompts for confirmation, if necessary.

INCLUDE IDENTIFIER:

```
#define INCL_WINWORKPLACE
```

FUNCTION PROTOTYPE:

```
ULONG wpDelete(WPObject *somSelf,
               ULONG ulConfirmations);
```

PARAMETERS:

```
somSelf          - Points to object where method invoked
ulConfirmations- Confirmation flags. Values:  NULL
                     CONFIRM_DELETE
                     CONFIRM_DELETEFOLDER
```

RETURNS:

```
NO_DELETE        - Error occurred
CANCEL_DELETE    - User canceled operation
OK_DELETE        - No confirmations
```

RETURNS:

The confirmation flags are passed to wpConfirmDelete. If it returns OK_DELETE, wpFree is called on the object.

METHOD USAGE:

This method can be called any time to delete an object.

METHOD OVERRIDE:

This method is not usually overridden.

RELATED METHODS:

```
wpConfirmDelete                 Page 164
wpFree                          Page 206
wpQueryConfirmations            Page 280
```

wpDeleteAllJobs

This instance method deletes all jobs in a printer object.

INCLUDE IDENTIFIER:

```
#define INCL_WINWORKPLACE
```

FUNCTION PROTOTYPE:

```
BOOL wpDeleteAllJobs(WPPrinter *somSelf);
```

PARAMETERS:

```
somSelf  - Pointer to the object to delete all jobs
```

RETURNS:

```
TRUE   - Successful completion
FALSE  - Error occurred
```

METHOD OVERRIDE:

```
This method is not usually overridden.
```

RELATED METHODS:

```
wpDeleteJob                    Page 183
```

wpDeleteContents

This instance method deletes the contents of a folder.

INCLUDE IDENTIFIER:

```
#define INCL_WINWORKPLACE
```

FUNCTION PROTOTYPE:

```
ULONG wpDeleteContents(WPFolder *somSelf,
                       ULONG ulConfirmations);
```

PARAMETERS:

```
somSelf           - Pointer to the object on which the
                    method is invoked.
ulConfirmations   - Confirmation flags. Values:
                      CONFIRM_DELETE
                      CONFIRM_DELETEFOLDER
                      NULL
```

RETURNS:

```
OK_DELETE       - All objects were deleted
NO_DELETE       - Error occurred
CANCEL_DELETE   - User canceled operation
```

REMARKS:

The wpDelete and wpFree methods automatically call this
instance method for folder objects.

METHOD USAGE:

This method can be called any time to delete the contents
of a folder.

METHOD OVERRIDE:

This method is not usually overridden.

RELATED METHODS:

wpDelete   Page 177
wpFree   Page 206

wpDeleteFromContent

This instance method removes an object from a folder's content list.

INCLUDE IDENTIFIER:

```
#define INCL_WINWORKPLACE
```

FUNCTION PROTOTYPE:

```
BOOL wpDeleteFromContent(WPFolder *somSelf,
                         WPObject *Object);
```

PARAMETERS:

```
somSelf - Pointer to the object on which the method
          is invoked
Object  - Pointer to the object to be deleted from
          folder's content list
```

RETURNS:

```
TRUE    - Successful completion
FALSE   - Error occurred
```

METHOD OVERRIDE:

This method should be overridden to intercept the notification of the "removed an object from a folder" event for subclasses that define their own folder views. The parent method must always be called.

RELATED METHODS:

wpAddToContent   Page 150

wpDeleteFromObjUseList

This instance method removes an item type from an object's in-use list.

INCLUDE IDENTIFIER:

#define INCL_WINWORKPLACE

FUNCTION PROTOTYPE:

```
BOOL wpDeleteFromObjUseList(WPObject *somSelf,
                           PUSEITEM pUseItem);
```

PARAMETERS:

somSelf   - Pointer to the object on which the method
            is invoked
pUseItem - Pointer to a USEITEM

RETURNS:

TRUE   - Successful completion
FALSE   - Error occurred

REMARKS:

This method removes a specified item type from an
object's in-use list. If the item being removed is of
type USAGE_OPENVIEW, the in-use emphasis bit is turned
off for all inserted records for this object.

METHOD USAGE:

wpDeleteFromObjUseList should be called when a particular usage item, added to the in-use list with wpAddToObjUseList, is no longer needed.

This method must be called before the USEITEM memory is
freed.

METHOD OVERRIDE:

This method is not usually overridden.

RELATED METHODS:

wpDeleteJob

This instance method deletes a job object.

INCLUDE IDENTIFIER:

```
#define INCL_WINWORKPLACE
```

FUNCTION PROTOTYPE:

```
BOOL wpDeleteJob(WPJob *somSelf);
```

PARAMETERS:

```
somSelf  - Pointer to the object to be deleted
```

RETURNS:

```
TRUE    - Successful completion
FALSE   - Error occurred
```

METHOD OVERRIDE:

```
This method is not usually overridden.
```

RELATED METHODS:

```
wpDeleteAllJobs                 Page 178
```

wpDisplayHelp

This instance method allows the object to display a help panel.

INCLUDE IDENTIFIER:

```
#define INCL_WINWORKPLACE
```

FUNCTION PROTOTYPE:

```
BOOL wpDisplayHelp(WPObject *somSelf,
                   ULONG ulHelpPanelId,
                   PSZ pszHelpLibrary);
```

PARAMETERS:

somSelf	– Pointer to the object on which the method is invoked
ulHelpPanelId	– Object's help panel id
pszHelpLibrary	– Pointer to a zero-terminated string that contains help library name

RETURNS:

TRUE	– Successful completion
FALSE	– Error occurred

REMARKS:

This method allows each object class to display a help panel in response to a user's request for help.

METHOD USAGE:

This method can be called at any time to display help.

METHOD OVERRIDE:

This method is not usually overridden.

RELATED METHODS:

wpMenuItemHelpSelected	Page 232
wpQueryDefaultHelp	Page 286
wpSetDefaultHelp	Page 416
wpclsQueryDefaultHelp	Page 513

wpDisplayMenu

This instance method creates and displays the pop-up menu of an object.

INCLUDE IDENTIFIER:

```
#define INCL_WINWORKPLACE
```

FUNCTION PROTOTYPE:

```
HWND wpDisplayMenu(WPObject *somSelf, HWND hwndOwner,
                   HWND hwndClient,
                   POINTL *ptlPopupPt,
                   ULONG ulMenuType,
                   ULONG ulReserved);
```

PARAMETERS:

somSelf   - Pointer to the object on which the
method is invoked.

hwndOwner   - Handle of window that menu is owned
by. Required and must be NULL.

hwndClient   - Handle of window on which menu is
displayed. Must be owned by *hwndOwner*.
If *hwndClient* is supplied, it is given
focus before displaying the menu.
If hwndClient is not supplied,
hwndOwner is given focus before
displaying menu.

ptlPopupPt   - Coordinates of starting position for
menu. For MENU_OBJECTPOPUP requests
where *hwndOwner* is the icon or tree
view of the container that contains the
object, this parameter is ignored and
the menu is displayed at lower-right
corner of object's icon. This parameter
is also ignored for MENU_TITLEBARPULL-
DOWNxxx requests.

ulMenuType   - Type of menu to display. Values:
     MENU_OBJECTPOPUP
     MENU_OPENVIEWPOPUP
     MENU_TITLEBARPULLDOWN

ulReserved   - Reserved value

RETURNS:

Return value of NULLHANDLE indicates that either an invalid *ulMenuType* or an invalid *hwndClient* or *hwndOwner* was given.

METHOD USAGE:

This method can be called at any time.

METHOD OVERRIDE:

This method should not be overridden.

RELATED METHODS:

wpDoesObjectMatch

This instance method allows the object to determine if it matches
the specified criteria.

INCLUDE IDENTIFIER:

```
#define INCL_WINWORKPLACE
```

FUNCTION PROTOTYPE:

```
BOOL wpDoesObjectMatch(WPObject *Object,
                       PVOID pExtendedCriteria);
```

PARAMETERS:

Object	- Pointer to the object to be examined
pExtendedCriteria	- Pointer to a buffer that contains the class-specific extended-search criteria

RETURNS:

TRUE	- Object matches the specified criteria
FALSE	- Object does not match the specified criteria

REMARKS:

If the object class has extended search criteria, this
method gets called to determine if the object found
matches the extended-search criteria.

METHOD USAGE:

This method can be called at any time to determine if
an object matches some extended-search criteria.

METHOD OVERRIDE:

This method should be overridden by classes that
introduce extended-search criteria for use by the Find
and Include facilities.

wpDragCell

This instance method is called to drag-apply a value in a cell.

INCLUDE IDENTIFIER:

```
#define INCL_WINWORKPLACE
```

FUNCTION PROTOTYPE:

```
BOOL wpDragCell(WPPalette *somSelf, PCELL pCell,
                HWND hwndPal, POINTL ptlDrag);
```

PARAMETERS:

```
somSelf   - Pointer to the object on which the method
            is invoked
pCell     - Pointer to CELL structure to be dragged
hwndPal   - Palette window handle
ptlDrag   - Pointer in hwndPal coordinates from which
            drag was initiated
```

RETURNS:

```
TRUE    - Successful completion
FALSE   - Error occurred
```

REMARKS:

The default processing for this method by WPPalette is to return FALSE.

METHOD USAGE:

This method is usually called only by the palette window after it receives the WM_BEGINDRAG message.

METHOD OVERRIDE:

This method should be overridden to handle the drag-apply action. Override processing should include capturing the mouse and waiting for and processing the WM_ENDDRAG message.

wpDraggedOverObject

This instance method can be called on an object that is currently being dragged with the mouse to tell it what the current target object is. The return code from this method lets the system know whether the object being dragged can be dropped on the specified target.

INCLUDE IDENTIFIER:

```
#define INCL_WINWORKPLACE
```

FUNCTION PROTOTYPE:

```
MRESULT wpDraggedOverObject(WPObject *somSelf,
                            WPObject *
                            DraggedOverObject);
```

PARAMETERS:

somSelf	- Pointer to an object being dragged
DraggedOverObject	- Pointer to the object that the drag cursor is over; the current target object for the drag operation

RETURNS:

Low WORD	- *DropIndicator*; a DOR_* constant, such as DOR_DROP or DOR_NODROP, that indicates if a drop is allowed on current target.
High WORD	- *DropOperation*; current drag operation code. For example, DO_COPY, DO_MOVE, or DO_LINK indicate that the drag action over this target should be a copy, move or link.

REMARKS:

When a target object is dragged by the mouse, it always receives a wpDragOver call. Many target objects choose to decide the current drag operation and whether a drop is possible based upon their own rules. For instance, the WPShredder object returns DO_DROP and DO_MOVE if it decides that all the source objects can be deleted. However, some targets require the source or sources to participate in the decision over whether they can accept the drop. The way that a target allows a source object to have a say in what the drop action will be by calling wpDraggedOverObject on each source object.

This method may be invoked on an object that is being dragged (source object) at any time to see if it can support a drop on the current target. If the object being dragged responds favorably to this method, it may later receive a wpDroppedOnObject call so that it can process the drop action.

METHOD USAGE:

This method is typically called by objects that require participation from the source object when a drop occurs. It can be called at any time; however, it would normally only be called by a target object on one of the source objects during a drag or drop operation.

METHOD OVERRIDE:

Override this method if your object class wishes to allow itself to be used as a source object that can perform a drop operation. A favorable return code from this method may lead to wpDroppedOnObject being invoked on the source object that would be overridden to actually do the drop operation.

RELATED METHODS:

wpDragOver

This instance method informs an object that other objects are being dragged over it.

INCLUDE IDENTIFIER:

```
#define INCL_WINWORKPLACE
```

FUNCTION PROTOTYPE:

```
MRESULT wpDragOver(WPObject *somSelf, HWND hwndCnr,
                   PDRAGINFO pDragInfo);
```

PARAMETERS:

```
somSelf     - Pointer to the object on which the
              method is invoked
hwndCnr     - Handle to the container-control window
pDragInfo   - Pointer to drag information
```

RETURNS:

Refer to the DM_DRAGOVER message in Volume 2 for a description of the return value.

REMARKS:

This method is sent for each DM_DRAGOVER message received by the object.

METHOD USAGE:

This method usually is called only by the system as the folder containing the object processes DM_DRAGOVER.

METHOD OVERRIDE:

This method should be overridden to determine if the objects being dragged can be dropped on this object.

RELATED METHODS:

wpDrop   Page 192
wpFormatDragItem   Page 205

wpDrop

This instance method informs an object that another object has been dropped on it.

INCLUDE IDENTIFIER:

```
#define INCL_WINWORKPLACE
```

FUNCTION PROTOTYPE:

```
MRESULT wpDrop(WPObject *somSelf, HWND hwndCnr,
               PDRAGINFO pDragInfo,
               PDRAGITEM pDragItem);
```

PARAMETERS:

```
somSelf     - Pointer to the object on which the
              method is invoked
hwndCnr     - Handle to the container-control window
pDragInfo   - Pointer to a PDRAGINFO structure
pDragItem   - Pointer to a PDRAGITEM structure
```

RETURNS:

```
RC_DROP_DROPCOMPLETE    - Objects dropped successfully
RC_DROP_ERROR           - Error occurred
RC_DROP_ITEMCOMPLETE    - One item dropped successfully
RC_DROP_RENDERING       - Rendering of source object has
                          been requested by object
                          being dropped
```

REMARKS:

This method is called when a DM_DROP message is received.

METHOD USAGE:

This method usually is called only by the system as a folder containing the object processed by DM_DROP.

METHOD OVERRIDE:

This method should be overridden to process the action of the dragged object or objects being dropped on it.

RELATED METHODS:

wpDragOver   Page 191
wpFormatDragItem   Page 205

wpDroppedOnObject

This instance method is called on an object that has just been dragged (a source object) when the target object that it was dropped on does not know what action to perform.

This method is called only on a source object when that source object has previously responded favorably to a wpDraggedOverObject call.

INCLUDE IDENTIFIER:

```
#define INCL_WINWORKPLACE
```

FUNCTION PROTOTYPE:

```
BOOL wpDroppedOnObject(WPObject *somSelf,
                       WPObject *DroppedOnObject);
```

PARAMETERS:

```
somSelf          - Pointer to an object being dragged.
DroppedOnObject  - Pointer to the object that was
                   dropped on. The current target
                   object for the drag operation.
```

RETURNS:

```
TRUE   - Successful
FALSE  - Error occurred
```

REMARKS:

```
When you drop on a target object and the source object
indicates that it knows how to handle the drop operation,
this method is invoked on the source object. For example,
the program object class supports being dropped on
certain other classes of object where the drop action
is taken by the program itself. The drop action provided
in WPProgram's override of wpDroppedOnObject would be
to execute itself as a viewer of the target object. This
method is called as a result of sending a DM_DROP
message.
```

METHOD USAGE:

Target objects that do not know how to handle the current drop operation can call this method on the source object that was dropped on it. This method would not normally be called outside the scope of a drag or drop operation.

METHOD OVERRIDE:

Object classes that override wpDraggedOverObject would normally be expected to also override this method.

RELATED METHODS:

wpEditCell

This instance method edits a value in a cell.

INCLUDE IDENTIFIER:

```
#define INCL_WINWORKPLACE
```

FUNCTION PROTOTYPE:

```
BOOL wpEditCell(WPPalette *somSelf, PCELL pCell,
                HWND hwndPal);
```

PARAMETERS:

```
somSelf  - Pointer to the object on which the method
           is invoked
pCell    - Pointer to the CELL structure to be edited
hwndPal  - Palette-window handle
```

RETURNS:

```
TRUE   - Successful completion
FALSE  - Error occurred
```

REMARKS:

The default processing for this method by WPPalette is to return FALSE.

METHOD USAGE:

This method usually is called only by the palette window when the user requests to edit the value in the cell. This request is made by selecting a cell and pressing the **Enter** key or **Edit** push button, or by double-clicking on the cell.

METHOD OVERRIDE:

This method should be overridden to handle the edit action.

wpEjectDisk

This instance method ejects media from drives that support software eject of removable media.

INCLUDE IDENTIFIER:

```
#define INCL_WINWORKPLACE
```

FUNCTION PROTOTYPE:

```
ULONG wpEjectDisk(WPDisk *somSelf);
```

PARAMETERS:

```
somSelf - Pointer to the object on which the method
          is invoked
```

RETURNS:

```
 0  - Successful
>0  - Return code from DosDevIoctl Category 8
      Function 40
```

METHOD USAGE:

```
This method can be called at any time.
```

METHOD OVERRIDE:

```
This method should not be overridden.
```

RELATED METHODS:

wpEndConversation

This instance method notifies the object that the drag or drop operation is complete.

INCLUDE IDENTIFIER:

```
#define INCL_WINWORKPLACE
```

FUNCTION PROTOTYPE:

```
MRESULT wpEndConversation(WPObject *somSelf,
                          ULONG ulItemId,
                          ULONG ulResult);
```

PARAMETERS:

```
somSelf    - Pointer to the object on which the method
             is invoked
ulItemId   - ulItemId from the DRAGITEM contained in
             DRAGINFO structure when object was dropped
ulResult   - Flag indicating whether the operation was
             performed successfully
```

RETURNS:

Refer to the DM_ENDCONVERSATION message in Volume 2 for a description of the return value.

METHOD USAGE:

This method usually is called as the folder containing the object is processed by DM_ENDCONVERSATION.

METHOD OVERRIDE:

This method should be overridden if the object must do any actions once the drag or drop operation is complete.

RELATED METHODS:

```
wpDragOver                      Page 191
wpDrop                          Page 192
wpFormatDragItem                Page 205
wpRender                        Page 366
wpRenderComplete                Page 367
```

wpFilterPopupMenu

This instance method modifies the context menu of an object.

INCLUDE IDENTIFIER:

```
#define INCL_WINWORKPLACE
```

FUNCTION PROTOTYPE:

```
ULONG wpFilterPopupMenu(WPObject *somSelf,
                        ULONG ulFlags, HWND hwndCnr,
                        BOOL fMultiSelect);
```

PARAMETERS:

somSelf   - Pointer to the object on which the
               method is invoked.
ulFlags   - If set, the corresponding pop-up menu
               is available. These flags are ORed
               together with flags already defined by
               ancestor classes to specify standard
               pop-up menu items that apply to this
               object. Values:
                 CTXT_ARRANGE
                 CTXT_CLOSE
                 CTXT_COPY
                 CTXT_DELETE
                 CTXT_DETAILS
                 CTXT_FIND
                 CTXT_HELP
                 CTXT_ICON
                 CTXT_LINK
                 CTXT_LOCKUP
                 CTXT_MOVE
                 CTXT_NEW
                 CTXT_OPEN
                 CTXT_PALETTE
                 CTXT_PRINT
                 CTXT_PROGRAM
                 CTXT_REFRESH
                 CTXT_SELECT
                 CTXT_SETTINGS
                 CTXT_SHUTDOWN
                 CTXT_SWITCHTO
                 CTXT_TREE
                 CTXT_WINDOW

```
hwndCnr        - Handle to container control window.
fMultiSelect   - Multiple menu items flag.
```

RETURNS:

New pop-up menu flags for this object.

METHOD USAGE:

This method usually is called only by the system when a
request is made to display the object's pop-up window.

METHOD OVERRIDE:

This method should be overridden to remove undesired
pop-up menu actions that were added by ancestor classes.
The parent method should be called prior to any override
processing.

RELATED METHODS:

wpInsertPopupMenuItems	Page 216
wpMenuItemHelpSelected	Page 232
wpMenuItemSelected	Page 235
wpModifyPopupMenu	Page 240

wpFindUseItem

This instance method retrieves an use item from the object's in-use list.

INCLUDE IDENTIFIER:

#define INCL_WINWORKPLACE

FUNCTION PROTOTYPE:

```
PUSEITEM wpFindUseItem(WPObject *somSelf,
                       ULONG ulType,
                       PUSEITEM pCurrentUseItem);
```

PARAMETERS:

```
somSelf           - Pointer to the object on which the
                    method is invoked.
ulType            - Specifies usage type of the item
                    to be located. Values:
                        USAGE_ANY
                        USAGE_LINK
                        USAGE_MEMORY
                        USAGE_OPENVIEW
                        USAGE_RECORD
pCurrentUseItem   - Pointer to a USEITEM structure.
                    Values:
                        NULL
                        Other
```

RETURNS:

```
NULL    - No items matching the specified find
          criteria were found in the in-use list for
          this object
Other   - Pointer to a USEITEM structure that matches
          the specified find criteria
```

REMARKS:

This method searches the object's in-use list for all items that were added by previous calls to wpAddToObjUseList.

METHOD USAGE:

This method should be called to determine how the object is currently being used, for example, which views are currently open and what container window it is inserted into.

METHOD OVERRIDE:

This method is not usually overridden.

RELATED METHODS:

wpAddToObjUseList	Page 151
wpDeleteFromObjUseList	Page 181

wpFindMinWindow

This instance method returns the minimized window object that corresponds to the given frame window handle.

INCLUDE IDENTIFIER:

```
#define INCL_WINWORKPLACE
```

FUNCTION PROTOTYPE:

```
WPObject *wpFindMinWindow(WPMinWinViewer *somSelf,
                          HWND hwndFrame);
```

PARAMETERS:

```
somSelf     - Pointer to the object on which the
              method is invoked
hwndFrame   - Frame window handle
```

RETURNS:

```
Object   - Pointer to the object representing the
           minimized window
NULL     - No object exists
```

METHOD OVERRIDE:

This method usually is not overridden.

RELATED METHODS:

wpQueryMinWindow   Page 327
wpSetMinWindow   Page 445

wpFindViewItem

This instance method locates either the first or next occurrence of one of the specified views in the in-use list.

INCLUDE IDENTIFIER:

```
#define INCL_WINWORKPLACE
```

FUNCTION PROTOTYPE:

```
PVIEWITEM wpFindViewItem(WPObject *somSelf,
                         ULONG flViews,
                         PUSEITEM pCurrentItem);
```

PARAMETERS:

```
somSelf        - Pointer to the object on which the
                 method is invoked.
flViews        - Flag indicating views to search for.
pCurrentItem   - Pointer to previous view item in
                 in-use list. Value of NULL indicates
                 that current view item is first item
                 in list.
```

RETURNS:

```
Pointer to the view item that was found.
```

METHOD USAGE:

```
This method can be called at any time to find either the
first or next view item.
```

METHOD OVERRIDE:

```
This method usually is not overridden.
```

wpFormatDragItem

This instance method formats the drag information of an object when the user starts to drag it.

INCLUDE IDENTIFIER:

```
#define INCL_WINWORKPLACE
```

FUNCTION PROTOTYPE:

```
BOOL wpFormatDragItem(WPObject *somSelf,
                      PDRAGITEM pDragItem);
```

PARAMETERS:

```
somSelf    - Pointer to the object on which the
             method is invoked
pDragItem  - Address of the drag item
```

RETURNS:

```
TRUE   - Successful completion
FALSE  - Error occurred
```

REMARKS:

This method enables the direct manipulation of this object by initializing the DRAGITEM structure.

METHOD USAGE:

This method usually is called only by the system when the user first starts to drag the object.

METHOD OVERRIDE:

This method is usually overridden by classes that require special processing to initiate a drag or drop operation.

RELATED METHODS:

wpDragOver	Page 191
wpDrop	Page 192

wpFree

This instance method destroys the object and deallocates its associated resources.

INCLUDE IDENTIFIER:

```
#define INCL_WINWORKPLACE
```

FUNCTION PROTOTYPE:

```
BOOL wpFree(WPObject *somSelf);
```

PARAMETERS:

```
somSelf  - Pointer to the object on which the method
           is invoked
```

RETURNS:

```
TRUE   - Successful completion
FALSE  - Error occurred
```

REMARKS:

This method destroys the persistent form of the object and then frees the memory that represented that object. If confirmations are on, wpDelete prompts the user before calling wpFree.

METHOD USAGE:

Destruction of an object should be done with wpDelete. This method usually is called only by the system.

METHOD OVERRIDE:

This method is usually overridden by storage classes that permanently remove this object and its associated data or by any objects that need to do special processing before deletion.

RELATED METHODS:

wpFreeMem

This instance method deallocates memory allocated by a call to wpAllocMem.

INCLUDE IDENTIFIER:

```
#define INCL_WINWORKPLACE
```

FUNCTION PROTOTYPE:

```
BOOL wpFreeMem(WPObject *somSelf, PBYTE pbMemory);
```

PARAMETERS:

```
somSelf    - Pointer to the object on which the method
             is invoked
pbMemory   - Pointer to the memory to be deallocated
```

RETURNS:

```
TRUE    - Successful completion
FALSE   - Error occurred
```

REMARKS:

This method deallocates memory for an object. wpFreeMem should always be called when the memory allocated by wpAllocMem is no longer needed.

METHOD USAGE:

This method should be called when the memory allocated by a call to wpAllocMem is no longer needed.

METHOD OVERRIDE:

This method should only be overridden to provide the deallocation of memory allocated by an override method of wpAllocMem.

RELATED METHODS:

wpAllocMem   Page 153

wpGetFattrsFromPSZ

This instance method returns the font attributes from a PresParam string.

INCLUDE IDENTIFIER:

```
#define INCL_WINWORKPLACE
```

FUNCTION PROTOTYPE:

```
VOID wpGetFattrsFromPSZ(WPFontPalette *somSelf,
                        PSZ pszFont, PFATTRS pFattrs);
```

PARAMETERS:

```
somSelf  - Pointer to the object on which the method
           is invoked
pszFont  - PresParam string
pFattrs  - Pointer to font attribute structure
```

RETURNS:

```
This is no return value for this method.
```

METHOD OVERRIDE:

```
This method usually is not overridden.
```

wpHide

This instance method hides or minimizes open views of this object.

INCLUDE IDENTIFIER:

```
#define INCL_WINWORKPLACE
```

FUNCTION PROTOTYPE:

```
BOOL wpHide(WPObject *somSelf);
```

PARAMETERS:

```
somSelf  - Pointer to the object on which the method
           is invoked
```

RETURNS:

```
TRUE   - Successful completion
FALSE  - Error occurred
```

REMARKS:

This method turns all windows owned by this object invisible or, if the system setting is set to provide minimized windows instead of hidden windows, minimizes all windows owned by this object.

METHOD USAGE:

This method can be called to hide an object's window.

METHOD OVERRIDE:

This method is not usually overridden.

RELATED METHODS:

wpRestore   Page 370

wpHideFldrRunObjs

This instance method hides or minimizes the open objects of a folder.

INCLUDE IDENTIFIER:

```
#define INCL_WINWORKPLACE
```

FUNCTION PROTOTYPE:

```
BOOL wpHideFldrRunObjs(WPFolder *somSelf, BOOL fHide);
```

PARAMETERS:

```
somSelf- Pointer to the object on which the method is
         invoked.
fHide  - Flag to indicate hide or show of open
         objects. Values:
            TRUE
            FALSE
```

RETURNS:

```
TRUE    - Successful completion
FALSE   - Error occurred
```

REMARKS:

Open objects in this folder either are hidden or minimized, depending on the current system setting. This method is called automatically on folders with the work area flag (FOI_WORKAREA) set when it is hidden or minimized.

METHOD USAGE:

This method can be called at any time to hide or minimize all objects in this folder that are currently open.

METHOD OVERRIDE:

This method is not usually overridden.

wpHoldJob

This instance method holds a job object.

INCLUDE IDENTIFIER:

```
#define INCL_WINWORKPLACE
```

FUNCTION PROTOTYPE:

```
BOOL wpHoldJob(WPJob *somSelf);
```

PARAMETERS:

```
somSelf  - Pointer to the object to be held
```

RETURNS:

```
TRUE   - Successful completion
FALSE  - Error occurred
```

METHOD OVERRIDE:

```
This method is not usually overridden.
```

RELATED METHODS:

```
wpReleaseJob                    Page 364
```

wpHoldPrinter

This instance method holds a printer object.

INCLUDE IDENTIFIER:

```
#define INCL_WINWORKPLACE
```

FUNCTION PROTOTYPE:

```
BOOL wpHoldPrinter(WPPrinter *somSelf);
```

PARAMETERS:

```
somSelf  - Pointer to the object to be held
```

RETURNS:

```
TRUE   - Successful completion
FALSE  - Error occurred
```

METHOD OVERRIDE:

```
This method is not usually overridden.
```

RELATED METHODS:

```
wpReleasePrinter              Page 365
```

wpInitCellStructs

This instance method sets up the cell dimensions of a palette object based upon the current count of rows and columns. This method also allocates the cell structures if they are not present.

INCLUDE IDENTIFIER:

```
#define WINWORKPLACE
```

FUNCTION PROTOTYPE:

```
BOOL wpInitCellStructs(WPPalette *somSelf);
```

PARAMETERS:

```
somSelf  - Pointer to the object on which the method
           is invoked
```

RETURNS:

```
TRUE   - Successful completion
FALSE  - Error occurred
```

METHOD OVERRIDE:

```
This method usually is not overridden.
```

RELATED METHODS:

```
wpRedrawCell                 Page 360
wpSetupCell                  Page 474
```

wpInitData

This instance method initializes the instance data of an object.

INCLUDE IDENTIFIER:

```
#define INCL_WINWORKPLACE
```

FUNCTION PROTOTYPE:

```
VOID wpInitData(WPObject *somSelf);
```

PARAMETERS:

```
somSelf  - Pointer to the object on which the method
           is invoked
```

RETURNS:

```
The return value is VOID.
```

REMARKS:

This method is called when the object is created or when it is awakened from the dormant state so that it can initialize all of its instance variables to a known state.

Note that this method is called before the object's state is known, so it is very important that the object does not try to process any other method while processing this method. Should an object require extra initialization that requires it to invoke other methods, this should be done from wpRestoreState. When the object is first created, wpSetupOnce should be overridden to perform initialization that is only required once.

METHOD USAGE:

This method usually is called only by the system when the object is made awake.

METHOD OVERRIDE:

Any class that has instance variables should override this method so that those variables are all initially in a known state.

It is essential to pass this method onto the parent class. If this method is overridden, wpUnInitData should also be overridden to deallocate resources that were allocated by the override processing of wpInitData.

RELATED METHODS:

wpInsertPopupMenuItems

This instance method inserts items into the pop-up menu of an object.

INCLUDE IDENTIFIER:

```
#define INCL_WINWORKPLACE
```

FUNCTION PROTOTYPE:

```
BOOL wpInsertPopupMenuItems(WPObject *somSelf,
                            HWND hwndMenu,
                            ULONG ulPosition,
                            HMODULE hmod,
                            ULONG ulMenuId,
                            ULONG ulSubMenuId);
```

PARAMETERS:

```
somSelf      - Pointer to the object on which the
               method is invoked.
hwndMenu     - Handle to the pop-up menu.
ulPosition   - Position at which to start inserting
               items.
hmod         - Module handle where ulMenuId is found.
ulMenuId     - Id of menu to put into pop-up menu.
               Values:
                   WPMENUID_ACCESSNEW
                   WPMENUID_ARRANGE
                   WPMENUID_ASSIGN
                   WPMENUID_CLOSE
                   WPMENUID_CHKDSK
                   WPMENUID_CREATEANOTHER
                   WPMENUID_COPY
                   WPMENUID_COPYDSK
                   WPMENUID_CREATESHADOW
                   WPMENUID_DELETE
                   WPMENUID_DESELALL
                   WPMENUID_DETAILS
                   WPMENUID_EJECTDISK
                   WPMENUID_EXTENDEDHELP
                   WPMENUID_FIND
                   WPMENUID_FIXDSK
                   WPMENUID_HELP
                   WPMENUID_HELP_FOR_HELP
                   WPMENUID_HELPINDEX
                   WPMENUID_HELPKEYS
```

```
                    WPMENUID_HOWTOGETHELP
                    WPMENUID_ICON
                    WPMENUID_LOCKDISK
                    WPMENUID_LOCKUP
                    WPMENUID_LOGIN
                    WPMENUID_LOGOUT
                    WPMENUID_MOVE
                    WPMENUID_OPEN
                    WPMENUID_PALETTE
                    WPMENUID_PICKUP
                    WPMENUID_PRIMARY
                    WPMENUID_PRINT
                    WPMENUID_PROGRAM
                    WPMENUID_PROPERTIES
                    WPMENUID_PUTDOWN
                    WPMENUID_PUTDOWN_CANCEL
                    WPMENUID_PUTDOWN_COPY
                    WPMENUID_PUTDOWN_CREATE
                    WPMENUID_PUTDOWN_LINK
                    WPMENUID_PUTDOWN_MOVE
                    WPMENUID_REFRESH
                    WPMENUID_RESERVED1
                    WPMENUID_RESERVED2
                    WPMENUID_SELALL
                    WPMENUID_SELECT
                    WPMENUID_SHUTDOWN
                    WPMENUID_SORT
                    WPMENUID_SYSTEMSETUP
                    WPMENUID_TREE
                    WPMENUID_UNASSIGN
                    WPMENUID_UNLOCKDISK
                    WPMENUID_USER
ulSubMenuId  - Id of submenu to put into pop-up menu.
```

RETURNS:

```
TRUE    - Successful completion
FALSE   - Error occurred
```

REMARKS:

This instance method inserts all menu items in ulMenuId
into the pop-up menu.

Menu item ids in open cascade must match THE corresponding open view. Class-specific menu ids should be above
WPMENUID_USER.

METHOD USAGE:

This method can be called only during the processing of wpModifyPopupMenu.

METHOD OVERRIDE:

This method is not usually overridden.

RELATED METHODS:

wpInsertSettingsPage

This instance method inserts a page into the Settings notebook of an object.

INCLUDE IDENTIFIER:

```
#define INCL_WINWORKPLACE
```

FUNCTION PROTOTYPE:

```
ULONG wpInsertSettingsPage(WPObject *somSelf,
                           HWND hwndNotebook,
                           PPAGEINFO pPageInfo);
```

PARAMETERS:

```
somSelf       - Pointer to the object on which the
                method is invoked
hwndNotebook  - Handle to the Settings notebook
pPageInfo     - Pointer to the notebook page
                information
```

RETURNS:

```
0        - Error occurred
PageId   - Page identifier for the inserted page
```

METHOD USAGE:

This method can be called only during the processing of wpAddSettingsPages.

METHOD OVERRIDE:

This method is not usually overridden.

RELATED METHODS:

wpIsCurrentDesktop

This instance method allows the Desktop to specify whether it is the active Desktop folder on the system.

INCLUDE IDENTIFIER:

```
#define INCL_WINWORKPLACE
```

FUNCTION PROTOTYPE:

```
BOOL wpIsCurrentDesktop(WPDesktop *somSelf);
```

PARAMETERS:

```
somSelf  - Pointer to the object on which the method
           is invoked
```

RETURNS:

```
TRUE   - Object is the active Desktop
FALSE  - Object is not the active Desktop and should
         behave as a normal folder
```

REMARKS:

The active Desktop is set by the system every time the Workplace Shell is initialized or the user profile is reset by a call to the PrfReset function. Because there can only be one active Desktop and objects cannot change their class, Desktop objects and descendants must call wpIsCurrentDesktop to determine if it is the current Desktop. Desktop folders that are not active take on the behavior of standard folder objects.

METHOD USAGE:

This method is called at the beginning of every overridden WPDesktop method. If the return is FALSE, the override method should call its parent without doing any override processing. If the return is TRUE, override processing can be made.

METHOD OVERRIDE:

This method is not usually overridden.

wpIsDeleteable

This instance method determines whether the object can be deleted by the Shredder.

INCLUDE IDENTIFIER:

```
#define WINWORKPLACE
```

FUNCTION PROTOTYPE:

```
BOOL wpIsDeleteable(WPObject *somSelf);
```

PARAMETERS:

```
somSelf  - Pointer to the object on which the method
           is invoked
```

RETURNS:

```
TRUE   - Object can be deleted by shredder
FALSE  - Object cannot be deleted by shredder
```

wpIsDetailsColumnVisible

This instance method determines whether any hidden column data exists for the current object.

Note: This method is used only in a details view.

INCLUDE IDENTIFIER:

```
#define INCL_WINWORKPLACE
```

FUNCTION PROTOTYPE:

```
BOOL wpIsDetailsColumnVisible(WPFolder *somSelf,
                             ULONG index);
```

PARAMETERS:

```
somSelf - Pointer to the object on which the method
          is invoked
index   - Column index for current details view
```

RETURNS:

```
TRUE    - Details column is visible
FALSE   - Details column is hidden
```

METHOD OVERRIDE:

```
This method usually is not overridden.
```

RELATED METHODS:

```
wpSetDetailsColumnVisibility    Page 422
```

wpIsDiskSwapped

This instance method checks if the removable media on which the file system object resides has been swapped.

INCLUDE IDENTIFIER:

```
#define INCL_WINWORKPLACE
```

FUNCTION PROTOTYPE:

```
BOOL wpIsDiskSwapped(WPFileSystem *somSelf);
```

PARAMETERS:

```
somSelf   - Pointer to the object on which the method
            is invoked
```

RETURNS:

```
TRUE    - Removable media has been swapped
FALSE   - Removable media has not been swapped
```

METHOD USAGE:

```
This method can be called at any time.
```

METHOD OVERRIDE:

```
This method usually is not overridden.
```

wpIsLocked

This instance method indicates whether the object can be made dormant.

INCLUDE IDENTIFIER:

```
#define INCL_WINWORKPLACE
```

FUNCTION PROTOTYPE:

```
BOOL wpIsLocked(WPObject *somSelf);
```

PARAMETERS:

```
somSelf - Pointer to the object on which the method
          is invoked
```

RETURNS:

```
TRUE   - Object is locked and cannot be made dormant
FALSE  - Object is not locked and can be made dormant
```

METHOD USAGE:

```
This method can be overridden at any time.
```

METHOD OVERRIDE:

```
This method usually is not overridden.
```

RELATED METHODS:

```
wpLockObject                    Page 231
```

wpIsObjectInititalized

This instance method determines whether an object has been completely initialized.

INCLUDE IDENTIFIER:

```
#define INCL_WINWORKPLACE
```

FUNCTION PROTOTYPE:

```
BOOL wpIsObjectInititalized(WPObject *somSelf);
```

PARAMETERS:

```
somSelf  - Pointer to the object on which the method
           is invoked
```

RETURNS:

```
TRUE   - Object is completely initialized
FALSE  - Object is not initialized
```

REMARKS:

Certain methods, such as wpSaveDeferred and wpSaveImmediate, are only valid on initialized objects.

wpIsObjectInitialized can be used within wpSetup to determine if wpSetup is being called during object creation (wpIsObjectInitialized returns FALSE) or after the object has been created, for example from WinSetObjectData (wpIsObjectInitialized returns TRUE.)

RELATED METHODS:

wpObjectReady   Page 246
wpSetup   Page 474

wpIsSortAttribAvailable

This instance method determines whether sort attributes are available for the current folder object.

INCLUDE IDENTIFIER:

```
#define INCL_WINWORKPLACE
```

FUNCTION PROTOTYPE:

```
BOOL wpIsSortAttribAvailable(WPFolder *somSelf,
                             ULONG Index);
```

PARAMETERS:

```
somSelf - Pointer to the object on which the method
          is invoked
Index   - Column index for current details view
```

RETURNS:

```
TRUE   - Sort attributes are visible
FALSE  - Sort attributes are hidden
```

METHOD OVERRIDE:

This method usually is not overridden.

RELATED METHODS:

```
wpSetSortAttribAvailable        Page 468
```

wpJobAdded

This instance method notifies the printer object that a job has been added to the print queue.

INCLUDE IDENTIFIER:

```
#define INCL_WINWORKPLACE
```

FUNCTION PROTOTYPE:

```
BOOL wpJobAdded(WPPrinter *somSelf, ULONG ulJobId);
```

PARAMETERS:

```
somSelf  - Pointer to the object on which the method
           is invoked
ulJobId  - Id of job added to print queue
```

RETURNS:

```
TRUE   - Successful completion
FALSE  - Error occurred
```

METHOD USAGE:

```
This method can be called at any time.
```

METHOD OVERRIDE:

```
This method can be overridden, but the parent must be
called for proper functioning of the printer object.
```

RELATED METHODS:

wpJobChanged   Page 228
wpJobDeleted   Page 229

wpJobChanged

This instance method notifies the printer object that a job in the print queue has been changed in some way.

INCLUDE IDENTIFIER:

```
#define INCL_WINWORKPLACE
```

FUNCTION PROTOTYPE:

```
BOOL wpJobChanged(WPPrinter *somSelf, ULONG ulJobId,
                  ULONG ulReserved);
```

PARAMETERS:

```
somSelf     - Pointer to the object on which the
              method is invoked
ulJobId     - Id of job that was changed
ulReserved  - Reserved value
```

RETURNS:

```
TRUE   - Successful completion
FALSE  - Error occurred
```

METHOD USAGE:

This method can be called at any time.

METHOD OVERRIDE:

This method can be overridden, but the parent must be called for proper functioning of the printer object.

RELATED METHODS:

wpJobAdded   Page 227
wpJobDeleted   Page 229

wpJobDeleted

This instance method notifies the printer object that a job has been deleted from the print queue.

INCLUDE IDENTIFIER:

```
#define INCL_WINWORKPLACE
```

FUNCTION PROTOTYPE:

```
BOOL wpJobDeleted(WPPrinter *somSelf, ULONG ulJobId);
```

PARAMETERS:

```
somSelf  - Pointer to the object on which the method
           is invoked
ulJobId  - Id of job deleted from print queue
```

RETURNS:

```
TRUE   - Successful completion
FALSE  - Error occurred
```

METHOD USAGE:

```
This method can be called at any time.
```

METHOD OVERRIDE:

```
This method can be overridden, but the parent must be
called for proper functioning of the printer object.
```

RELATED METHODS:

```
wpJobAdded                    Page 227
wpJobChanged                  Page 228
```

wpLockDrive

This instance method locks and unlocks removable media in drives that support this feature.

INCLUDE IDENTIFIER:

```
#define INCL_WINWORKPLACE
```

FUNCTION PROTOTYPE:

```
ULONG wpLockDrive(WPDisk *somSelf, BOOL fLock);
```

PARAMETERS:

```
somSelf - Pointer to the object on which the method
          is invoked.
fLock   - Lock flag. Values:
             TRUE
             FALSE
```

RETURNS:

```
 0  - Successful
>0  - Return code from DosDevIoctl Category 8
      Function 40
```

METHOD USAGE:

```
This method can be called at any time.
```

METHOD OVERRIDE:

```
This method should not be overridden.
```

RELATED METHODS:

wpLockObject

This instance method locks an object by incrementing the lock count of the receiving object so that it cannot be made dormant.

INCLUDE IDENTIFIER:

```
#define INCL_WINWORKPLACE
```

FUNCTION PROTOTYPE:

```
VOID wpLockObject(WPObject *somSelf);
```

PARAMETERS:

```
somSelf  - Pointer to the object on which the method
           is invoked
```

RETURNS:

None.

METHOD USAGE:

This method can be called at any time to lock the object.

METHOD OVERRIDE:

This method usually is not overridden.

RELATED METHODS:

wpIsLocked   Page 224

wpMenuItemHelpSelected

This instance method displays the requested help panel of an object.

INCLUDE IDENTIFIER:

```
#define INCL_WINWORKPLACE
```

FUNCTION PROTOTYPE:

```
BOOL wpMenuItemHelpSelected(WPObject *somSelf,
                            ULONG ulMenuId);
```

PARAMETERS:

```
somSelf   - Pointer to the object on which the method
            is invoked.
ulMenuId  - Unsigned SHORT containing the object's
            menu id. Values:
                WPMENUID_ACCESSNEW
                WPMENUID_ARRANGE
                WPMENUID_ASSIGN
                WPMENUID_CLOSE
                WPMENUID_CHKDSK
                WPMENUID_CREATEANOTHER
                WPMENUID_COPY
                WPMENUID_COPYDSK
                WPMENUID_CREATESHADOW
                WPMENUID_DELETE
                WPMENUID_DESELALL
                WPMENUID_DETAILS
                WPMENUID_EJECTDISK
                WPMENUID_EXTENDEDHELP
                WPMENUID_FIND
                WPMENUID_FIXDSK
                WPMENUID_HELP
                WPMENUID_HELP_FOR_HELP
                WPMENUID_HELPINDEX
                WPMENUID_HELPKEYS
                WPMENUID_HOWTOGETHELP
                WPMENUID_ICON
                WPMENUID_LOCKDISK
                WPMENUID_LOCKUP
                WPMENUID_LOGIN
                WPMENUID_LOGOUT
                WPMENUID_MOVE
                WPMENUID_OPEN
```

```
                    WPMENUID_PALETTE
                    WPMENUID_PICKUP
                    WPMENUID_PRIMARY
                    WPMENUID_PRINT
                    WPMENUID_PROGRAM
                    WPMENUID_PROPERTIES
                    WPMENUID_PUTDOWN
                    WPMENUID_PUTDOWN_CANCEL
                    WPMENUID_PUTDOWN_COPY
                    WPMENUID_PUTDOWN_CREATE
                    WPMENUID_PUTDOWN_LINK
                    WPMENUID_PUTDOWN_MOVE
                    WPMENUID_REFRESH
                    WPMENUID_RESERVED1
                    WPMENUID_RESERVED2
                    WPMENUID_SELALL
                    WPMENUID_SELECT
                    WPMENUID_SHUTDOWN
                    WPMENUID_SORT
                    WPMENUID_SYSTEMSETUP
                    WPMENUID_TREE
                    WPMENUID_UNASSIGN
                    WPMENUID_UNLOCKDISK
                    WPMENUID_USER
```

RETURNS:

```
TRUE    - Successful completion
FALSE   - Error occurred
```

REMARKS:

The default WPObject class does not process this method
other than to return FALSE.

METHOD USAGE:

This method usually is called only by the system when
help on a pop-up menu item is requested.

METHOD OVERRIDE:

This method should be overridden to display an appropriate help panel for a user-defined menu item. This is
usually done by issuing a call to wpDisplayHelp.

RELATED METHODS:

wpMenuItemSelected

This instance method enables an object to process a menu selection.

INCLUDE IDENTIFIER:

```
#define INCL_WINWORKPLACE
```

FUNCTION PROTOTYPE:

```
BOOL wpMenuItemSelected(WPObject *somSelf,
                        HWND hwndFrame,
                        ULONG ulMenuId);
```

PARAMETERS:

```
somSelf    - Pointer to the object on which the
             method is invoked.
hwndFrame  - Handle to the frame window.
ulMenuId   - Id of pop-up menu selected. Values:
                WPMENUID_ACCESSNEW
                WPMENUID_ARRANGE
                WPMENUID_ASSIGN
                WPMENUID_CLOSE
                WPMENUID_CHKDSK
                WPMENUID_CREATEANOTHER
                WPMENUID_COPY
                WPMENUID_COPYDSK
                WPMENUID_CREATESHADOW
                WPMENUID_DELETE
                WPMENUID_DESELALL
                WPMENUID_DETAILS
                WPMENUID_EJECTDISK
                WPMENUID_EXTENDEDHELP
                WPMENUID_FIND
                WPMENUID_FIXDSK
                WPMENUID_HELP
                WPMENUID_HELP_FOR_HELP
                WPMENUID_HELPINDEX
                WPMENUID_HELPKEYS
                WPMENUID_HOWTOGETHELP
                WPMENUID_ICON
                WPMENUID_LOCKDISK
                WPMENUID_LOCKUP
                WPMENUID_LOGIN
                WPMENUID_LOGOUT
                WPMENUID_MOVE
```

```
WPMENUID_OPEN
WPMENUID_PALETTE
WPMENUID_PICKUP
WPMENUID_PRIMARY
WPMENUID_PRINT
WPMENUID_PROGRAM
WPMENUID_PROPERTIES
WPMENUID_PUTDOWN
WPMENUID_PUTDOWN_CANCEL
WPMENUID_PUTDOWN_COPY
WPMENUID_PUTDOWN_CREATE
WPMENUID_PUTDOWN_LINK
WPMENUID_PUTDOWN_MOVE
WPMENUID_REFRESH
WPMENUID_RESERVED1
WPMENUID_RESERVED2
WPMENUID_SELALL
WPMENUID_SELECT
WPMENUID_SHUTDOWN
WPMENUID_SORT
WPMENUID_SYSTEMSETUP
WPMENUID_TREE
WPMENUID_UNASSIGN
WPMENUID_UNLOCKDISK
WPMENUID_USER
```

RETURNS:

```
TRUE    - Successful completion
FALSE   - Error occurred
```

REMARKS:

Class-specific menu ids should be above WPMENUID_USER.

METHOD USAGE:

This method usually is called only by the system when a pop-up menu item is selected.

METHOD OVERRIDE:

This method should be overridden to process class-specific menu item actions or to modify the behavior of a menu item action provided by an ancestor class.

RELATED METHODS:

wpModifyFldrFlags

This instance method sets or removes folder-status flags from a given folder.

INCLUDE IDENTIFIER:

```
#define INCL_WINWORKPLACE
```

FUNCTION PROTOTYPE:

```
BOOL wpModifyFldrFlags(WPFolder *somSelf,
                       ULONG ulFlags,
                       ULONG ulFlagMask);
```

PARAMETERS:

```
somSelf      - Pointer to the object on which the
               method is invoked.
ulFlags      - Status flags to be set or cleared.
               Values:
                   FOI_POPULATEWITHALL
                   FOI_POPULATEWITHFOLDERS
                   FOI_WORKAREA
                   FOI_CHANGEFONT
                   FOI_WAMINIMIZE
                   FOI_WASTARTONRESTORE
                   FOI_NOREFRESHVIEWS
                   FOI_ASYNCREFRESHONOPEN
                   FOI_TREEPOPULATE
                   FOI_POPULATEINPROGRESS
                   FOI_REFRESHINPROGRESS
                   FOI_FIRSTPOPULATE
                   FOI_WAMCRINPROGRESS
                   FOI_CNRBKGNDOLDFORMAT
                   FOI_CHANGEICONBGNDCOLOR
ulFlagMask   - Flag indicating whether to set or clear
               ulFlags. Values:
                   0
                   1
```

RETURNS:

```
TRUE    - Successful completion
FALSE   - Error occurred
```

REMARKS:

This method sets or clears the corresponding folder flags as an atomic operation. This method can be used instead of wpQueryFldrFlags and wpSetFldrFlags.

METHOD USAGE:

This instance method can be called at any time to change a folder's status.

METHOD OVERRIDE:

This method usually is not overridden.

RELATED METHODS:

wpQueryFldrFlags   Page 308
wpSetFldrFlags   Page 434

wpModifyPopupMenu

This instance method adds additional items to the pop-up menu of an object.

INCLUDE IDENTIFIER:

```
#define INCL_WINWORKPLACE
```

FUNCTION PROTOTYPE:

```
BOOL wpModifyPopupMenu(WPObject *somSelf,
                       HWND hwndMenu,
                       HWND hwndCnr,
                       ULONG ulPosition);
```

PARAMETERS:

```
somSelf      - Pointer to the object on which the
               method is invoked
hwndMenu     - Menu handle
hwndCnr      - Handle to container-control window
ulPosition   - Position to insert menu items
```

RETURNS:

```
TRUE    - Successful completion
FALSE   - Error occurred
```

REMARKS:

Class-specific menu ids should be above WPMENUID_USER. This method is called only if the current pop-up menu applies to objects of the same class.

METHOD USAGE:

This method usually is called by the system when a request to display the object's pop-up menu is made. It is called following a call to wpFilterPopupMenu.

METHOD OVERRIDE:

This method should be overridden to add class-specific actions to the object's pop-up menu. Descendant classes can remove these actions by processing wpFilterPopup-Menu.

RELATED METHODS:

wpModifyStyle

This instance method modifies the current object style for the given object.

INCLUDE IDENTIFIER:

```
#define INCL_WINWORKPLACE
```

FUNCTION PROTOTYPE:

```
BOOL wpModifyStyle(WPObject *somSelf,
                   ULONG ulStyleFlag,
                   ULONG ulStyleMask);
```

PARAMETERS:

somSelf   – Pointer to the object on which the
               method is invoked.
ulStyleFlag – Flag indicating object's styles to be
               affected. Values:
                   OBJSTYLE_NOMOVE
                   OBJSTYLE_LINK
                   OBJSTYLE_NOCOPY
                   OBJSTYLE_NOTDEFAULTICON
                   OBJSTYLE_TEMPLATE
                   OBJSTYLE_NODELETE
                   OBJSTYLE_NOPRINT
                   OBJSTYLE_NODRAG
                   OBJSTYLE_NOTVISIBLE
                   OBJSTYLE_NORENAME
                   OBJSTYLE_NODROP
ulStyleMask – Flag indicating whether to set or
               clear *ulStyleFlag*. Values:
                   0
                   1

RETURNS:

TRUE   – Successful completion
FALSE   – Error occurred

REMARKS:

This method sets and clears corresponding style flags as an atomic operation. It can be used in place of wpQueryStyle and wpSetStyle.

METHOD USAGE:

This method can be called at any time to change the style
of an object.

METHOD OVERRIDE:

This method usually is not overridden.

RELATED METHODS:

wpQueryStyle	Page 356
wpSetStyle	Page 469
wpclsQueryStyle	Page 547

wpModuleForClass

This instance method returns the module name for a given class.

INCLUDE IDENTIFIER:

```
#define INCL_WINWORKPLACE
```

FUNCTION PROTOTYPE:

```
PSZ wpModuleForClass(SOMClassMgr *somSelf,
                     PSZ pszClass);
```

PARAMETERS:

```
somSelf    - Pointer to the object on which the method
             is invoked
pszClass   - Class for which module name is returned
```

RETURNS:

Module name for *pszClass*.

METHOD USAGE:

This method can be called at any time. It is invoked using SOMClassMgrObject.

METHOD OVERRIDE:

This method should not be overridden.

RELATED METHODS:

wpInsertPopupMenuItems	Page 216
wpModifyPopupMenu	Page 240

wpMoveObject

This instance method moves the object to a different location.

INCLUDE IDENTIFIER:

```
#define INCL_WINWORKPLACE
```

FUNCTION PROTOTYPE:

```
BOOL wpMoveObject(WPObject *somSelf,WPFolder *Folder);
```

PARAMETERS:

```
somSelf - Pointer to the object on which the method
          is invoked.
Folder  - Pointer to a folder object in which to move
          this object into. This pointer can be
          determined by issuing a call to wpclsQuery-
          Folder.
```

RETURNS:

```
TRUE   - Successful completion
FALSE  - Error occurred
```

METHOD USAGE:

```
This method can be called at any time to move an object
to a new location.
```

METHOD OVERRIDE:

```
This method is not usually overridden except by storage
classes. The parent should be called last unless special
actions must take place when an object is moved.
```

RELATED METHODS:

```
wpCopyObject                    Page 170
wpCreateShadowObject            Page 174
```

wpObjectReady

This instance method is a notification of when a Workplace Shell object has been completely initialized. The Workplace Shell invokes this method against an object when the object has been completely initialized by the Workplace Shell.

INCLUDE IDENTIFIER:

```
#define INCL_WINWORKPLACE
```

FUNCTION PROTOTYPE:

```
VOID wpObjectReady(WPObject *somSelf, ULONG ulCode,
                WPObject *refObject);
```

PARAMETERS:

somSelf   - Pointer to the object on which the
             method is invoked.
ulCode   - Code indicating how object was made
             ready. Values:
                 OR_NEW
                 OR_AWAKE
                 OR_FROMTEMPLATE
                 OR_FROMCOPY
                 OR_SHADOW
                 OR_REFERENCE
refObject - Reference to another object that is
             basis for creation of an object described
             by *somSelf*. If *ulCode* is OR_FROMTEMPLATE,
             refObject contains the template that the
             object was created from. If *ulCode* is
             OR_FROMCOPY, *refObject* contains the
             object that the object was copied from.
             If *ulCode* is OR_SHADOW, *refObject*
             contains the object that the object is a
             shadow of.

RETURNS:

None.

METHOD USAGE:

This method is not intended to be called. It is meant to be overridden.

METHOD OVERRIDE:

This method must be overridden by a subclass so that the instance of the subclass can be notified when the instance is initialized by the Workplace Shell. The instance is ready when the object has all of its instance data.

This is the earliest point in an object's life cycle that wpSaveDeferred can be called against the object.

RELATED METHODS:

wpIsObjectInitialized   Page 225

wpOpen

This instance method opens a view to the object.

INCLUDE IDENTIFIER:

```
#define INCL_WINWORKPLACE
```

FUNCTION PROTOTYPE:

```
HWND wpOpen(WPObject *somSelf, HWND hwndCnr,
            ULONG ulView, ULONG ulParam);
```

PARAMETERS:

```
somSelf  - Pointer to the object on which the method
           is invoked.
hwndCnr  - Handle of the container window from which
           object is opened; can be NULLHANDLE.
ulView   - Specifies which view to open. Values:
               OPEN_CONTENTS
               OPEN_DEFAULT
               OPEN_DETAILS
               OPEN_HELP
               OPEN_RUNNING
               OPEN_SETTINGS
               OPEN_TREE
               OPEN_USER
ulParam  - Open view parameter.
```

RETURNS:

```
NULLHANDLE  - Error occurred
Other       - Handle to window created or program
              executed
```

METHOD USAGE:

This method can be called at any time to open a view of
an object.

METHOD OVERRIDE:

This method should be overridden to process any class-
specific open views. It also can be overridden to modify
the behavior defined in an ancestor class.

When wpOpen is overridden to implement a user-defined view, it should call wpAddObjToUseList and wpRegisterView to ensure that the new view is recognized by the Workplace Shell as a view of the object.

RELATED METHODS:

wpClose   Page 156

wpPaintCell

This instance method paints a cell.

INCLUDE IDENTIFIER:

```
#define INCL_WINWORKPLACE
```

FUNCTION PROTOTYPE:

```
BOOL wpPaintCell(WPPalette *somSelf, PCELL pCell,
                HPS hps, PRECTL pprcl, BOOL fHilite);
```

PARAMETERS:

```
somSelf  - Pointer to the object on which the method
           is invoked.
pCell    - Pointer to CELL structure to be painted.
hps      - Presentation space handle for the cell.
pprcl    - Pointer to RECTL structure for area to be
           painted.
fHilite  - Flag to indicate selected state. Values:
              TRUE
              FALSE
```

RETURNS:

```
TRUE   - Successful completion
FALSE  - Error occurred
```

REMARKS:

The default processing for this method by WPPalette is
to paint a SYSCLR_WINDOW background. If the cell is
highlighted, a SYSCLR_HIGHLITEBACKGROUND background is
painted.

METHOD USAGE:

This method can be called at any time to paint a cell.

METHOD OVERRIDE:

This method should be overridden by all subclasses that
want to display visual information in the cell window.
The parent method should be called first.

wpPaintPalette

This instance method paints the specified palette window.

INCLUDE IDENTIFIER:

```
#define INCL_WINWORKPLACE
```

FUNCTION PROTOTYPE:

```
BOOL wpPaintPalette(WPPalette *somSelf, HPS hps,
                    PRECTL prcl);
```

PARAMETERS:

```
somSelf  - Pointer to the object on which the method
           is invoked
hps      - Handle to paint presentation space
prcl     - Pointer to coordinates of palette window to
           be painted
```

RETURNS:

```
TRUE   - Successful completion
FALSE  - Error occurred
```

METHOD OVERRIDE:

```
This method usually is not overridden.
```

RELATED METHODS:

```
wpPaintCell                    Page 250
```

wpPopulate

This instance method enables a folder to populate itself.

INCLUDE IDENTIFIER:

```
#define INCL_WINWORKPLACE
```

FUNCTION PROTOTYPE:

```
BOOL wpPopulate(WPFolder *somSelf, ULONG ulReserved,
                WPFolder *Folder, BOOL fFoldersOnly);
```

PARAMETERS:

```
somSelf        - Pointer to the object on which the
                 method is invoked.
ulReserved     - Reserved value; must be 0.
Folder         - Real name of the folder to populate.
fFoldersOnly   - ORed flag indicating type of contents
                 with which to populate the folder.
                 Values:
                     TRUE
                     FALSE
```

RETURNS:

```
TRUE    - Successful completion
FALSE   - Error occurred
```

REMARKS:

This method sets the folder flags, depending upon the value of fFoldersOnly.

The following folder flags indicate what the current population state of the folder is:

```
FOI_POPULATEDWITHALL       - Folder totally populated
FOI_POPULATEDWITHFOLDERS   - Folder is populated only
                             with subfolders
```

If the folder is re-populated when it has already been populated (as determined by inspecting the folder flags), no action is taken on this message apart from returning the notification message.

wpPopulate locks each object it instantiates as a result of the call.

METHOD USAGE:

This method is usually called only by the system when the folder is opened.

METHOD OVERRIDE:

This method can be overridden to alter the contents of a folder. To filter contents added by ancestor classes, call the parent method first.

wpPrintJobNext

This instance method prints a job next.

INCLUDE IDENTIFIER:

```
#define INCL_WINWORKPLACE
```

FUNCTION PROTOTYPE:

```
BOOL wpPrintJobNext(WPJob *somSelf);
```

PARAMETERS:

```
somSelf  - Pointer to the object to be printed next
```

RETURNS:

```
TRUE    - Successful completion
FALSE   - Error occurred
```

METHOD OVERRIDE:

```
This method is not usually overridden.
```

wpPrintMetaFile

This instance method prints an object of type *metafile*.

INCLUDE IDENTIFIER:

```
#define INCL_WINWORKPLACE
```

FUNCTION PROTOTYPE:

```
BOOL wpPrintMetaFile(WPDataFile *somSelf,
                     PPRINTDEST pPrintDest);
```

PARAMETERS:

```
somSelf     - Pointer to the object on which the
              method is invoked
pPrintDest  - Pointer to the print data; it contains
              all the parameters required to issue
              DevPostDeviceModes and DevOpenDC calls
```

RETURNS:

```
TRUE   - Successful completion
FALSE  - Error occurred
```

METHOD USAGE:

```
This method usually is called asynchronously as a result
of a call to wpPrintObject.
```

METHOD OVERRIDE:

```
This method can be overridden by any object class that
wants to replace the system-supplied metafile print
method.
```

RELATED METHODS:

```
wpPrintObject                    Page 256
```

wpPrintObject

This instance method prints a view of the object.

INCLUDE IDENTIFIER:

```
#define INCL_WINWORKPLACE
```

FUNCTION PROTOTYPE:

```
BOOL wpPrintObject(WPObject *somSelf,
                   PPRINTDEST pPrintDest,
                   ULONG ulReserved);
```

PARAMETERS:

somSelf   – Pointer to the object on which the
               method is invoked
pPrintDest   – Pointer to print data; it contains all
               the parameters required to issue
               DevPostDeviceModes and DevOpenDC calls
ulReserved   – Reserved value; must be 0

RETURNS:

TRUE   – Successful completion
FALSE   – Error occurred

METHOD USAGE:

This method can be called at any time to print a view
of an object.

METHOD OVERRIDE:

This method should be overridden to modify the print
behavior supported by an ancestor class.

RELATED METHODS:

wpPrintPifFile

This instance method prints an object of type *PIF*.

INCLUDE IDENTIFIER:

```
#define INCL_WINWORKPLACE
```

FUNCTION PROTOTYPE:

```
BOOL wpPrintPifFile(WPDataFile *somSelf,
                    PPRINTDEST pPrintDest);
```

PARAMETERS:

somSelf   - Pointer to the object on which the
              method is invoked
pPrintDest - Pointer to the print data; it contains
              all the parameters required to issue
              DevPostDeviceModes and DevOpenDC

RETURNS:

TRUE   - Successful completion
FALSE - Error occurred

METHOD USAGE:

This method usually is called asynchronously as a result
of a call to wpPrintObject.

METHOD OVERRIDE:

This method can be overridden by any object class that
wants to replace the system-supplied PIF file print
method.

RELATED METHODS:

wpPrintObject   Page 256

wpPrintPlainTextFile

This instance method prints a file that contains only ASCII text.

INCLUDE IDENTIFIER:

```
#define INCL_WINWORKPLACE
```

FUNCTION PROTOTYPE:

```
BOOL wpPrintPlainTextFile(WPFileSystem *somSelf,
                          PPRINTDEST pPrintDest);
```

PARAMETERS:

somSelf   - Pointer to the object on which the
              method is invoked
pPrintDest - Pointer to the print data; it contains
              all the parameters required to issue
              DevPostDeviceModes and DevOpenDC calls

RETURNS:

TRUE   - Successful completion
FALSE - Error occurred

METHOD USAGE:

This method usually is called asynchronously as a result
of a call to wpPrintObject.

METHOD OVERRIDE:

This method can be overridden to replace or remove the
system-supplied Plain Text file print algorithm. An
override of this method does not call the parent method.

RELATED METHODS:

wpPrintObject   Page 256

wpPrintPrinterSpecificFile

This instance method prints an object of type *printer-specific data*.

INCLUDE IDENTIFIER:

```
#define INCL_WINWORKPLACE
```

FUNCTION PROTOTYPE:

```
BOOL wpPrintPrinterSpecificFile(WPDataFile *somSelf,
                               PPRINTDEST
                               pPrintDest);
```

PARAMETERS:

```
somSelf      - Pointer to the object on which the
               method is invoked
pPrintDest   - Pointer to the print data; it contains
               all the parameters required to issue
               DevPostDeviceModes and DevOpenDC calls
```

RETURNS:

```
TRUE    - Successful completion
FALSE   - Error occurred
```

METHOD USAGE:

```
This method usually is called asynchronously as a result
of a call to wpPrintObject.
```

METHOD OVERRIDE:

```
This method can be overridden by any object class that
wants to replace the system-supplied, printer-specific,
data-file print method.
```

RELATED METHODS:

```
wpPrintObject                 Page 256
```

wpPrintUnknownFile

This instance method prints an object of unknown type.

INCLUDE IDENTIFIER:

```
#define INCL_WINWORKPLACE
```

FUNCTION PROTOTYPE:

```
BOOL wpPrintUnknownFile(WPDataFile *somSelf,
                        PPRINTDEST pPrintDest);
```

PARAMETERS:

```
somSelf      - Pointer to the object on which the
               method is invoked
pPrintDest   - Pointer to the print data; it contains
               all the parameters required to issue
               DevPostDeviceMode and DevOpenDC calls
```

RETURNS:

```
TRUE    - Successful completion
FALSE   - Error occurred
```

METHOD USAGE:

This method usually is called asynchronously as a result of a call to wpPrintObject.

METHOD OVERRIDE:

This method can be overridden by any object class that wants to replace the system-supplied unknown file print method.

RELATED METHODS:

wpPrintObject   Page 256

wpQueryActionButtons

This instance method returns a list of action buttons displayed on the LaunchPad.

INCLUDE IDENTIFIER:

```
#define INCL_WINWORKPLACE
```

FUNCTION PROTOTYPE:

```
PACTIONS wpQueryActionButtons(WPLaunchPad *somSelf,
                             PULONG pulNumActions);
```

PARAMETERS:

somSelf   - Pointer to the object on which the
                   method is invoked
pulNumActions   - Pointer to number of actions
                   returned

RETURNS:

Pointer to an array of actions displayed on the LaunchPad.

METHOD OVERRIDE:

This method can be overridden to add or change actions.

If you want to modify the set of actions returned, call the parent wpQueryActionButtons first.

If you want to return a completely different set of actions, you do not need to call the parent first. If you are adding actions which are not provided or the *ulMenuId* is not a menu id of the WPDesktop class, then you need to also override WPDesktop, using wpMenuItem-Selected, to respond to your defined actions.

RELATED METHODS:

wpRefreshDrawer   Page 362

wpQueryActionButtonStyle

This instance method determines how the action buttons are displayed on the LaunchPad.

INCLUDE IDENTIFIER:

```
#define INCL_WINWORKPLACE
```

FUNCTION PROTOTYPE:

```
ULONG wpQueryActionButtonStyle(WPLaunchPad *somSelf);
```

PARAMETERS:

```
somSelf  - Pointer to the object on which the method
           is invoked
```

RETURNS:

One of the following flags, indicating the style of the action buttons:

```
ACTION_BUTTONS_MINI
ACTION_BUTTONS_NORMAL
ACTION_BUTTONS_OFF
ACTION_BUTTONS_TEXT
```

METHOD OVERRIDE:

This method can be overridden to know when the action display button display style is being queried.

RELATED METHODS:

wpQueryAssociatedFileIcon

This instance method returns the icon of the program associated with the current data file.

INCLUDE IDENTIFIER:

```
#define INCL_WINWORKPLACE
```

FUNCTION PROTOTYPE:

```
HPOINTER wpQueryAssociatedFileIcon
                              (WPDataFile *somSelf);
```

PARAMETERS:

```
somSelf  - Pointer to the object on which the method
           is invoked
```

RETURNS:

```
A return value of NULLHANDLE indicates that there is no
associated program icon.
```

RELATED METHODS:

wpQueryAssociatedProgram   Page 264
wpSetAssociatedFileIcon   Page 398

wpQueryAssociatedProgram

This instance method returns the WPProgram or WPProgramFile object that is associated with this data file for the specified view.

INCLUDE IDENTIFIER:

```
#define INCL_WINWORKPLACE
```

FUNCTION PROTOTYPE:

```
WPObject *wpQueryAssociatedProgram
                        (WPDataFile *somSelf,
                         ULONG ulView,
                         PULONG pulHowMatched,
                         PSZ pszMatchString,
                         ULONG cbMatchString,
                         PSZ pszDefaultType);
```

PARAMETERS:

somSelf	– Pointer to the object on which the method is invoked.
ulView	– View of data file whose association is being queried; normally this is the result of a call to wpQueryDefaultView.

pulHowMatched	– Flag indicating association type. Values:
	    0
	    1
	    2

pszMatchString	– Type or name filter. If *pulHowMatched* is 0, the first byte is set to NULL.
cbMatchString	– Size of pszMatchString.

pszDefaultType	– Default data type. Values:
	    string
	    NULL
	    -1

RETURNS:

Class	– WPProgram or WPProgramFile class of object associated with this data file for this view
NULL	– No WPProgram or WPProgramFile object is associated with this view

METHOD OVERRIDE:

This method must be overridden if your class introduces a new form of association for a range of views not known to the Workplace Shell.

RELATED METHODS:

wpQueryAssociatedFileIcon   Page 263
wpSetAssociatedFileIcon   Page 398

wpQueryAssociationFilter

This WPProgram instance method determines which file-title filters are used to associate data-file objects to this program object.

INCLUDE IDENTIFIER:

```
#define INCL_WINWORKPLACE
```

FUNCTION PROTOTYPE:

```
PSZ wpQueryAssociationFilter(WPProgram *somSelf);
```

PARAMETERS:

```
somSelf   - Pointer to the object on which the method
            is invoked
```

RETURNS:

```
NULL    - Error occurred
Other   - Pointer to a string containing file-title
          filters, which can contain several filters
          separated by a comma
```

REMARKS:

The association filter is used to designate this program as an available open view for data-file objects that have a title that matches one of the association filters that are set. If a data-file object matches a filter in a program object or program-file object, the title of that object appears in the data-file object's Open cascade of its pop-up menu.

This method returns the filter string set by the last call to wpSetAssociationFilter. The wpQueryAssociation-Type method can be called to determine which file types are used to associate data-file objects to this program object.

METHOD USAGE:

This method can be called at any time to determine which file-title filters are used to associate data-file objects to this program object.

METHOD OVERRIDE:

This method is not usually overridden.

RELATED METHODS:

wpQueryAssociationFilter

This WPProgramFile instance method determines which file-title filters are used to associate data-file objects to this program object.

INCLUDE IDENTIFIER:

#define INCL_WINWORKPLACE

FUNCTION PROTOTYPE:

PSZ wpQueryAssociationFilter(WPProgramFile *somSelf);

PARAMETERS:

somSelf   - Pointer to the object on which the method
            is invoked

RETURNS:

NULL   - Error occurred
Other   - Pointer to a string containing file title
          filters, which can contain several filters
          separated by a comma

REMARKS:

The association filter is used to designate this program as an available open view for data-file objects that have a title that matches one of the association filters that are set. If a data-file object matches a filter in a program object or program-file object, the title of that object appears in the data-file object's Open cascade of its pop-up menu.

This method returns the filter string set by the last call to wpSetAssociationFilter. The wpQueryAssocation-Type method can be called to determine which file types are used to associate data-file objects to this program object.

METHOD USAGE:

This method can be called at any time to determine which file-title filters are used to associate data-file objects to this program object.

METHOD OVERRIDE:

This method is not usually overridden.

RELATED METHODS:

wpQueryAssociationType

This WPProgram instance method determines which file types are used to associate data-file objects to this program object.

INCLUDE IDENTIFIER:

```
#define INCL_WINWORKPLACE
```

FUNCTION PROTOTYPE:

```
PSZ wpQueryAssociationType(WPProgram *somSelf);
```

PARAMETERS:

```
somSelf   - Pointer to the object on which the method
            is invoked
```

RETURNS:

```
NULL    - Error occurred
Other   - Pointer to a string containing file types;
          can contain several filters separated by a
          comma (for example: "Plain Text,C Code")
```

REMARKS:

The association type is used to designate this program as an available open view for data-file objects that have a type that matches one of the association types that are set. If a data-file object matches a type in a program object or program-file object, the title of that object appears in the data-file object's Open cascade of its pop-up menu.

This method returns the type string set by the last call to wpSetAssociationType. The wpQueryAssociationFilter method can be called to determine which file-title filters are used to associate data-file objects to this program object.

METHOD USAGE:

This method can be called at any time to determine which file types are used to associate data-file objects to this program object.

METHOD OVERRIDE:

This method is not usually overridden.

RELATED METHODS:

wpQueryAssociationType

This WPProgramFile instance method determines which file types are used to associate data-file objects to this program object.

INCLUDE IDENTIFIER:

```
#define INCL_WINWORKPLACE
```

FUNCTION PROTOTYPE:

```
PSZ wpQueryAssociationType(WPProgramFile *somSelf);
```

PARAMETERS:

somSelf   - Pointer to the object on which the method
            is invoked

RETURNS:

NULL   - Error occurred
Other   - Pointer to a string containing file types;
          can contain several filters separated by a
          comma

REMARKS:

The association type is used to designate this program as an available open view for data-file objects that have a type that matches one of the association types that are set. If a data-file object matches a type in a program object or program-file object, the title of that object appears in the data-file object's Open cascade of its pop-up menu.

This method returns the type string set by the last call to wpSetAssociationType. The wpQueryAssociationFilter method can be called to determine which file-title filters are used to associate data-file objects to this program object.

METHOD USAGE:

This method can be called at any time to determine which file types are used to associate data-file objects to this program object.

METHOD OVERRIDE:

This method is not usually overridden.

RELATED METHODS:

wpQueryAttr

This instance method queries the file attributes of a file-system-based object

INCLUDE IDENTIFIER:

#define INCL_WINWORKPLACE

FUNCTION PROTOTYPE:

ULONG wpQueryAttr(WPFileSystem *somSelf);

PARAMETERS:

somSelf   - Pointer to the object on which the method
            is invoked

RETURNS:

File attributes of a file-system-based object.

METHOD OVERRIDE:

This method usually is not overridden.

RELATED METHODS:

wpSetAttr   Page 408

wpQueryAutoRefresh

This instance method queries the current automatic refresh value
for the Power object's status window.

INCLUDE IDENTIFIER:

```
#define INCL_WINWORKPLACE
```

FUNCTION PROTOTYPE:

```
BOOL wpQueryAutoRefresh(WPPower *somSelf);
```

PARAMETERS:

```
somSelf  - Pointer to the object on which the method
           is invoked
```

RETURNS:

```
TRUE   - Automatic refresh is enabled
FALSE  - Automatic refresh is disabled
```

RELATED METHODS:

wpQueryButtonAppearance

This instance method returns the Frame Control button appearance of an object.

INCLUDE IDENTIFIER:

```
#define INCL_WINWORKPLACE
```

FUNCTION PROTOTYPE:

```
ULONG wpQueryButtonAppearance(WPObject *somSelf);
```

PARAMETERS:

```
somSelf  - Pointer to the object on which the method
           is invoked
```

RETURNS:

```
One of the following flags, indicating type of control
button:

  DEFAULTBUTTON
  HIDEBUTTON
  MINBUTTON
```

METHOD USAGE:

This method is usually called by the system to retrieve the appearance of the object's Frame Control button.

METHOD OVERRIDE:

This method usually is not overridden.

RELATED METHODS:

```
wpSetButtonAppearance            Page 410
wpclsQueryButtonAppearance       Page 512
```

wpQueryCloseDrawer

This instance method determines whether the drawer closes after an object in the drawer is opened.

INCLUDE IDENTIFIER:

```
#define INCL_WINWORKPLACE
```

FUNCTION PROTOTYPE:

```
BOOL wpQueryCloseDrawer(WPLaunchPad *somSelf);
```

PARAMETERS:

somSelf   - Pointer to the object on which the method
            is invoked

RETURNS:

TRUE   - Drawer closes
FALSE   - Drawer does not close

METHOD OVERRIDE:

This method can be overridden to force a particular value.

RELATED METHODS:

wpSetCloseDrawer   Page 411

wpQueryComputerName

This instance method queries the name of the computer on which the printer object resides.

INCLUDE IDENTIFIER:

```
#define INCL_WINWORKPLACE
```

FUNCTION PROTOTYPE:

```
ULONG wpQueryComputerName(WPPrinter *somSelf,
                          PSZ pszComputerName);
```

PARAMETERS:

```
somSelf            - Pointer to the object to be queried
pszComputerName    - Returned computer name of the
                     object queried
```

RETURNS:

```
0  - Error occurred
1  - Successful; computer name is local (NULL)
2  - Successful; computer name is on network (see
              pszComputerName for value)
```

METHOD OVERRIDE:

This method is not usually overridden.

RELATED METHODS:

wpQueryPrinterName   Page 340
wpSetComputerName   Page 412

wpQueryConcurrentView

This instance method queries the concurrent-view behavior of an object.

INCLUDE IDENTIFIER:

```
#define INCL_WINWORKPLACE
```

FUNCTION PROTOTYPE:

```
ULONG wpQueryConcurrentView(WPObject *somSelf);
```

PARAMETERS:

somSelf - Pointer to the object on which the method
          is invoked

RETURNS:

Flag that indicates the concurrent view mode. Possible
values:

```
CCVIEW_ON
CCVIEW_OFF
CCVIEW_DEFAULT
```

METHOD OVERRIDE:

This method should not be overridden.

RELATED METHODS:

wpSetConcurrentView   Page 413

wpQueryConfirmations

This instance method determines which confirmations are set on this object.

INCLUDE IDENTIFIER:

```
#define INCL_WINWORKPLACE
```

FUNCTION PROTOTYPE:

```
ULONG wpQueryConfirmations(WPObject *somSelf);
```

PARAMETERS:

```
somSelf  - Pointer to the object on which the method
           is invoked
```

RETURNS:

```
One of the following confirmation flags:
```

```
   NULL
   CONFIRM_ACTION
   CONFIRM_DELETE
   CONFIRM_DELETEFOLDER
   CONFIRM_KEEPASSOC
   CONFIRM_RENAMEFILESWITHEXT
   CONFIRM_PROGRESS
```

METHOD USAGE:

```
This method can be called at any time to determine the
confirmations set on an object.
```

METHOD OVERRIDE:

```
This method is not usually overridden.
```

RELATED METHODS:

```
wpConfirmDelete                 Page 164
wpDelete                        Page 177
wpFree                          Page 206
```

wpQueryContainerFlagPtr

This instance method returns a pointer to the flag indication object that has a container.

INCLUDE IDENTIFIER:

```
#define INCL_WINWORKPLACE
```

FUNCTION PROTOTYPE:

```
PULONG wpQueryContainerFlagPtr(WPObject *somSelf);
```

PARAMETERS:

```
somSelf  - Pointer to the object on which the method
           is invoked
```

RETURNS:

```
Pointer to flag-indication object that has a container.
```

METHOD USAGE:

```
This method can be called at any time to query the flag
indication object.
```

METHOD OVERRIDE:

```
This method usually is not overridden.
```

wpQueryContent

This instance method enables a folder to specify its contents.

INCLUDE IDENTIFIER:

```
#define INCL_WINWORKPLACE
```

FUNCTION PROTOTYPE:

```
WPObject *wpQueryContent(WPFolder *somSelf,
                         WPObject *Object,
                         ULONG ulOption);
```

PARAMETERS:

somSelf   - Pointer to the object on which the method
            is invoked.
Object   - Pointer to a workplace object; ignored
            unless QC_NEXT is specified in *ulOption*.
ulOption - Flag indicating the object to query.
            Values:
               QC_FIRST
               QC_LAST
               QC_NEXT

RETURNS:

A pointer to the correct item in folder's content list.

REMARKS:

This method allows the user to query the folder's content
in various ways using ulOption. QC_FIRST returns the
first item in the content list, QC_LAST returns the last,
and QC_NEXT returns the next item after "Object" in the
list.

METHOD USAGE:

This method is usually called to look for a specific
object or to query the contents in a specific folder.

METHOD OVERRIDE:

This method is not usually overridden.

wpQueryCoreRecord

This instance method returns information about records in the container control for the given object.

INCLUDE IDENTIFIER:

```
#define INCL_WINWORKPLACE
```

FUNCTION PROTOTYPE:

```
PMINIRECORDCORE wpQueryCoreRecord(WPObject *somSelf);
```

PARAMETERS:

```
somSelf   - Pointer to the object on which the method is
            invoked
```

RETURNS:

```
Pointer to mini-record data structure containing infor-
mation about an object's container control record.
```

METHOD OVERRIDE:

```
This method usually is not overridden.
```

wpQueryCreation

This instance method returns the creation data and time of a file.

INCLUDE IDENTIFIER:

```
#define INCL_WINWORKPLACE
```

FUNCTION PROTOTYPE:

```
ULONG wpQueryCreation(WPFileSystem *somSelf, FDATE
                      *fDate, FTIME, *fTime);
```

PARAMETERS:

```
somSelf - Pointer to the object on which the method
          is invoked
fDate   - Pointer to date structure in which file's
          creation date is returned
fTime   - Pointer to time structure in which file's
          creation time is returned
```

RETURNS:

```
0       - No error
Other   - Error occurred
```

METHOD OVERRIDE:

```
This method usually is not overridden.
```

RELATED METHODS:

```
wpQueryLastAccess               Page 322
wpQueryLastWrite                Page 323
```

wpQueryDateInfo

This instance method returns the date information from the given file object.

INCLUDE IDENTIFIER:

```
#define INCL_WINWORKPLACE
```

FUNCTION PROTOTYPE:

```
ULONG wpQueryDateInfo(WPFileSystem *somSelf,
                      FILEFINDBUF4 *pstFileFindBuf);
```

PARAMETERS:

```
somSelf          - Pointer to the object on which the
                   method is invoked
pstFileFindBuf   - Pointer to the buffer of file
                   information
```

RETURNS:

```
Date information for the specified file.
```

METHOD OVERRIDE:

```
This method usually is not overridden.
```

RELATED METHODS:

```
wpSetDateInfo              Page 415
```

wpQueryDefaultHelp

This instance method specifies the default help panel of an object.

INCLUDE IDENTIFIER:

```
#define INCL_WINWORKPLACE
```

FUNCTION PROTOTYPE:

```
BOOL wpQueryDefaultHelp(WPObject *somSelf,
                        PULONG pHelpPanelId,
                        PSZ pszHelpLibrary);
```

PARAMETERS:

```
somSelf         - Pointer to the object on which the
                  method is invoked.
pHelpPanelId    - Pointer to the help panel id.
pszHelpLibrary  - Pointer to a buffer in which to
                  place the name of the help library.
                  This buffer should be the length of
                  CCHMAXPATH bytes.
```

RETURNS:

```
TRUE   - Successful completion
FALSE  - Error occurred
```

REMARKS:

The default help panel for this class can be determined
by calling wpclsQueryDefaultHelp.

METHOD USAGE:

This method can be called at any time to determine the
default panel for this object.

METHOD OVERRIDE:

This method is not usually overridden.

RELATED METHODS:

wpQueryDefaultIconPos

This instance method returns the default icon position of the current object within a folder.

INCLUDE IDENTIFIER:

```
#define INCL_WINWORKPLACE
```

FUNCTION PROTOTYPE:

```
BOOL wpQueryDefaultIconPos(WPObject *somSelf,
                           PPOINTL pPointl);
```

PARAMETERS:

```
somSelf - Pointer to the object on which the method
          is invoked.
pPointl - Pointer to coordinates of the default icon
          position. x and y values represent position
          in object's folder in percentage
          coordinates.
```

RETURNS:

```
TRUE    - Successful completion
FALSE   - Error occurred
```

REMARKS:

Refer to wpSetup for more information about the initial icon position.

METHOD USAGE:

This method can be called at any time to set the default icon position within a folder.

METHOD OVERRIDE:

This method usually is not overridden.

RELATED METHODS:

wpSetDefaultIconPos   Page 417

wpQueryDefaultView

This instance method queries the current default open view of an object.

INCLUDE IDENTIFIER:

```
#define INCL_WINWORKPLACE
```

FUNCTION PROTOTYPE:

```
ULONG wpQueryDefaultView(WPObject *somSelf);
```

PARAMETERS:

```
somSelf   - Pointer to the object on which the method
            is invoked
```

RETURNS:

```
OPEN_CONTENTS   - Open content view
OPEN_DEFAULT    - Open default view (double-click)
OPEN_DETAILS    - Open details view
OPEN_HELP       - Display help panel
OPEN_RUNNING    - Execute object
OPEN_SETTINGS   - Open Settings notebook
OPEN_TREE       - Open tree view
OPEN_UNKNOWN    - Unknown view
OPEN_USER       - Class specific views have a greater
                  value than this
```

REMARKS:

This method returns the default open view for this instance. This view is displayed when a user double-clicks on the object or when the user selects *Open* without selecting an item in the open cascade.

METHOD USAGE:

This method can be called at any time to determine its default open view.

METHOD OVERRIDE:

This method is not usually overridden.

RELATED METHODS:

wpQueryDefStatusView

This instance method returns the default status view of the current Power object when Advanced Power Management (APM) is enabled.

INCLUDE IDENTIFIER:

```
#define INCL_WINWORKPLACE
```

FUNCTION PROTOTYPE:

```
ULONG wpQueryDefStatusView(WPPower *somSelf);
```

PARAMETERS:

```
somSelf  - Pointer to the object on which the method
           is invoked
```

RETURNS:

```
OPEN_STATUS    - Full status (including the battery
                 life, power source, and battery
                 state) is shown
OPEN_BATTERY   - Only battery life indicator is shown.
```

REMARKS:

When APM is enabled, this method returns the current default view of the Power object.

When APM is not enabled, this method still returns the status but it is not the default view because APM is disabled. The status returned will be the default the next time APM is enabled.

METHOD OVERRIDE:

This method should not be overridden.

RELATED METHODS:

wpQueryDetailsData

This instance method queries the current details data of an object.

INCLUDE IDENTIFIER:

```
#define INCL_WINWORKPLACE
```

FUNCTION PROTOTYPE:

```
BOOL wpQueryDetailsData(WPObject *somSelf,
                        PVOID *ppDetailsData,
                        PULONG pcb);
```

PARAMETERS:

```
somSelf          - Pointer to the object on which the
                   method is invoked.
*ppDetailsData   - Pointer to detail data information.
pcb              - Length of *ppDetailsData buffer. If
                   ppDetailsData is set to NULL, the
                   actual size of ppDetailsData is
                   returned in pcb.
```

RETURNS:

```
TRUE    - Successful completion
FALSE   - Error occurred
```

REMARKS:

All objects that have information to display in details view must override this method. *ppDetailsData is a pointer to the beginning of the buffer into which details data should be written. The override should write whatever data it is responsible for and then increment the pointer to the beginning of the area of the next class in the hierarchy (1 byte past the last field for which it is responsible).

*ppDetailsData *must* be modified so that the subclasses write in the appropriate place.

The details data returned by a class must match the information returned in wpclsQueryDetailsInfo.

METHOD USAGE:

This method can be called at any time to determine the current object details.

METHOD OVERRIDE:

All objects that have information to display in details view must override this method.

The parent method must *always* be called before writing the data an adjusting the pointer.

RELATED METHODS:

wpQueryDisk

This instance method returns the disk object for the drive on which
the file system is located.

INCLUDE IDENTIFIER:

```
#define INCL_WINWORKPLACE
```

FUNCTION PROTOTYPE:

```
WPFileSystem *wpQueryDisk(WPFileSystem *somSelf);
```

PARAMETERS:

```
somSelf  - Pointer to the object on which the method
           is invoked
```

RETURNS:

```
Disk object of the drive on which the file system is
located.
```

wpQueryDisplaySmallIcons

This instance method determines whether the small icons are displayed on the LaunchPad.

INCLUDE IDENTIFIER:

```
#define INCL_WINWORKPLACE
```

FUNCTION PROTOTYPE:

```
BOOL wpQueryDisplaySmallIcons(WPLaunchPad *somSelf);
```

PARAMETERS:

```
somSelf  - Pointer to the object on which the method
           is invoked
```

RETURNS:

```
TRUE   - Small icons are displayed
FALSE  - Normal-sized icons are displayed
```

METHOD OVERRIDE:

This method can be overridden to force a particular value.

RELATED METHODS:

```
wpRefreshDrawer              Page 362
wpSetDisplaySmallIcons       Page 423
```

wpQueryDisplayText

This instance method determines whether the text is displayed under icons on the LaunchPad.

INCLUDE IDENTIFIER:

```
#define INCL_WINWORKPLACE
```

FUNCTION PROTOTYPE:

```
BOOL wpQueryDisplayText(WPLaunchPad *somSelf);
```

PARAMETERS:

```
somSelf   - Pointer to the object on which the method
            is invoked
```

RETURNS:

```
TRUE    - Text is displayed
FALSE   - Text is not displayed
```

METHOD OVERRIDE:

This method can be overridden to force a particular value.

RELATED METHODS:

wpQueryDisplayTextInDrawers

This instance method determines whether the text is displayed under icons in drawers.

INCLUDE IDENTIFIER:

```
#define INCL_WINWORKPLACE
```

FUNCTION PROTOTYPE:

```
BOOL wpQueryDisplayTextInDrawers
                            (WPLaunchPad *somSelf);
```

PARAMETERS:

```
somSelf  - Pointer to the object on which the method
           is invoked
```

RETURNS:

```
TRUE   - Text is displayed
FALSE  - Text is not displayed
```

METHOD OVERRIDE:

This method can be overridden to force a particular value.

RELATED METHODS:

```
wpQueryDisplayText              Page 296
wpRefreshDrawer                 Page 362
wpSetDisplayText                Page 424
wpSetDisplayTextInDrawers       Page 425
```

wpQueryDisplayVertical

This instance method returns the orientation of the LaunchPad.

INCLUDE IDENTIFIER:

```
#define INCL_WINWORKPLACE
```

FUNCTION PROTOTYPE:

```
BOOL wpQueryDisplayVertical(WPLaunchPad *somSelf);
```

PARAMETERS:

```
somSelf   - Pointer to the object on which the method
            is invoked
```

RETURNS:

```
TRUE    - LaunchPad is displayed vertically
FALSE   - LaunchPad is displayed horizontally
```

REMARKS:

```
Drawers are displayed in the opposite direction.
```

METHOD OVERRIDE:

```
This  method  can  be  overridden  to  force  a  particular
value.
```

RELATED METHODS:

```
wpRefreshDrawer              Page 362
wpSetDisplayVertical         Page 426
```

wpQueryDrawerHWND

This instance method returns the handle associated with the open
LaunchPad or drawer.

INCLUDE IDENTIFIER:

```
#define INCL_WINWORKPLACE
```

FUNCTION PROTOTYPE:

```
HWND wpQueryDrawerHWND(WPLaunchPad *somSelf,
                       ULONG ulDrawer);
```

PARAMETERS:

```
somSelf    - Pointer to the object on which the method
             is invoked.
ulDrawer   - LaunchPad or drawer being queried. Values:
                0 - LaunchPad
               >0 - Drawer id
```

RETURNS:

```
hwnd   - Handle of frame window for LaunchPad or drawer
NULL   - View handle is closed
```

METHOD OVERRIDE:

This method can be overridden to know when the slideup
view handle is being requested.

RELATED METHODS:

wpRefreshDrawer   Page 362
wpSetDrawerHWND   Page 427

wpQueryDriveLockStatus

This instance method queries the lock status of a drive.

INCLUDE IDENTIFIER:

```
#define INCL_WINWORKPLACE
```

FUNCTION PROTOTYPE:

```
ULONG wpQueryDriveLockStatus(WPDisk *somSelf
                             PULONG pulLockStatus
                             PULONG pulLockCount);
```

PARAMETERS:

```
somSelf        - Pointer to the object on which the
                 method is invoked.
pulLockStatus  - Pointer to lock status of drive.
                 Values:
                     0 - No media exists in drive, which
                         is unlocked
                     1 - Media exists in drive
                     2 - Drive is locked
                     3 - Media exists in locked drive
pulLockCount   - Number of locks against the drive.
```

RETURNS:

```
 0  - Successful.
>0  - Return code from DosDevIoctl Category 8
      Function 66. If error returned, assume
      lock is not supported by drive and eject.
```

METHOD USAGE:

This method can be called at any time.

METHOD OVERRIDE:

This method should not be overridden.

RELATED METHODS:

wpEjectDisk	Page 197
wpLockDrive	Page 216

wpQueryEASize

This instance method returns the size of a file's extended attributes (EAs).

INCLUDE IDENTIFIER:

```
#define INCL_WINWORKPLACE
```

FUNCTION PROTOTYPE:

```
ULONG wpQueryEASize(WPFileSystem *somSelf);
```

PARAMETERS:

```
somSelf  - Pointer to the object on which the method
           is invoked
```

RETURNS:

```
Size of the extended attributes of the file.
```

METHOD OVERRIDE:

```
This method usually is not overridden.
```

RELATED METHODS:

```
wpQueryFileSize              Page 305
wpSetFileSizeInfo            Page 429
```

wpQueryError

This instance method retrieves the error identity of the last error condition.

INCLUDE IDENTIFIER:

```
#define INCL_WINWORKPLACE
```

FUNCTION PROTOTYPE:

```
ULONG wpQueryError(WPObject *somSelf);
```

PARAMETERS:

```
somSelf  - Pointer to the object on which the method
           is invoked
```

RETURNS:

```
Any of the following error codes:
```

```
WPERR_ALREADY_EXIST
WPERR_BUFFER_OVERFLOW
WPERR_BUFFER_TOO_SMALL
WPERR_CNT_REPLACE_METACLS
WPERR_CLSLOADMOD_FAILED
WPERR_CLSPROCADDR_FAILED
WPERR_INI_FILE_WRITE
WPERR_INVALID_BUFFER
WPERR_INVALID_CLASS
WPERR_INVALID_COUNT
WPERR_INVALID_FLAGS
WPERR_INVALID_FOLDER
WPERR_INVALID_HFIND
WPERR_INVALID_MODULE
WPERR_INVALID_NEWCLASS
WPERR_INVALID_OBJECT
WPERR_INVALID_OBJECTID
WPERR_INVALID_OLDCLASS
WPERR_INVALID_TARGET_OBJECT
WPERR_MEMORY_CLEANUP
WPERR_NO_MEMORY
WPERR_NOT_IMMEDIATE_CHILD
WPERR_NOT_WORKPLACE_CLASS
WPERR_OBJECT_NOT_FOUND
WPERR_OBJWORD_LOCATION
```

WPERR_PROTECTED_CLASS
WPERR_SEMAPHORE_ERROR

REMARKS:

This method retrieves the error identity that was set on this object by the last call to wpSetError.

METHOD USAGE:

This method can be called at any time to determine the identity of the last error that occurred. This method usually is called after calling a method that returned a failure.

METHOD OVERRIDE:

This method is not usually overridden.

RELATED METHODS:

wpSetError   Page 428

wpQueryFilename

This instance method copies the unqualified, or fully-qualified, file name to a buffer.

INCLUDE IDENTIFIER:

```
#define INCL_WINWORKPLACE
```

FUNCTION PROTOTYPE:

```
PSZ wpQueryFilename(WPFileSystem *somSelf,
                    PSZ pszFilename,
                    BOOL fQualified);
```

PARAMETERS:

```
somSelf       - Pointer to the object on which the
                method is invoked.
pszFileName   - String containing the file name.
fQualified    - Qualification requested flag. Values:
                    TRUE
                    FALSE
```

RETURNS:

```
Buffer in which the file name is returned.
```

REMARKS:

The buffer supplied with this call, *pszBuf,* must be as least CCHMAXPATH characters in length, currently defined as 256.

METHOD OVERRIDE:

This method should not be overridden.

wpQueryFileSize

This instance method returns the size of a specified file.

INCLUDE IDENTIFIER:

```
#define INCL_WINWORKPLACE
```

FUNCTION PROTOTYPE:

```
ULONG wpQueryFileSize(WPFileSystem *somSelf);
```

PARAMETERS:

```
somSelf  - Pointer to the object on which the method
           is invoked
```

RETURNS:

```
Size of the specified file.
```

METHOD OVERRIDE:

```
This method usually is not overridden.
```

RELATED METHODS:

wpQueryFldrAttr

This instance method queries a folder's current view attributes for the WC_CONTAINER window that used in each view window.

INCLUDE IDENTIFIER:

```
#define INCL_WINWORKPLACE
```

FUNCTION PROTOTYPE:

```
ULONG wpQueryFldrAttr(WPFolder *somSelf,
                      ULONG ulView);
```

PARAMETERS:

```
somSelf - Pointer to the object on which the method
          is invoked.
ulView  - Flag indicating the view to query. Values:
              OPEN_CONTENTS
              OPEN_DETAILS
              OPEN_HELP
              OPEN_TREE
```

RETURNS:

```
Flag containing current folder-view attribute. These are
the CV_* attributes defined by the container-control
window. See the CNRINFO data structure in Appendix A.
```

METHOD USAGE:

```
This method can be called at any time to determine the
view attributes currently set.
```

METHOD OVERRIDE:

```
This method is not usually overridden.
```

RELATED METHODS:

wpQueryFldrFlags	Page 308
wpQueryFldrFont	Page 309
wpSetFldrAttr	Page 430
wpSetFldrFlags	Page 434
wpSetFldrFont	Page 435

wpQueryFldrDetailsClass

This instance method determines which class of details are set for a folder.

INCLUDE IDENTIFIER:

#define INCL_WINWORKPLACE

FUNCTION PROTOTYPE:

M_WPObject *wpQueryFldrDetailsClass
                              (WPFolder *somSelf);

PARAMETERS:

somSelf - Pointer to the object on which the method
           is invoked

RETURNS:

NULL   - Error occurred
Other - Pointer to the class object for which
         details are to be displayed

REMARKS:

Because folders can contain objects of different classes with different details, the user must often specify which class of details should be displayed. The value set by this method is not used until a details view of the folder is opened. wpSetFldrDetailsClass can be called to set the class of details to be displayed.

METHOD USAGE:

This method can be called at any time to determine the current class of details to be displayed.

METHOD OVERRIDE:

This method is not usually overridden.

RELATED METHODS:

wpSetFldrDetailsClass   Page 432

wpQueryFldrFlags

This instance method queries the current flags of a folder.

INCLUDE IDENTIFIER:

```
#define INCL_WINWORKPLACE
```

FUNCTION PROTOTYPE:

```
ULONG wpQueryFldrFlags(WPFolder *somSelf);
```

PARAMETERS:

```
somSelf  - Pointer to the object on which the method
           is invoked
```

RETURNS:

```
FOI_POPULATEDWITHALL        - Folder was populated with
                              all its contents
FOI_POPULATEDWITHFOLDERS    - Folder was populated only
                              with folders it contains
FOI_WORKAREA                - User sets the work area
                              property
```

METHOD USAGE:

```
This method is called at any time to determine a folder's
flag state.
```

METHOD OVERRIDE:

```
This method is not usually overridden.
```

RELATED METHODS:

wpQueryFldrFont

This instance method queries the current font of a folder.

INCLUDE IDENTIFIER:

```
#define INCL_WINWORKPLACE
```

FUNCTION PROTOTYPE:

```
PSZ wpQueryFldrFont(WPFolder *somSelf, ULONG ulView);
```

PARAMETERS:

```
somSelf - Pointer to object on which method is invoked
ulView  - Flag indicating the view to query. Values:
            OPEN_CONTENTS
            OPEN_DETAILS
            OPEN_TREE
```

RETURNS:

Pointer to font string for specified open view in the format: point size, period, face name (ex:"12.Courier").

REMARKS:

One font for each view; concurrent views have same font.

METHOD USAGE:

This method can be called any time to determine the current font for a view.

METHOD OVERRIDE:

This method is not usually overridden.

RELATED METHODS:

wpQueryFldrAttr	Page 306
wpQueryFldrFlags	Page 308
wpSetFldrAttr	Page 430
wpSetFldrFlags	Page 434
wpSetFldrFont	Page 435

wpQueryFldrSort

This instance method returns a pointer to the sort record for the specified open view and type.

INCLUDE IDENTIFIER:

```
#define INCL_WINWORKPLACE
```

FUNCTION PROTOTYPE:

```
PVOID wpQueryFldrSort(WPFolder *somSelf, ULONG ulView,
                      ULONG ulType);
```

PARAMETERS:

```
somSelf - Pointer to the object on which the method
          is invoked.
ulView  - Flag indicating folder view. Values:
             OPEN_CONTENTS
             OPEN_DETAILS
             OPEN_TREE
ulType  - Flag indicating folder type.
```

RETURNS:

```
Pointer to the SORTFASTINFO structure containing sort
record information for the open view.
```

METHOD OVERRIDE:

```
This method should not be overridden.
```

RELATED METHODS:

wpQueryFldrSortClass

This instance method returns the sort class object whose details are currently being used as sort criteria for a given folder.

INCLUDE IDENTIFIER:

```
#define INCL_WINWORKPLACE
```

FUNCTION PROTOTYPE:

```
M_WPObject *wpQueryFldrSortClass(WPFolder *somSelf);
```

PARAMETERS:

```
somSelf  - Pointer to the object on which the method
           is invoked
```

REMARKS:

The sort class for a particular folder determines what class's sort details appear as active sort criteria for the folder's Settings page and sort submenu. The default sort class for all folders is WPFileSystem. The sort class can be changed through the folder's Settings page or through wpSetFldrSortClass.

METHOD OVERRIDE:

This method usually is not overridden.

RELATED METHODS:

wpQueryFldrSort	Page 310
wpSetFldrSort	Page 436
wpSetFldrSortClass	Page 438

wpQueryFloatOnTop

This instance method determines whether the LaunchPad floats on top of all other windows.

INCLUDE IDENTIFIER:

```
#define INCL_WINWORKPLACE
```

FUNCTION PROTOTYPE:

```
BOOL wpQueryFloatOnTop(WPLaunchPad *somSelf);
```

PARAMETERS:

```
somSelf  - Pointer to the object on which the method
           is invoked
```

RETURNS:

```
TRUE   - LaunchPad floats on top
FALSE  - LaunchPad does not float on top
```

METHOD OVERRIDE:

This method can be overridden to force a particular value.

RELATED METHODS:

wpRefreshDrawer   Page 362
wpSetFloatOnTop   Page 439

wpQueryFolder

This instance method returns the folder that this object resides in.

INCLUDE IDENTIFIER:

```
#define INCL_WINWORKPLACE
```

FUNCTION PROTOTYPE:

```
WPObject *wpQueryFolder(WPObject *somSelf);
```

PARAMETERS:

```
somSelf   - Pointer to the object on which the method
            is invoked
```

RETURNS:

```
Pointer to a container object that contains the speci-
fied object. All objects are contained by a folder except
for a drive object (root direction folder) for which
this method returns NULL.
```

METHOD USAGE:

```
This method can be called at any time to query the folder
that contains the current object.
```

METHOD OVERRIDE:

```
This method usually is not overridden.
```

RELATED METHODS:

```
wpclsQueryFolder                Page 525
```

wpQueryHandle

This instance method returns a persistent object handle for the specified object instance.

INCLUDE IDENTIFIER:

```
#define INCL_WINWORKPLACE
```

FUNCTION PROTOTYPE:

```
HOBJECT wpQueryHandle(WPObject *somSelf);
```

PARAMETERS:

```
somSelf  - Pointer to object on which method invoked
```

RETURNS:

```
Persistent handle for this object.
```

REMARKS:

The object handle returned is the same as that used from WinCreateObject, WinSetObjectData, or WinDestroyObject. The handle is unique on a given machine so the returned object handle can be passed to other processes or stored.

This method should be used sparingly on file-based object classes because OS/2 tracks the current location of every single file object that is allocated an object handle. Performance can be adversely affected if handles are obtained to every single file object awakened.

METHOD USAGE:

This method can be called any time to get a handle that is persistent across restarts and unique on a machine.

METHOD OVERRIDE:

This method should not be overridden.

RELATED METHODS:

wpclsQueryObject   Page 536

wpQueryHideLaunchPadFrame-Ctls

This instance method determines whether the system menu and the title bar for the LaunchPad are hidden.

INCLUDE IDENTIFIER:

```
#define INCL_WINWORKPLACE
```

FUNCTION PROTOTYPE:

```
BOOL wpQueryHideLaunchPadFrameCtls
                        (WPLaunchPad *somSelf);
```

PARAMETERS:

```
somSelf  - Pointer to the object on which the method
           is invoked
```

RETURNS:

```
TRUE   - Frame controls are hidden
FALSE  - Frame controls are not hidden
```

METHOD OVERRIDE:

```
This method can be overridden to force a particular
value.
```

RELATED METHODS:

```
wpRefreshDrawer                  Page 362
wpSetHideLaunchPadFrameCtls      Page 440
```

wpQueryIcon

This instance method queries the current icon of an object.

INCLUDE IDENTIFIER:

```
#define INCL_WINWORKPLACE
```

FUNCTION PROTOTYPE:

```
HPOINTER wpQueryIcon(WPObject *somSelf);
```

PARAMETERS:

```
somSelf  - Pointer to the object on which the method
           is invoked
```

RETURNS:

```
NULLHANDLE  - Error occurred
Other       - Handle to an icon
```

METHOD USAGE:

```
This method can be called at any time to get the handle
to the current icon for this object.
```

METHOD OVERRIDE:

```
This method is not usually overridden. The default icon
for a class is typically set from an override of
wpclsQueryIcon and the instance's icon may be altered
with wpSetIcon.
```

RELATED METHODS:

wpQueryIconData	Page 317
wpSetIcon	Page 441
wpSetIconData	Page 442
wpclsQueryIcon	Page 527

wpQueryIconData

This instance method queries the data to be used for the current icon of an object.

INCLUDE IDENTIFIER:

```
#define INCL_WINWORKPLACE
```

FUNCTION PROTOTYPE:

```
ULONG wpQueryIconData(WPObject *somSelf,
                      PICONINFO pIconInfo);
```

PARAMETERS:

```
somSelf     - Pointer to the object on which the
              method is invoked
pIconInfo   - Pointer to an ICONINFO structure
              containing an icon specification
```

RETURNS:

```
Other   - Successful completion
0       - Error occurred
```

METHOD USAGE:

This method is called at any time to query the data for the current icon for this object.

METHOD OVERRIDE:

This method is not usually overridden.

RELATED METHODS:

wpQueryIconViewPos

This instance method returns the initial icon view position of a given folder.

INCLUDE IDENTIFIER:

```
#define INCL_WINWORKPLACE
```

FUNCTION PROTOTYPE:

```
CHAR *wpQueryIconViewPos(WPFolder *somSelf);
```

PARAMETERS:

```
somSelf  - Pointer to the object on which the method
           is invoked
```

RETURNS:

```
Pointer to the string containing the initial icon view
position x, y, cx, and cy.
```

METHOD OVERRIDE:

```
This method usually is not overridden.
```

wpQueryJobFile

This instance method returns the spool file name for the local print jobs.

INCLUDE IDENTIFIER:

```
#define INCL_WINWORKPLACE
```

FUNCTION PROTOTYPE:

```
BOOL wpQueryJobFile(WPJob *somSelf, PSZ pBuf,
                    PULONG pcbBuf);
```

PARAMETERS:

```
somSelf - Pointer to the object on which the method
          is invoked.
pBuf    - Buffer in which complete path to spool file
          is returned. Return value of NULL indicates
          that pcbBuf is too small to hold network Id.
pcbBuf  - Pointer to length, in bytes of pBuf buffer.
          If either pBuf is NULL or this call fails,
          length of required buffer plus one is
          returned in this parameter.
```

RETURNS:

```
TRUE   - Successful completion
FALSE  - Error occurred
```

METHOD USAGE:

```
This method can be called at any time.
```

METHOD OVERRIDE:

```
This method usually is not overridden.
```

RELATED METHODS:

wpQueryJobId

This instance method returns the job id of the current job.

INCLUDE IDENTIFIER:

```
#define INCL_WINWORKPLACE
```

FUNCTION PROTOTYPE:

```
ULONG wpQueryJobId(WPJob *somSelf);
```

PARAMETERS:

```
somSelf  - Pointer to the object on which the method
           is invoked
```

RETURNS:

```
Job id of the current object.
```

METHOD USAGE:

```
This method can be called at any time.
```

METHOD OVERRIDE:

```
This method usually is not overridden.
```

RELATED METHODS:

wpQueryJobType

This instance method returns the data type of the given job.

INCLUDE IDENTIFIER:

```
#define INCL_WINWORKPLACE
```

FUNCTION PROTOTYPE:

```
BOOL wpQueryJobType(WPJob *somSelf, PSZ pBuf,
                    PULONG pcbBuf);
```

PARAMETERS:

```
somSelf - Pointer to the object on which the method
          is invoked.
pBuf    - Buffer in which data type of spooled job is
          returned. Return value of NULL indicates
          that pcbBuf is too small to hold data-type
          string. Example data types are "PM_Q_STD"
          or "PM_Q_RAW."
pcbBuf  - Pointer to length, in bytes of pBuf buffer.
          If either pBuf is NULL or this call fails,
          the length of the required buffer + 1 is
          returned in this parameter.
```

RETURNS:

```
TRUE   - Successful completion
FALSE  - Error occurred
```

METHOD OVERRIDE:

This method usually is not overridden.

RELATED METHODS:

wpQueryLastAccess

This instance method returns the last date and time a given file was accessed.

INCLUDE IDENTIFIER:

```
#define INCL_WINWORKPLACE
```

FUNCTION PROTOTYPE:

```
ULONG wpQueryLastAccess(WPFileSystem *somSelf,
                        FDATE *fDate, FTIME *fTime);
```

PARAMETERS:

```
somSelf - Pointer to the object on which the method
          is invoked
fDate   - Pointer to date structure containing last
          date the file was accessed
fTime   - Pointer to time structure containing last
          time the file was accessed
```

RETURNS:

```
0       - No error
Other   - Error occurred
```

METHOD OVERRIDE:

```
This method usually is not overridden.
```

RELATED METHODS:

```
wpQueryCreation              Page 284
wpQueryLastWrite             Page 323
```

wpQueryLastWrite

This instance method returns the last date and time a given file was written to.

INCLUDE IDENTIFIER:

```
#define INCL_WINWORKPLACE
```

FUNCTION PROTOTYPE:

```
ULONG wpQueryLastWrite(WPFileSystem *somSelf,
                       FDATE *fDate, FTIME *fTime);
```

PARAMETERS:

```
somSelf - Pointer to the object on which the method
          is invoked
fDate   - Pointer to date structure containing last
          date the file was written to
fTime   - Pointer to time structure containing last
          time the file was written to
```

RETURNS:

```
0      - No error
Other  - Error occurred
```

METHOD OVERRIDE:

```
This method usually is not overridden.
```

RELATED METHODS:

```
wpQueryCreation                Page 284
wpQueryLastAccess              Page 323
```

wpQueryLocalAlias

This instance method returns the local alias associated with the network printer object. This alias is the local print queue name as defined in Settings notebook of the OS/2 Spooler.

INCLUDE IDENTIFIER:

```
#define INCL_WINWORKPLACE
```

FUNCTION PROTOTYPE:

```
BOOL wpQueryLocalAlias(WPRPrinter *somSelf, PSZ pBuf,
                       PULONG pcbBuf);
```

PARAMETERS:

```
somSelf - Pointer to the object on which the method
          is invoked.
pBuf     - Buffer in which local print queue name is
          returned.
pcbBuf   - Size, in bytes, of pBuf buffer. If 0 or this
          call fails, the length of the required
          buffer + 1 is returned in this parameter.
```

RETURNS:

```
TRUE    - Successful completion
FALSE   - Error occurred
```

REMARKS:

The returned local print queue name can be used to submit print jobs to the network printer. If there is no local print queue that references this network printer object, *pcbBuf* is set to 0 and FALSE is returned.

METHOD USAGE:

This method can be called at any time.

METHOD OVERRIDE:

This method usually is not overridden.

RELATED METHODS:

wpQueryLogicalDrive

This instance method returns the logical drive number that is represented by this disk object.

INCLUDE IDENTIFIER:

```
#define INCL_WINWORKPLACE
```

FUNCTION PROTOTYPE:

```
ULONG wpQueryLogicalDrive(WPDisk *somSelf);
```

PARAMETERS:

```
somSelf  - Pointer to the object on which the method
           is invoked
```

RETURNS:

```
Logical drive identifier.
```

REMARKS:

Every instance of WPDisk that is created in the system must represent a logical drive partition. There should never be more than one disk object per logical drive.

METHOD USAGE:

This method can be called at any time.

METHOD OVERRIDE:

This method should not be overridden.

wpQueryMinWindow

This instance method returns the minimized window behavior of an object.

INCLUDE IDENTIFIER:

```
#define INCL_WINWORKPLACE
```

FUNCTION PROTOTYPE:

```
ULONG wpQueryMinWindow(WPObject *somSelf);
```

PARAMETERS:

```
somSelf  - Pointer to the object on which the method
           is invoked
```

RETURNS:

```
One of the following flags, indicating minimized window
behavior:

  MINWIN_DEFAULT
  MINWIN_DESKTOP
  MINWIN_HIDDEN
  MINWIN_VIEWER
```

METHOD USAGE:

```
This method is usually called by the system in order to
retrieve an object's minimized window behavior.
```

METHOD OVERRIDE:

```
This method usually is not overridden.
```

RELATED METHODS:

```
wpSetMinWindow                Page 445
```

wpQueryNameClashOptions

This instance method returns the options that will not be available on the name clash dialog.

INCLUDE IDENTIFIER:

```
#define INCL_WINWORKPLACE
```

FUNCTION PROTOTYPE:

```
ULONG wpQueryNameClashOptions(WPObject *somSelf,
                              ULONG menuId);
```

PARAMETERS:

```
somSelf - Pointer to the object on which the method
          is invoked
menuId  - Id of selected menu item that caused the
          name clash options to be queried
```

RETURNS:

```
NO_NAMECLASH_RENAME    - Renames are not allowed
NO_NAMECLASH_DIALOG    - Dialogs are not shown
NO_NAMECLASH_APPEND    - Appends are not allowed
NO_NAMECLASH_REPLACE   - Replacements are not allowed
```

METHOD OVERRIDE:

This method usually is not overridden.

wpQueryNetIdentity

This instance method returns the fully qualified network name of this network group.

INCLUDE IDENTIFIER:

```
#define INCL_WINWORKPLACE
```

FUNCTION PROTOTYPE:

```
PSZ wpQueryNetIdentity(WPNetgrp *somSelf);
```

PARAMETERS:

```
somSelf  - Pointer to the object on which the method
           is invoked
```

RETURNS:

```
Fully qualified network name of this network group.
```

METHOD OVERRIDE:

```
This method usually is not overridden.
```

RELATED METHODS:

wpQueryNetworkId

This instance method returns the fully qualified network id of the remote print queue for the network printer object.

INCLUDE IDENTIFIER:

```
#define INCL_WINWORKPLACE
```

FUNCTION PROTOTYPE:

```
BOOL wpQueryNetworkId(WPRPrinter *somSelf, PSZ pBuf,
                      PULONG pcbBuf);
```

PARAMETERS:

```
somSelf - Pointer to the object on which the method
          is invoked.
pBuf    - Buffer in which network id is returned.
          Network id must be following form:
          <NetworkId>;\\<ServerId>\<Resource>
          For example, LS:\\DEPTSERV\DEPTPRNT.
          A return value of NULL indicates that
          pcbBuf is too small to hold network id.
pcbBuf  - Size, in bytes, of pBuf buffer. If pBuf is
          NULL or this call fails, length of required
          buffer is returned in this parameter.
```

RETURNS:

```
TRUE    - Successful completion
FALSE   - Error occurred
```

METHOD OVERRIDE:

```
This method usually is not overridden.
```

RELATED METHODS:

wpQueryNextIconPos

This instance method queries the next icon position of a folder.

INCLUDE IDENTIFIER:

```
#define INCL_WINWORKPLACE
```

FUNCTION PROTOTYPE:

```
PPOINTL wpQueryNextIconPos(WPFolder *somSelf);
```

PARAMETERS:

```
somSelf  - Pointer to the object on which the method
           is invoked
```

RETURNS:

A pointer to the next position at which icons will be inserted.

REMARKS:

The next icon is the next available *parking space* within the folder's client area.

METHOD USAGE:

This method can be called at any time to determine the next position where objects will be inserted in the file.

METHOD OVERRIDE:

This method is not usually overridden.

RELATED METHODS:

wpSetNextIconPos   Page 447

wpQueryObjectID

This instance method returns the unique, text object id that was assigned to the given object when it was installed or changed (with wpSetup).

INCLUDE IDENTIFIER:

```
#define INCL_WINWORKPLACE
```

FUNCTION PROTOTYPE:

```
PSZ wpQueryObjectID(WPObject *somSelf);
```

PARAMETERS:

```
somSelf  - Pointer to the object on which the method
           is invoked
```

RETURNS:

```
String containing a unique object id.
```

REMARKS:

The install routine uses this variable to ensure that a given object is never re-installed, thereby avoiding duplication of objects.

The object id is always lost when the object is copied; therefore, only one object ever exists for a given object id.

RELATED METHODS:

wpSetObjectID   Page 448

wpQueryObjectList

This instance method returns a list of object buttons displayed on the LaunchPad or drawer.

INCLUDE IDENTIFIER:

```
#define INCL_WINWORKPLACE
```

FUNCTION PROTOTYPE:

```
HOBJECT wpQueryObjectList(WPLaunchPad *somSelf,
                          ULONG ulDrawer,
                          PULONG pulNumActions);
```

PARAMETERS:

somSelf	- Pointer to the object on which the method is invoked.
ulDrawer	- LaunchPad or drawer being queried. Values:
	0
	>0
pulNumActions	- Pointer to number of objects returned.

RETURNS:

Pointer to array of objects displayed on LaunchPad or drawers.

METHOD OVERRIDE:

This method can be overridden to add or change objects.

RELATED METHODS:

wpRefreshDrawer   Page 362

wpQueryObjectNetId

This instance method returns the network id of the shared-directory
object that this object is linked to.

INCLUDE IDENTIFIER:

```
#define INCL_WINWORKPLACE
```

FUNCTION PROTOTYPE:

```
PSZ wpQueryObjectNetId(WPNetLink *somSelf);
```

PARAMETERS:

```
somSelf  - Pointer to the object on which the method
           is invoked
```

RETURNS:

Pointer to network id string. Network name is in the
following format:

```
"<NetworkId>\<ServerId>\<Share Name>"
```

REMARKS:

The shared-directory object uses this id to make its
network calls. This id is not stored in the object's
data.

METHOD USAGE:

This method can be called at any time to retrieve the
network id of an object.

METHOD OVERRIDE:

This method usually is not overridden.

RELATED METHODS:

wpQueryPaletteHelp

This instance method returns the help panel id that is displayed when the **Help** push button is used from an open palette view.

INCLUDE IDENTIFIER:

```
#define INCL_WINWORKPLACE
```

FUNCTION PROTOTYPE:

```
ULONG wpQueryPaletteHelp(WPPalette *somSelf);
```

PARAMETERS:

```
somSelf  - Pointer to the object on which the method
           is invoked
```

RETURNS:

The help panel id within this class's help module as specified by wpQueryDefaultHelp for this object instance.

REMARKS:

This method returns the help panel id that is visible from the open palette view. That panel should describe what the palette cells represent, how to edit them, and how to apply the cell values to other windows or objects. The palette object can specify class default and instance specific helps for the object in addition to this specialized help that only applies to the palette view.

METHOD USAGE:

This method can be called at any time.

METHOD OVERRIDE:

All subclasses of WPPalette need to override this method to provide help about their open palette view window.

RELATED METHODS:

wpQueryPaletteInfo

This instance method determines current information about the palette.

INCLUDE IDENTIFIER:

```
#define INCL_WINWORKPLACE
```

FUNCTION PROTOTYPE:

```
BOOL wpQueryPaletteInfo(WPPalette *somSelf,
                        PPALINFO pPalInfo);
```

PARAMETERS:

somSelf   - Pointer to the object on which the method
            is invoked
pPalInfo - Pointer to a PALINFO structure

RETURNS:

TRUE   - Successful completion
FALSE   - Error occurred

REMARKS:

The palette information can be set by issuing a call to
wpSetPaletteInfo.

METHOD USAGE:

This method can be called at any time to get current
information about the palette.

METHOD OVERRIDE:

This method is not usually overridden.

RELATED METHODS:

wpSetPaletteInfo   Page 453

wpQueryPowerConfirmation

This instance method queries the current confirmation-message control value for the Power object. This message is displayed when power-status changes are requested from the pop-up menu of the Power object.

INCLUDE IDENTIFIER:

```
#define INCL_WINWORKPLACE
```

FUNCTION PROTOTYPE:

```
BOOL wpQueryPowerConfirmation(WPPower *somSelf);
```

PARAMETERS:

```
somSelf - Pointer to the object on which the method
          is invoked
```

RETURNS:

```
TRUE   - Confirmation enabled
FALSE  - Confirmation disabled
```

RELATED METHODS:

wpQueryPowerManagement

This instance method queries the enable or disable state of the OS/2 Power Management support.

INCLUDE IDENTIFIER:

```
#define INCL_WINWORKPLACE
```

FUNCTION PROTOTYPE:

```
BOOL wpQueryPowerManagement(WPPower *somSelf);
```

PARAMETERS:

```
somSelf - Pointer to the object on which the method
          is invoked
```

RETURNS:

```
TRUE    - Power management enabled
FALSE   - Power management disabled
```

RELATED METHODS:

wpQueryPrinterName

This instance method queries the name of the printer.

INCLUDE IDENTIFIER:

```
#define INCL_WINWORKPLACE
```

FUNCTION PROTOTYPE:

```
BOOL wpQueryPrinterName(WPPrinter *somSelf,
                        PSZ pszPrinterName);
```

PARAMETERS:

```
somSelf         - Pointer to the object to be queried
pszPrinterName  - Returned printer name of the object
                  queried
```

RETURNS:

```
TRUE   - Successful completion
FALSE  - Error occurred
```

REMARKS:

If this is a printer object, the printer queue name is defined on the computer specified by wpQueryComputer-Name. Use wpQueryLocalAlias to retrieve the local print queue name for network printer objects.

METHOD OVERRIDE:

This method is not usually overridden.

RELATED METHODS:

340

wpQueryPrintObject

This instance method returns a pointer to the printer object that contains the current job.

INCLUDE IDENTIFIER:

```
#define INCL_IDENTIFIER:
```

FUNCTION PROTOTYPE:

```
WPObject wpQueryPrintObject(WPJob *somSelf);
```

PARAMETERS:

```
somSelf  - Pointer to the object on which the method
           is invoked
```

RETURNS:

```
Pointer to the printer object.
```

METHOD USAGE:

```
This method can be called at any time.
```

METHOD OVERRIDE:

```
This method usually is not overridden.
```

wpQueryProgDetails

This WPProgram instance method queries the program details of an object.

INCLUDE IDENTIFIER:

```
#define INCL_WINWORKPLACE
```

FUNCTION PROTOTYPE:

```
BOOL wpQueryProgDetails(WPProgram *somSelf,
                        PPROGDETAILS pProgDetails,
                        PULONG pSize);
```

PARAMETERS:

somSelf   - Pointer to the object on which the
                 method is invoked.
pProgDetails   - Pointer to the program details.
pSize   - Pointer to size of pProgDetails
                 buffer. If NULL, the size of the
                 current pProgDetails is returned in
                 Size.

RETURNS:

TRUE   - Successful completion
FALSE - Error occurred

METHOD USAGE:

This method can be called at any time to determine the details on this object.

METHOD OVERRIDE:

This method is not usually overridden.

RELATED METHODS:

wpSetProgDetails   Page 457

wpQueryProgDetails

This WPProgramFile instance method queries the program details of an object.

INCLUDE IDENTIFIER:

```
#define INCL_WINWORKPLACE
```

FUNCTION PROTOTYPE:

```
BOOL wpQueryProgDetails(WPProgramFile *somSelf,
                        PPROGDETAILS pProgDetails,
                        PULONG pSize);
```

PARAMETERS:

somSelf
- Pointer to the object on which the method is invoked.

pProgDetails
- Pointer to the program details.

pSize
- Pointer to size of pProgDetails buffer. If NULL, the size of the current pProgDetails is returned in *Size*.

RETURNS:

TRUE   - Success completion
FALSE - Error occurred

METHOD USAGE:

This method can be called at any time to determine the details on this object.

METHOD OVERRIDE:

This method is not usually overridden.

RELATED METHODS:

wpSetProgDetails   Page 457

wpQueryProgramAssociations

This instance method returns the program associations from the .INI file.

INCLUDE IDENTIFIER:

```
#define INCL_WINWORKPLACE
```

FUNCTION PROTOTYPE:

```
PSZ wpQueryProgramAssociations(WPProgram *somSelf,
                               PBYTE ptr,
                               PSZ pszAssoc,
                               BOOL fFilter);
```

PARAMETERS:

somSelf   - Pointer to the object on which the method
            is invoked.
ptr   - Pointer.
pszAssoc - Pointer to string of data-file association
            types or filters, separated by commas. If
            fFilter is TRUE, pszAssoc should contain
            filters instead of types.
fFilter   - Filter flag. Values:
                 TRUE
                 FALSE

RETURNS:

Pointer to association string.

METHOD USAGE:

This method can be called at any time.

METHOD OVERRIDE:

This method usually is not overridden.

RELATED METHODS:

wpSetProgramAssociations   Page 461

wpQueryProgramAssociations

This instance method returns the program associations from the .INI file.

INCLUDE IDENTIFIER:

```
#define INCL_WINWORKPLACE
```

FUNCTION PROTOTYPE:

```
PSZ wpQueryProgramAssociations(WPProgramFile *somSelf,
                               PBYTE ptr,
                               PSZ pszAssoc,
                               BOOL fFilter);
```

PARAMETERS:

somSelf	- Pointer to the object on which the method is invoked.
ptr	- Pointer.
pszAssoc	- Pointer to string of data-file association types or filters, separated by commas. If fFilter is TRUE, pszAssoc should contain filters instead of types.
fFilter	- Filter flag. Values: TRUE FALSE

RETURNS:

Pointer to association string.

METHOD USAGE:

This method can be called at any time.

METHOD OVERRIDE:

This method usually is not overridden.

RELATED METHODS:

wpQueryProgramAssociations   Page 344

wpQueryQueueOptions

This instance method returns the queue options of the printer object.

INCLUDE IDENTIFIER:

```
#define INCL_WINWORKPLACE
```

FUNCTION PROTOTYPE:

```
ULONG wpQueryQueueOptions(WPPrinter *somSelf);
```

PARAMETERS:

```
somSelf  - Pointer to the object on which the method
           is invoked
```

RETURNS:

Flag indicating queue option settings. The following flags can be ORed together:

```
PO_PRINTERSPECIFIC        - If set, printer object spools
                            print jobs in PM_Q_RAW
                            format. If cleared,
                            printer object spools print
                            jobs in PM_Q_STD format.
PO_PRINTWHILESPOOLING     - If set, printing is enabled
                            while job is spooling. If
                            cleared, printing occurs
                            only after job is spooled.
PO_APPDEFAULT             - If set, this printer object
                            becomes the application's
                            default printer object. If
                            cleared, the application's
                            default printer object is not
                            changed.
PO_DIALOGBEFOREPRINT      - If set, the Job Properties
                            dialog is displayed when job
                            is submitted to this
                            printer object. If cleared,
                            the dialog is not displayed.
```

METHOD USAGE:

This method can be called at any time.

METHOD OVERRIDE:

This method usually is not overridden.

RELATED METHODS:

wpSetQueueOptions   Page 463

wpQueryRealName

This instance method queries the physical file name of an object.

INCLUDE IDENTIFIER:

```
#define INCL_WINWORKPLACE
```

FUNCTION PROTOTYPE:

```
BOOL wpQueryRealName(WPFileSystem *somSelf,
                     PSZ pszFilename, PULONG pcb,
                     BOOL fQualified);
```

PARAMETERS:

somSelf   – Pointer to the object on which the
                method is invoked.
pszFilename   – Pointer to the buffer in which to
                place the real file name of the object.
pcb   – Size of the file name buffer. If
                pszFileName is set to NULL, the actual
                length of the file is returned.
fQualified   – Indicates if the fully qualified path
                is queried. Values:
                    TRUE
                    FALSE

RETURNS:

TRUE   – Successful completion
FALSE   – Error occurred

REMARKS:

This method returns the fully qualified path name for
this object. Generally, the object's real name and title
are the same. For file systems that do not support the
features of a title, the title is stored in the .LONGNAME
extended attribute and then the title and real name may
differ. The real name of the file object can be used
with any of the DOS*xxx* functions that act on file names.

METHOD USAGE:

This method can be called at any time to determine the
physical file name for this object.

METHOD OVERRIDE:

This method is not usually overridden.

RELATED METHODS:

wpQueryRefreshRate

This instance method queries the current status-window update rate used by the Power object when automatic refresh is enabled.

INCLUDE IDENTIFIER:

```
#define INCL_WINWORKPLACE
```

FUNCTION PROTOTYPE:

```
ULONG wpQueryRefreshRate(WPPower *somSelf);
```

PARAMETERS:

```
somSelf - Pointer to the object on which the method
          is invoked
```

RELATED METHODS:

wpQueryRemoteOptions

This instance method returns the remote options of a printer object.

INCLUDE IDENTIFIER:

```
#define INCL_WINWORKPLACE
```

FUNCTION PROTOTYPE:

```
BOOL wpQueryRemoteOptions(WPPrinter *somSelf,
                          ULONG ulRefreshIntervals,
                          PULONG pflAllJobs);
```

PARAMETERS:

somSelf   – Pointer to the object on which
                      the method is invoked.
ulRefreshIntervals – Time interval, in seconds, when
                      printer object is refreshed.
pflAllJobs   – Flag indicating which jobs to
                      display. Values:
                           TRUE
                           FALSE

RETURNS:

TRUE   – Successful completion
FALSE – Error occurred

METHOD USAGE:

This method can be called at any time.

METHOD OVERRIDE:

This method usually is not overridden.

RELATED METHODS:

wpSetRemoteOptions   Page 466

wpQueryRootFolder

This instance method returns the root folder object for the logical drive represented by the WPDisk object.

INCLUDE IDENTIFIER:

```
#define INCL_WINWORKPLACE
```

FUNCTION PROTOTYPE:

```
WPRootFolder *wpQueryRootFolder(WPDisk *somSelf);
```

PARAMETERS:

```
somSelf   - Pointer to the object on which the method
            is invoked
```

RETURNS:

```
The root folder object; NULL if an error occurred.
```

REMARKS:

```
Every instance of WPDisk that is created in the system
points to a root folder, the root directory of the
logical device that the disk object represents.
```

METHOD USAGE:

```
This method can be called at any time.
```

METHOD OVERRIDE:

```
This method should not be overridden.
```

wpQueryScreenGroupID

This instance method returns the screen group id of the running application for a specified object.

INCLUDE IDENTIFIER:

```
#define INCL_WINWORKPLACE
```

FUNCTION PROTOTYPE:

```
USHORT wpQueryScreenGroupID(WPObject *somSelf,
                                USHORT usPrevSgld);
```

PARAMETERS:

```
somSelf      - Pointer to the object on which the
               method is invoked
usPrevSgld   - Previous screen group Id
```

RETURNS:

```
0       - First id is returned
Other   - Next id after usPrevSgld is returned
```

METHOD USAGE:

```
This method can be called at any time.
```

METHOD OVERRIDE:

```
This method should not be overridden.
```

wpQueryShadowedObject

This instance method enables the shadow object to query the object with which it is currently linked.

INCLUDE IDENTIFIER:

```
#define INCL_WINWORKPLACE
```

FUNCTION PROTOTYPE:

```
WPObject *wpQueryShadowedObject(WPShadow *somSelf,
                                BOOL fLock);
```

PARAMETERS:

```
somSelf - Pointer to the object on which the method
          is invoked.
fLock   - Lock object flag. If FALSE, the newly
          created object is made dormant whenever
          the object and folder containing the object
          are closed. If TRUE, the new flag remains
          awake until caller issues wpUnlockObject.
```

RETURNS:

```
NULL  - Error occurred
Other - Pointer to the object with which this shadow
        is linked
```

METHOD USAGE:

```
This method is called at any time to determine the object
with which this shadow is currently linked.
```

METHOD OVERRIDE:

```
This method is not usually overridden.
```

RELATED METHODS:

```
wpCreateShadowObject          Page 174
```

wpQuerySrvrIdentity

This instance method returns the fully qualified server name of this network group.

INCLUDE IDENTIFIER:

```
#define INCL_WINWORKPLACE
```

FUNCTION PROTOTYPE:

```
PSZ wpQuerySrvrIdentity(WPServer *somSelf);
```

PARAMETERS:

```
somSelf  - Pointer to the object on which the method
           is invoked
```

RETURNS:

```
Fully qualified server name of server group.
```

METHOD OVERRIDE:

```
This method usually is not overridden.
```

RELATED METHODS:

wpQueryStyle

This instance method queries the current class style of an object.

INCLUDE IDENTIFIER:

```
#define INCL_WINWORKPLACE
```

FUNCTION PROTOTYPE:

```
ULONG wpQueryStyle(WPObject *somSelf);
```

PARAMETERS:

```
somSelf  - Pointer to the object on which the method
           is invoked
```

RETURNS:

Object styles. The following flags can be ORed together to indicate the style of the object:

```
OBJSTYLE_CUSTOMICON
OBJSTYLE_NOCOPY
OBJSTYLE_NODELETE
OBJSTYLE_NODRAG
OBJSTYLE_NODROPON
OBJSTYLE_NOLINK
OBJSTYLE_NOMOVE
OBJSTYLE_NOPRINT
OBJSTYLE_NORENAME
OBJSTYLE_NOSETTINGS
OBJSTYLE_NOTVISIBLE
OBJSTYLE_TEMPLATE
```

METHOD USAGE:

This method can be called at any time to determine the current style for an object class. To determine the default style, wpclsQueryStyle should be called.

METHOD OVERRIDE:

This method is not usually overridden.

RELATED METHODS:

```
wpSetStyle                    Page  469
wpclsQueryStyle               Page  547
```

wpQueryTitle

This instance method queries the current title of an object.

INCLUDE IDENTIFIER:

```
#define INCL_WINWORKPLACE
```

FUNCTION PROTOTYPE:

```
PSZ wpQueryTitle(WPObject *somSelf);
```

PARAMETERS:

```
somSelf  - Pointer to the object on which the method
           is invoked
```

RETURNS:

```
Pointer to the object title.
```

REMARKS:

The object title can be altered by the user at any time. Objects should always use this method to access the current title and never store the string pointer that is returned.

METHOD USAGE:

This method can be called at any time to determine the current title of an object. To determine the default title, wpclsQueryTitle should be called.

METHOD OVERRIDE:

This method is not usually overridden.

RELATED METHODS:

wpQueryType

This instance method queries the file type of an object.

INCLUDE IDENTIFIER:

```
#define INCL_WINWORKPLACE
```

FUNCTION PROTOTYPE:

```
PSZ wpQueryType(WPFileSystem *somSelf);
```

PARAMETERS:

```
somSelf  - Pointer to the object on which the method
           is invoked
```

RETURNS:

The pointer to a buffer containing file type. This string can contain a list of types delineated by a line feed character.

REMARKS:

This method returns the type of a file-system-based object. The type of a file is designated by its .TYPE extended attribute value.

METHOD USAGE:

This method can be called at any time to determine the type of the file object.

METHOD OVERRIDE:

This method is not usually overridden.

RELATED METHODS:

wpRedrawCell

This instance method forces a palette object to repaint the specified cell area.

INCLUDE IDENTIFIER:

```
#define INCL_WINWORKPLACE
```

FUNCTION PROTOTYPE:

```
BOOL wpRedrawCell(WPPalette *somSelf, PCELL pCell);
```

PARAMETERS:

```
somSelf   - Pointer to the object on which the method
            is invoked
pCell     - Pointer to the cell within the palette
            that needs repainting
```

RETURNS:

```
TRUE    - Successful
FALSE   - Unsuccessful
```

REMARKS:

This method is used as cell values within the palette are altered. For example, when the color selector dialog is changing the color of a palette cell in the color palette, this method is invoked to refresh the color back in the open views of the color palette object.

METHOD USAGE:

This method may be called at any time to force the palette object to repaint the specified cell in all of its currently open views.

METHOD OVERRIDE:

Overriding this method is not recommended.

RELATED METHODS:

wpPaintCell   Page 250

360

wpRefresh

This instance method refreshes the contents of a folder.

INCLUDE IDENTIFIER:

```
#define INCL_WINWORKPLACE
```

FUNCTION PROTOTYPE:

```
BOOL wpRefresh(WPFileSystem *somSelf, ULONG ulView,
               PVOID pReserved);
```

PARAMETERS:

```
somSelf    - Pointer to the object on which the
             method is invoked.
ulView     - Flag indicating which view to refresh.
             Values:
                 OPEN_CONTENT
                 OPEN_DETAILS
                 OPEN_TREE
pReserved  - Reserved value; must be 0.
```

RETURNS:

```
TRUE   - Successful completion
FALSE  - Error occurred
```

METHOD USAGE:

This method can be called at any time to refresh the
contents of a folder.

METHOD OVERRIDE:

This method is not usually overridden.

RELATED METHODS:

wpPopulate   Page 252

wpRefreshDrawer

This instance method updates the drawer after changes have been
made in the set of objects in the LaunchPad or drawer.

INCLUDE IDENTIFIER:

```
#define INCL_WINWORKPLACE
```

FUNCTION PROTOTYPE:

```
VOID wpRefreshDrawer(WPLaunchPad *somSelf,
                     ULONG ulDrawer);
```

PARAMETERS:

```
somSelf    - Pointer to the object on which the method
             is invoked.
ulDrawer   - LaunchPad or drawer is being refreshed.
             Values:
                0
                >0
```

RETURNS:

```
There is no return value for this method.
```

METHOD OVERRIDE:

```
This method can be overridden to know when the drawer
is being refreshed.

During the processing of wpRefreshDrawer, wpSetDraw-
erHWND is called to set hwnd to NULLHANDLE while the
objects are being recreated. It then calls wpSetDraw-
erHWND to set hwnd back to handle of the frame window
for the drawer.
```

RELATED METHODS:

```
wpQueryDrawerHWND              Page 299
wpSetDrawerHWND                Page 427
```

wpRegisterView

This instance method registers a new open view of an object.

INCLUDE IDENTIFIER:

```
#define INCL_WINWORKPLACE
```

FUNCTION PROTOTYPE:

```
BOOL wpRegisterView(WPObject *somSelf, HWND hwndFrame,
                PSZ pszViewTitle);
```

PARAMETERS:

```
somSelf      - Pointer to the object on which the
               method is invoked
hwndFrame    - Handle to the frame window containing
               the new view
pszViewTitle - Pointer to string containing view name
```

RETURNS:

```
TRUE   - Successful completion
FALSE  - Error occurred
```

REMARKS:

Registering a view sets the object title as the frame-window title and adds a view title as the current view in the Window List and title bar. In-use emphasis is managed by wpAddToObjUseList.

METHOD USAGE:

This method is usually called during the processing of wpOpen to register a new view with the object.

METHOD OVERRIDE:

This method is not usually overridden.

RELATED METHODS:

wpAddToObjUseList   Page 151
wpOpen   Page 248

wpReleaseJob

This instance method releases a job object.

INCLUDE IDENTIFIER:

```
#define INCL_WINWORKPLACE
```

FUNCTION PROTOTYPE:

```
BOOL wpReleaseJob(WPJob *somSelf);
```

PARAMETERS:

```
somSelf  - Pointer to the object to be released
```

RETURNS:

```
TRUE   - Successful completion
FALSE  - Error occurred
```

METHOD OVERRIDE:

```
This method is not usually overridden.
```

RELATED METHODS:

```
wpHoldJob                      Page 211
```

wpReleasePrinter

This instance method releases a printer object.

INCLUDE IDENTIFIER:

```
#define INCL_WINWORKPLACE
```

FUNCTION PROTOTYPE:

```
BOOL wpReleasePrinter(WPPrinter *somSelf);
```

PARAMETERS:

```
somSelf  - Pointer to the object to be released
```

RETURNS:

```
TRUE   - Successful completion
FALSE  - Error occurred
```

METHOD OVERRIDE:

```
This method is not usually overridden.
```

RELATED METHODS:

```
wpHoldPrinter                 Page 212
```

wpRender

This instance method requests a drag or drop rendering format from the object.

INCLUDE IDENTIFIER:

```
#define INCL_WINWORKPLACE
```

FUNCTION PROTOTYPE:

```
MRESULT wpRender(WPObject *somSelf,
                 PDRAGTRANSFER ppdxfer);
```

PARAMETERS:

```
somSelf  - Pointer to the object on which the method
           is invoked
ppdxfer  - Pointer to a DRAGTRANSFER structure
```

RETURNS:

Refer to the DM_RENDER message in Volume 2 for a description of the return value.

METHOD USAGE:

This method is usually called only by the system as the folder containing the object processed by DM_RENDER.

METHOD OVERRIDE:

This method should be overridden to return a class-specific rendering mechanism and format.

RELATED METHODS:

wpRenderComplete

This instance method notifies the object that the drag or drop rendering request is complete.

INCLUDE IDENTIFIER:

```
#define INCL_WINWORKPLACE
```

FUNCTION PROTOTYPE:

```
MRESULT wpRenderComplete(WPObject *somSelf,
                         PDRAGTRANSFER ppdxfer,
                         ULONG ulResult);
```

PARAMETERS:

```
somSelf    - Pointer to the object on which the method
             is invoked
ppdxfer    - Pointer to a DRAGTRANSFER structure
ulResult   - Flag indicating whether the operation was
             performed successfully
```

RETURNS:

Refer to the DM_RENDERCOMPLETE message in Volume 2 for a description of the return value.

REMARKS:

This method is called when the object receives a DM_RENDERCOMPLETE message.

METHOD USAGE:

This method is usually called only by the system as the folder containing the object processed by DM_RENDERCOM-PLETE.

METHOD OVERRIDE:

This method should be overridden if the class has a special rendering mechanism and format.

RELATED METHODS:

wpReplacementIsInEffect

This instance method determines whether the given class is currently replaced by a specified class.

INCLUDE IDENTIFIER:

```
#define INCL_WINWORKPLACE
```

FUNCTION PROTOTYPE:

```
BOOL wpReplacementIsInEffect(SOMClassMgr *somSelf,
                            PSZ pszOldClass,
                            HWND pszNewClass);
```

PARAMETERS:

somSelf	– Pointer to the object on which the method is invoked
pszOldClass	– Old class
pszNewClass	– New class

RETURNS:

TRUE	– *pszOldClass* is currently replaced by *pszNewClass*
FALSE	– *pszOldClass* is not currently replaced by *pszNewClass*

METHOD USAGE:

This method can be called at any time. It is invoked using SOMClassMgrObject.

METHOD OVERRIDE:

This method usually is not overridden.

wpRestore

This instance method restores an object's views from the hidden or minimized states.

INCLUDE IDENTIFIER:

```
#define INCL_WINWORKPLACE
```

FUNCTION PROTOTYPE:

```
BOOL wpRestore(WPObject *somSelf);
```

PARAMETERS:

```
somSelf  - Pointer to the object on which the method
           is invoked
```

RETURNS:

```
TRUE   - Successful completion
FALSE  - Error occurred
```

REMARKS:

This method is the inverse of wpHide.

METHOD USAGE:

This method can be called at any time to restore all views of this object from the hidden or minimized state.

METHOD OVERRIDE:

This method is not usually overridden.

RELATED METHODS:

wpHide

Page 209

wpRestoreCellData

This instance method restores the data for the specified cell.

INCLUDE IDENTIFIER:

```
#define INCL_IDENTIFIER:
```

FUNCTION PROTOTYPE:

```
BOOL wpRestoreCellData(WPPalette *somSelf,
                       PCELL pCell, ULONG ulIndex,
                       ULONG ulCellSize);
```

PARAMETERS:

somSelf   - Pointer to the object on which the
              method is invoked.
pCell   - Pointer to cell whose data is to be
              restored.
ulIndex   - Cell index, which is the number of the
              cell; must be within the range 0 to
              xCellCount*yCellCount-1.
ulCellSize - Number of bytes to be allocated for
              cell. If 0 is specified, system
              allocates enough space to hold saved
              data.

RETURNS:

TRUE   - Successful completion
FALSE   - Error occurred

METHOD USAGE:

This method can be called at any time.

METHOD OVERRIDE:

This method must be overridden by all subclasses that
wish to save and restore part of their cell data. For
example, the scheme palette saves the name of the
background bit map for the scheme.

This method must be overridden by all subclasses that
change the size of their cell data.

RELATED METHODS:

wpSaveCellData   Page 381

wpRestoreData

This instance method restores the binary instance data of an object.

INCLUDE IDENTIFIER:

```
#define INCL_WINWORKPLACE
```

FUNCTION PROTOTYPE:

```
BOOL wpRestoreData(WPObject *somSelf, PSZ pszClass,
                   ULONG ulKey, PBYTE pbValue,
                   PULONG pcbValue);
```

PARAMETERS:

somSelf   - Pointer to the object on which the
              method is invoked.
pszClass   - Pointer to a zero-terminated string
              that contains any unique string. The
              class name is recommended but not
              enforced.
ulKey   - Class-defined identifier that correlates
              to a particular instance data variable.
pbValue   - Address of the data to be restored.
pcbValue   - Size of the data block to be restored.
              If pbValue is NULL, the actual size is
              returned in pcbValue.

RETURNS:

TRUE   - Successful completion
FALSE - Error occurred

REMARKS:

This method restores data that was saved by a call to
wpSaveData.

METHOD USAGE:

This method can be called only during the processing of
wpRestoreState.

METHOD OVERRIDE:

This method is not usually overridden.

RELATED METHODS:

wpRestoreLong

This instance method restores a 32-bit, instance-data value of an object.

INCLUDE IDENTIFIER:

```
#define INCL_WINWORKPLACE
```

FUNCTION PROTOTYPE:

```
BOOL wpRestoreLong(WPObject *somSelf, PSZ pszClass,
                   ULONG ulKey, PULONG pValue);
```

PARAMETERS:

```
somSelf    - Pointer to the object on which the method
             is invoked.
pszClass   - Pointer to a zero-terminated string that
             contains any unique string. The class
             name is recommended but not enforced.
ulKey      - Class-defined identifier that correlates
             to a particular instance data variable.
pValue     - Address of the LONG value.
```

RETURNS:

```
TRUE   - Successful completion
FALSE  - Error occurred
```

REMARKS:

This method restores a 32-bit data value that was saved by a call to wpSaveLong.

METHOD USAGE:

This method can be called only during the processing of wpRestoreState.

METHOD OVERRIDE:

This method is not usually overridden.

RELATED METHODS:

wpRestoreState

This method restores the state of the object that was saved during the processing of wpSaveState.

INCLUDE IDENTIFIER:

```
#define INCL_WINWORKPLACE
```

FUNCTION PROTOTYPE:

```
BOOL wpRestoreState(WPObject *somSelf,
                    ULONG ulReserved);
```

PARAMETERS:

```
somSelf     - Pointer to the object on which the
              method is invoked
ulReserved  - Reserved value; must be 0
```

RETURNS:

```
TRUE   - Successful completion
FALSE  - Error occurred
```

METHOD USAGE:

This method is usually called only by the system while it is processing wpInitData.

METHOD OVERRIDE:

This method should be overridden by all classes that provide settings that can be saved. An override of wpSaveState is a prerequisite if persistent instance data is desired.

Override processing of this method typically includes a series of calls to any combination of the following restore state methods:

- wpRestoreData
- wpRestoreLong
- wpRestoreString

RELATED METHODS:

wpRestoreString

This instance method restores an ASCIIZ instance-data string of an object.

INCLUDE IDENTIFIER:

```
#define INCL_WINWORKPLACE
```

FUNCTION PROTOTYPE:

```
BOOL wpRestoreString(WPObject *somSelf, PSZ pszClass,
                     ULONG ulKey, PSZ pszValue,
                     PULONG pulValue);
```

PARAMETERS:

```
somSelf    - Pointer to the object on which the method
             is invoked.
pszClass   - Pointer to a zero-terminated string that
             contains any unique string. The class
             name is recommended but not enforced.
ulKey      - Class-defined identifier that correlates
             to a particular instance data variable.
pszValue   - Address of the string to be restored
pulValue   - Size of the string to be restored. If
             pszValue is NULL, the actual size is
             returned in pulValue.
```

RETURNS:

```
TRUE   - Successful completion
FALSE  - Error occurred
```

REMARKS:

This method restores an ASCIIZ string that was saved by a call to wpSaveString.

METHOD USAGE:

This method can be called only during the processing of wpRestoreState.

METHOD OVERRIDE:

This method is not usually overridden.

RELATED METHODS:

wpSaveCellData

This instance method saves the data for the specified cell.

INCLUDE IDENTIFIER:

```
#define INCL_WINWORKPLACE
```

FUNCTION PROTOTYPE:

```
BOOL wpSaveCellData(WPPalette *somSelf, PCELL pCell,
                    ULONG ulIndex);
```

PARAMETERS:

```
somSelf  - Pointer to the object on which the method
           is invoked.
pCell    - Pointer to cell whose data is to be saved.
ulIndex  - Cell index, which is the number of the
           cell; must be within the range 0 to
           xCellCount*yCellCount-1.
```

RETURNS:

```
TRUE   - Successful completion
FALSE  - Error occurred
```

METHOD USAGE:

This method can be called at any time.

METHOD OVERRIDE:

This method should be overridden by all subclasses that wish to save and restore part of their cell data. For example, the scheme palette saves the name of the background bit map for the scheme.

RELATED METHODS:

```
wpRestoreCellData              Page 371
```

wpSaveData

This instance method saves the binary instance data of an object.

INCLUDE IDENTIFIER:

```
#define INCL_WINWORKPLACE
```

FUNCTION PROTOTYPE:

```
BOOL wpSaveData(WPObject *somSelf, PSZ pszClass,
               ULONG ulKey, PBYTE pbValue,
               ULONG ulValue);
```

PARAMETERS:

```
somSelf    - Pointer to the object on which the method
             is invoked.
pszClass   - Pointer to a zero-terminated string that
             contains any unique string. The class
             name is recommended but not enforced.
ulKey      - Class-defined identifier that correlates
             to a particular instance data variable.
pbValue    - Address of the block of data to be stored.
ulValue    - Size of the block of data to be stored.
```

RETURNS:

```
TRUE    - Successful completion
FALSE   - Error occurred
```

REMARKS:

The saved data can be restored by issuing a call to wpRestoreData.

METHOD USAGE:

This method can be called only during the processing of wpSaveState.

METHOD OVERRIDE:

This method is not usually overridden.

RELATED METHODS:

wpSaveDeferred

This instance method makes the object save itself asynchronously.

INCLUDE IDENTIFIER:

```
#define INCL_WINWORKPLACE
```

FUNCTION PROTOTYPE:

```
BOOL wpSaveDeferred(WPPalette *somSelf);
```

PARAMETERS:

```
somSelf  - Pointer to the object on which the method
           is invoked
```

RETURNS:

```
TRUE   - Save request was accepted
FALSE  - Save request was not accepted
```

REMARKS:

The system maintains a list of objects that currently must be saved and periodically asks those objects to save their state data to persistent storage using wpSaveImmediate.

To improve performance, wpSaveDeferred should always be used in preference to wpSaveImmediate unless the state data was changed in some critical way. For example, if the object wanted to save a new password, it would use wpSaveImmediate instead of wpSaveDeferred to guarantee that the password has been saved before continuing.

Note: wpSaveDeferred can be called only after an object has been initialized. It can be called from within wpObjectReady but not from wpRestoreState. To determine if an object is initialized, use wpIsObjectInitialized.

METHOD USAGE:

This method should be called by all object classes whenever state data is altered. The workplace classes invoke this method each time a wpSet*xxxx* method is used.

METHOD OVERRIDE:

This method should not be overridden.

RELATED METHODS:

wpSaveImmediate   Page 386

wpSaveImmediate

This instance method synchronously saves the current state of an object.

INCLUDE IDENTIFIER:

```
#define INCL_WINWORKPLACE
```

FUNCTION PROTOTYPE:

```
BOOL wpSaveImmediate(WPObject *somSelf);
```

PARAMETERS:

```
somSelf  - Pointer to the object on which the method
           is invoked
```

RETURNS:

```
TRUE   - Successful completion
FALSE  - Error occurred
```

REMARKS:

This method causes wpSaveState to be called.

METHOD USAGE:

This method is called automatically for all objects that are flagged as needing to save their data by wpSaveDeferred. An object can call this method on itself any time a critical instance variable is changed.

wpSaveDeferred should be used in most cases. However, if you use wpSaveImmediate, you should not call it from your user-interface thread; use a background thread instead.

This method will cause wpSaveState to be called.

METHOD OVERRIDE:

This method is not usually overridden.

RELATED METHODS:

wpSaveLong

This instance method saves a 32-bit, instance-data value of an object.

INCLUDE IDENTIFIER:

```
#define INCL_WINWORKPLACE
```

FUNCTION PROTOTYPE:

```
BOOL wpSaveLong(WPObject *somSelf, PSZ pszClass,
             ULONG ulKey, ULONG ulValue);
```

PARAMETERS:

```
somSelf   - Pointer to the object on which the method
            is invoked.
pszClass  - Pointer to a zero-terminated string that
            contains any unique string. The class
            name is recommended but not enforced.
ulKey     - Class-defined identifier that correlates
            to a particular instance data variable.
ulValue   - Value to be stored.
```

RETURNS:

```
TRUE   - Successful completion
FALSE  - Error occurred
```

REMARKS:

The saved 32-bit data value can be restored by issuing a call to wpRestoreLong.

METHOD USAGE:

This method can be called only during the processing of wpSaveState.

METHOD OVERRIDE:

This method is not usually overridden.

RELATED METHODS:

wpSaveState

This instance method saves the state of an object.

INCLUDE IDENTIFIER:

```
#define INCL_WINWORKPLACE
```

FUNCTION PROTOTYPE:

```
BOOL wpSaveState(WPObject *somSelf);
```

PARAMETERS:

```
somSelf  - Pointer to the object on which the method
           is invoked
```

RETURNS:

```
TRUE   - Successful completion
FALSE  - Error occurred
```

REMARKS:

This saved state of the object is restored during the processing of wpRestoreState.

METHOD USAGE:

This method is usually called by the system while it is processing wpClose or wpSaveImmediate. If an immediate save is required, wpSaveImmediate can be called, but it is not recommended. wpSaveDeferred should be used.

METHOD OVERRIDE:

This method should be overridden by all classes that provide savable settings. An override of wpRestoreState is a prerequisite. Override processing of this method typically includes a series of calls to any combination of the following save state methods:

- wpSaveData
- wpSaveLong
- wpSaveString

RELATED METHODS:

wpSaveString

This instance method saves an ASCIIZ instance-data string of an object.

INCLUDE IDENTIFIER:

```
#define INCL_WINWORKPLACE
```

FUNCTION PROTOTYPE:

```
BOOL wpSaveString(WPObject *somSelf, PSZ pszClass,
                  ULONG ulKey, PSZ pszValue);
```

PARAMETERS:

```
somSelf   - Pointer to the object on which the method
            is invoked.
pszClass  - Pointer to a zero-terminated string that
            contains any unique string. The class
            name is recommended but not enforced.
ulKey     - Class-defined identifier that correlates
            to a particular instance data variable.
pszValue  - String to be stored.
```

RETURNS:

```
TRUE    - Successful completion
FALSE   - Error occurred
```

REMARKS:

The saved ASCIIZ string can be restored by issuing a call to wpRestoreString.

METHOD USAGE:

This method can be called only during the processing of wpSaveState.

METHOD OVERRIDE:

This method is not usually overridden.

RELATED METHODS:

wpScanSetupString

This instance method parses the setup string that is passed when an object is created.

INCLUDE IDENTIFIER:

```
#define INCL_WINWORKPLACE
```

FUNCTION PROTOTYPE:

```
BOOL wpScanSetupString(WPObject *somSelf,
                       PSZ pszSetupString,
                       PSZ pszKey, PSZ pszValue,
                       PULONG pcbValue);
```

PARAMETERS:

somSelf	- Pointer to the object on which the method is invoked
pszSetupString	- Class-specific setup parameters for an object
pszKey	- Key to scan for
pszValue	- Buffer for the value
pcbValue	- If pszValue is NULL, the length of the string plus 1 is returned in pcbValue

RETURNS:

TRUE	- Successful completion
FALSE	- Error occurred

REMARKS:

If a comma or semicolon is needed in the setup string, the escape character (^) can be used.

METHOD USAGE:

This method is usually called from within an override of wpSetup.

METHOD OVERRIDE:

This method is not usually overridden.

RELATED METHODS:

wpSelectCell

This instance method selects a specified cell from a palette object.

INCLUDE IDENTIFIER:

```
#define INCL_WINWORKPLACE
```

FUNCTION PROTOTYPE:

```
VOID wpSelectCell(WPPalette *somSelf, HWND hwndPal,
                  PCELL pCell);
```

PARAMETERS:

```
somSelf   - Pointer to the object on which the method
            is invoked
hwndPal   - Palette window handle
pCell     - Cell pointer
```

RETURNS:

```
This is no return vale for this method.
```

METHOD OVERRIDE:

```
This method can be overridden by all subclasses that
wish to perform actions when a cell is selected.
```

RELATED METHODS:

wpSetActionButtonStyle

This instance method sets how the action buttons are displayed on the LaunchPad.

INCLUDE IDENTIFIER:

```
#define INCL_WINWORKPLACE
```

FUNCTION PROTOTYPE:

```
BOOL wpSetActionButtonStyle(WPLaunchPad *somSelf,
                           ULONG ulStyle);
```

PARAMETERS:

```
somSelf  - Pointer to the object on which the method
           is invoked.
ulStyle  - Flag indicating style of action buttons.
           Values:
               ACTION_BUTTONS_MINI
               ACTION_BUTTONS_NORMAL
               ACTION_BUTTONS_OFF
               ACTION_BUTTONS_TEXT
```

RETURNS:

```
TRUE   - Successful completion
FALSE  - Error occurred
```

METHOD OVERRIDE:

This method can be overridden to know when the action display button display style is being changed.

RELATED METHODS:

```
wpRefreshDrawer                Page 362
wpSetActionButtonStyle         Page 397
```

wpSetAssociatedFileIcon

This instance method sets the icon that corresponds to the data file's associated default view.

INCLUDE IDENTIFIER:

```
#define INCL_WINWORKPLACE
```

FUNCTION PROTOTYPE:

```
VOID wpSetAssociatedFileIcon(WPDataFile *somSelf);
```

PARAMETERS:

```
somSelf - Data file whose association is to be found
```

RETURNS:

```
None.
```

REMARKS:

This method is not called if the data file has a customized icon (the .ICON EA is set). It is called when associated information about a data file (such as the real name or type) has changed.

The following methods can be overridden in class WPDataFile:

- wpRestoreState
- wpSetDefaultView
- wpSetRealName
- wpSetType

Except for wpRestoreState, these methods are overridden to call _wpSetAssociatedFileIcon on the data file if the object is initialized and the icon on the data file is a default icon.

In class WPProgramFile, wpSetAssociatedFileIcon is overridden so that the program file icon that corresponds to the program, not to the associated view, can be set.

METHOD OVERRIDE:

This method should be overridden to prevent the Workplace Shell from changing the icon on your class of data
file objects or if to set your own icon for a set of
associations that fall outside of the range recognized
by the Workplace Shell.

To override this method to set the icon, use wpSetIcon.

wpSetAssociationFilter

This WPProgram instance method sets an association of the program object to a data-file object based on a file-title filter.

INCLUDE IDENTIFIER:

```
#define INCL_WINWORKPLACE
```

FUNCTION PROTOTYPE:

```
BOOL wpSetAssociationFilter(WPProgram *somSelf,
                           PSZ pszFilter);
```

PARAMETERS:

```
somSelf    - Pointer to the object on which the
             method is invoked
pszFilter  - Pointer to a string containing file-
             title filters to associate; can contain
             several filters separated by a comma (for
             example: "*.TXT, *.DOC")
```

RETURNS:

```
TRUE   - Successful completion
ERROR  - Error occurred
```

REMARKS:

The association filter is used to designate this program as an available open view for data-file objects that have a title that matches one of the association filters that are set. If a data-file object matches a filter in a program object or program file object, the title of that object appears in the data-file object's Open cascade of its pop-up menu.

This method causes the existing association filters for this object to be replaced. To determine the existing association filters that are set on this object, a call to wpQueryAssociationFilter can be made. The wpSetAssociationType method can be called to set an association based on the type of data-file object.

METHOD USAGE:

This method can be called at any time to set an association of the program object to a data-file object based on a file-title filter.

METHOD OVERRIDE:

This method is not usually overridden.

RELATED METHODS:

wpQueryAssociationType	Page 270
wpSetAssociationFilter	Page 400
wpSetAssociationType	Page 404

wpSetAssociationFilter

This WPProgramFile instance method sets an association of the program object to a data-file object based on a file-title filter.

INCLUDE IDENTIFIER:

```
#define INCL_WINWORKPLACE
```

FUNCTION PROTOTYPE:

```
BOOL wpSetAssociationFilter(WPProgramFile *somSelf,
                           PSZ pszFilter);
```

PARAMETERS:

```
somSelf    - Pointer to the object on which the
             method is invoked
pszFilter  - Pointer to a string containing file
             title filters to associate; can contain
             several filters separated by a comma
```

RETURNS:

```
TRUE   - Successful completion
ERROR  - Error occurred
```

REMARKS:

The association filter designates this program as an available open view for data-file objects that have a title that matches one of the association filters. If a data-file object matches a filter in a program object or program file object, the title of that object appears in the data-file object's Open view of its pop-up menu.

This method causes the existing association filters for this object to be replaced. To determine the existing association filters that are set on this object, a call to wpQueryAssociationFilter can be made. The wpSetAssociationType method can be called to set an association based on the type of data-file object.

METHOD USAGE:

This method can be called at any time to set an association of the program object to a data-file object based on a file-title filter.

METHOD OVERRIDE:

This method is not usually overridden.

RELATED METHODS:

wpQueryAssociationType	Page 270
wpSetAssociationType	Page 404

wpSetAssociationType

This WPProgram instance method sets an association of the program object to a data-file object based on a file type.

INCLUDE IDENTIFIER:

#define INCL_WINWORKPLACE

FUNCTION PROTOTYPE:

```
BOOL wpSetAssociationType(WPProgram *somSelf,
                          PSZ pszType);
```

PARAMETERS:

somSelf - Pointer to the object on which the method
           is invoked
pszType - Pointer to a string containing file
           types to associate; can contain several
           file types separated by a comma

RETURNS:

TRUE   - Successful completion
ERROR   - Error occurred

REMARKS:

The association type designates this program as an available open view for data-file objects that have a type that matches one of the association types. If a data-file object matches a type in a program object or program-file object, the title of that object appears in the data-file object's Open view of its pop-up menu.

This method causes the existing association types for this object to be replaced. To determine the existing association types that are set on this object, a call to wpQueryAssociationType can be made. The wpSetAssociationFilter method can be called to set an association based on the title of data-file object.

METHOD USAGE:

This method can be called at any time to set an association of the program object to a data-file object based on a file type.

METHOD OVERRIDE:

This method is not usually overridden.

RELATED METHODS:

wpSetAssociationType

This WPProgramFile instance method sets an association of the program object to a data-file object based on a file type.

INCLUDE IDENTIFIER:

#define INCL_WINWORKPLACE

FUNCTION PROTOTYPE:

```
BOOL wpSetAssociationType(WPProgramFile *somSelf,
                          PSZ pszType);
```

PARAMETERS:

```
somSelf  - Pointer to the object on which the method
           is invoked
pszType  - Pointer to a string containing file
           types to associate; can contain several
           file types separated by a comma
```

RETURNS:

```
TRUE   - Successful completion
ERROR  - Error occurred
```

REMARKS:

The association type designates this program as an available open view for data-file objects that have a type that matches one of the association types. If a data-file object matches a type in a program object or program-file object, the title of that object appears in the data-file object's Open view of its pop-up menu.

This method causes the existing association types for this object to be replaced. To determine the existing association types that are set on this object, a call to wpQueryAssociationType can be made. The wpSetAssociationFilter method can be called to set an association based on the title of data-file object.

METHOD USAGE:

This method can be called at any time to set an association of the program object to a data-file object based on a file type.

METHOD OVERRIDE:

This method is not usually overridden.

RELATED METHODS:

wpQueryAssociationType   Page 270
wpSetAssociationFilter   Page 402

wpSetAttr

This instance method sets the file attributes of a file-system-based object.

INCLUDE IDENTIFIER:

```
#define INCL_WINWORKPLACE
```

FUNCTION PROTOTYPE:

```
BOOL wpSetAttr(WPFileSystem *somSelf, ULONG attrFile);
```

PARAMETERS:

```
somSelf   - Pointer to the object on which the method
            is invoked
attrFile  - File attributes
```

RETURNS:

```
TRUE    - Successful completion
FALSE   - Errors occurred
```

METHOD OVERRIDE:

This method usually is not overridden.

RELATED METHODS:

wpQueryAttr   Page 274

wpSetAutoRefresh

This instance method enables or disables the automatic refresh option of the Power object status window.

INCLUDE IDENTIFIER:

```
#define INCL_WINWORKPLACE
```

FUNCTION PROTOTYPE:

```
BOOL wpSetAutoRefresh(WPPower *somSelf);
```

PARAMETERS:

```
somSelf - Pointer to the object on which the method
          is invoked
```

RETURNS:

```
TRUE   - Automatic refresh enabled
FALSE  - Automatic refresh disabled
```

RELATED METHODS:

wpSetButtonAppearance

This instance method sets the appearance of an object's Frame Control button.

INCLUDE IDENTIFIER:

```
#define INCL_WINWORKPLACE
```

FUNCTION PROTOTYPE:

```
VOID wpSetButtonAppearance(WPObject *somSelf,
                           ULONG ulButtonType);
```

PARAMETERS:

```
somSelf       - Pointer to the object on which the
                method is invoked.
ulButtonType  - Flag indicating type of control
                button. Values:
                    HIDEBUTTON
                    MINBUTTON
                    DEFAULTBUTTON
```

RETURNS:

```
There is no return value for this method.
```

REMARKS:

```
This method is usually called by the system.
```

METHOD OVERRIDE:

```
This method usually is not overridden.
```

RELATED METHODS:

```
wpQueryButtonAppearance            Page 276
wpclsQueryButtonAppearance         Page 512
```

wpSetCloseDrawer

This instance method sets whether the drawer closes after an object in the drawer is opened.

INCLUDE IDENTIFIER:

```
#define INCL_WINWORKPLACE
```

FUNCTION PROTOTYPE:

```
VOID wpSetCloseDrawer(WPLaunchPad *somSelf,
                      BOOL fClose);
```

PARAMETERS:

```
somSelf - Pointer to the object on which the method
          is invoked.
fClose  - Flag indicating whether to close the
          drawer. Values:
              TRUE
              FALSE
```

RETURNS:

None.

METHOD OVERRIDE:

This method can be overridden to force a particular value.

RELATED METHODS:

wpQueryCloseDrawer   Page 277
wpRefreshDrawer   Page 362

wpSetComputerName

This instance method sets the name of the computer on which the printer exists.

INCLUDE IDENTIFIER:

```
#define INCL_WINWORKPLACE
```

FUNCTION PROTOTYPE:

```
BOOL wpSetComputerName(WPPrinter *somSelf,
                       PSZ pszComputerName);
```

PARAMETERS:

```
somSelf          - Pointer to the object to set the
                   computer name
pszComputerName  - Computer name to be set
```

RETURNS:

```
TRUE   - Successful completion
FALSE  - Error occurred
```

METHOD OVERRIDE:

This method is not usually overridden.

RELATED METHODS:

wpSetConcurrentView

This instance method sets the multiple concurrent-view behavior of the object.

INCLUDE IDENTIFIER:

```
#define INCL_WINWORKPLACE
```

FUNCTION PROTOTYPE:

```
ULONG wpSetConcurrentView(WPObject *somSelf
                          ULONG ulCCView);
```

PARAMETERS:

```
somSelf  - Pointer to the object on which the method
           is invoked
ulCCView - Flag indicating concurrent view behavior
           of object. Values:
             CCVIEW_ON
             CCVIEW_OFF
             CCVIEW_DEFAULT
```

RETURNS:

```
None.
```

METHOD OVERRIDE:

```
This method should not be overridden.
```

RELATED METHODS:

```
wpQueryConcurrentView          Page 279
```

wpSetCorrectDiskIcon

This instance method sets the correct icon for a specified disk object.

INCLUDE IDENTIFIER:

```
#define INCL_WINWORKPLACE
```

FUNCTION PROTOTYPE:

```
BOOL wpSetCorrectDiskIcon(WPDisk *somSelf);
```

PARAMETERS:

```
somSelf  - Pointer to the object on which the method
           is invoked
```

RETURNS:

```
TRUE   - Successful completion
FALSE  - Error occurred
```

METHOD OVERRIDE:

This method can be overridden to set a different icon for the disk type.

wpSetDateInfo

This instance method changes the current date information of an object.

INCLUDE IDENTIFIER:

```
#define INCL_WINWORKPLACE
```

FUNCTION PROTOTYPE:

```
ULONG wpSetDateInfo(WPFileSystem *somSelf,
                    FILEFINDBUF4 *pstFileFindBuf);
```

PARAMETERS:

```
somSelf         - Pointer to the object on which the
                  method is invoked
pstFileFindBuf  - Pointer to file information buffer
```

RETURNS:

```
0      - No error
Other  - Error occurred
```

METHOD OVERRIDE:

```
This method usually is not overridden.
```

wpSetDefaultHelp

This instance method sets the default help panel for an object.

INCLUDE IDENTIFIER:

```
#define INCL_WINWORKPLACE
```

FUNCTION PROTOTYPE:

```
BOOL wpSetDefaultHelp(WPObject *somSelf,
                      ULONG ulPanelId,
                      PSZ pszHelpLibrary);
```

PARAMETERS:

```
somSelf        - Points to object where method invoked
ulPanelId      - Help panel identity
pszHelpLibrary - Pointer to help library name; NULL
                 implies the default should be used
```

RETURNS:

```
TRUE   - Successful completion
FALSE  - Error occurred
```

REMARKS:

The default help panel for this class can be determined by calling wpclsQueryDefaultHelp.

METHOD USAGE:

This method can be called at any time to set the default help panel for this object.

METHOD OVERRIDE:

This method is not usually overridden.

RELATED METHODS:

wpDisplayHelp	Page 184
wpMenuItemHelpSelected	Page 232
wpQueryDefaultHelp	Page 286
wpclsQueryDefaultHelp	Page 513

wpSetDefaultIconPos

This instance method sets the default icon position of an object within a folder.

INCLUDE IDENTIFIER:

```
#define INCL_WINWORKPLACE
```

FUNCTION PROTOTYPE:

```
BOOL wpSetDefaultIconPos(WPObject *somSelf,
                         PPOINTL pPoint):
```

PARAMETERS:

```
somSelf   - Pointer to the object on which the method
            is invoked.
pPointl   - Pointer to coordinates of default icon
            position. x and y values represent
            position in object's folder in percentage
            coordinates.
```

RETURNS:

```
TRUE    - Successful completion
FALSE   - Error occurred
```

REMARKS:

Refer to wpSetup for more information about the initial icon position (ICONPOS).

METHOD USAGE:

This method can be overridden at any time to set the default icon position.

METHOD OVERRIDE:

This method usually is not overridden.

RELATED METHODS:

wpQueryDefaultIconPos   Page 288

wpSetDefaultPrinter

This instance method sets a default printer object.

INCLUDE IDENTIFIER:

```
#define INCL_WINWORKPLACE
```

FUNCTION PROTOTYPE:

```
BOOL wpSetDefaultPrinter(WPPrinter *somSelf);
```

PARAMETERS:

```
somSelf  - Pointer to the object to be the default
```

RETURNS:

```
TRUE   - Successful completion
FALSE  - Error occurred
```

METHOD OVERRIDE:

```
This method is not usually overridden.
```

wpSetDefaultView

This instance method changes the current default open view of an object.

INCLUDE IDENTIFIER:

```
#define INCL_WINWORKPLACE
```

FUNCTION PROTOTYPE:

```
BOOL wpSetDefaultView(WPObject *somSelf,
                      ULONG ulView);
```

PARAMETERS:

```
somSelf - Pointer to the object on which the method
          is invoked.
ulView  - Specifies which view to open. Values:
              OPEN_CONTENTS
              OPEN_DEFAULT
              OPEN_DETAILS
              OPEN_HELP
              OPEN_RUNNING
              OPEN_SETTINGS
              OPEN_TREE
              OPEN_USER
```

RETURNS:

```
TRUE   - Successful completion
FALSE  - Error occurred
```

REMARKS:

The default open view for this class can be determined by calling wpclsQueryDefaultView.

METHOD USAGE:

This method can be called at any time to set the default open view for this object.

METHOD OVERRIDE:

This method is not usually overridden.

RELATED METHODS:

wpSetDefStatusView

This instance method sets the default status view when Advanced Power Management (APM) is enabled.

INCLUDE IDENTIFIER:

```
#define INCL_WINWORKPLACE
```

FUNCTION PROTOTYPE:

```
VOID wpSetDefStatusView(WPPower *somSelf,
                        ULONG ulDefStatus);
```

PARAMETERS:

```
somSelf     - Pointer to the object on which the
              method is invoked.
ulDefStatus - Setting for default status view. Values:
                OPEN_STATUS
                OPEN_BATTERY
```

RETURNS:

None.

REMARKS:

This method sets the default status view of the object when APM is enabled. If it is not enabled, this method sets the default status view for the next time APM is enabled.

METHOD USAGE:

This method can be called at any time to set the default status view for this object.

RELATED METHODS:

wpSetDetailColumnVisiblity

This instance method shows or hides the details column of a specified folder.

INCLUDE IDENTIFIER:

```
#define INCL_WINWORKPLACE
```

FUNCTION PROTOTYPE:

```
BOOL wpSetDetailColumnVisiblity(WPFolder *somSelf,
                                ULONG index,
                                BOOL Visible);
```

PARAMETERS:

```
somSelf  - Pointer to the object on which the method
           is invoked.
index    - Column index for current details view.
Visible  - Flag indicating whether to show or hide
           details column. Values:
               TRUE
               FALSE
```

RETURNS:

```
TRUE   - Successful completion
FALSE  - Error occurred
```

METHOD OVERRIDE:

This method usually is not overridden.

RELATED METHODS:

wpIsDetailsColumnVisible   Page 222

wpSetDisplaySmallIcons

This instance method sets whether small or normal sized icons are displayed on the LaunchPad and drawer.

INCLUDE IDENTIFIER:

```
#define INCL_WINWORKPLACE
```

FUNCTION PROTOTYPE:

```
VOID wpSetDisplaySmallIcons(WPLaunchPad *somSelf,
                            BOOL fState);
```

PARAMETERS:

```
somSelf - Pointer to the object on which the method
          is invoked.
fState  - Flag indicating whether to display small
          icons. Values:
             TRUE
             FALSE
```

RETURNS:

None.

METHOD OVERRIDE:

This method can be overridden to force a particular value.

RELATED METHODS:

wpQueryDisplaySmallIcons   Page 295
wpRefreshDrawer   Page 362

wpSetDisplayText

This instance method sets whether the text is displayed under the icons on the LaunchPad.

INCLUDE IDENTIFIER:

```
#define INCL_WINWORKPLACE
```

FUNCTION PROTOTYPE:

```
VOID wpSetDisplayText(WPLaunchPad *somSelf,
                      BOOL fState);
```

PARAMETERS:

```
somSelf - Pointer to the object on which the method
          is invoked.
fState  - Flag indicating whether to display text
          under icons.
              TRUE
              FALSE
```

RETURNS:

None.

METHOD OVERRIDE:

This method can be overridden to force a particular value.

RELATED METHODS:

wpSetDisplayTextInDrawers

This instance method sets whether the text is displayed under the icons in drawers.

INCLUDE IDENTIFIER:

```
#define INCL_WINWORKPLACE
```

FUNCTION PROTOTYPE:

```
VOID wpSetDisplayTextInDrawers(WPLaunchPad *somSelf,
                               BOOL fState);
```

PARAMETERS:

```
somSelf - Pointer to the object on which the method
          is invoked.
fState  - Flag indicating whether to display text
          under icons. Values:
              TRUE
              FALSE
```

RETURNS:

None.

METHOD OVERRIDE:

This method can be overridden to force a particular value.

RELATED METHODS:

wpSetDisplayVertical

This instance method sets the orientation of the LaunchPad.

INCLUDE IDENTIFIER:

```
#define INCL_WINWORKPLACE
```

FUNCTION PROTOTYPE:

```
VOID wpSetDisplayVertical(WPLaunchPad *somSelf,
                          BOOL fState);
```

PARAMETERS:

```
somSelf - Pointer to the object on which the method
          is invoked.
fState  - Flag indicating orientation of LaunchPad.
          Values:
             TRUE
             FALSE
```

RETURNS:

```
None.
```

METHOD OVERRIDE:

This method can be overridden to force a particular value.

RELATED METHODS:

wpSetDrawerHWND

This instance method stores the handle associated with the Launch-Pad or drawer into the instance data.

INCLUDE IDENTIFIER:

```
#define INCL_WINWORKPLACE
```

FUNCTION PROTOTYPE:

```
BOOL wpSetDrawerHWND(WPLaunchPad *somSelf,
                     ULONG ulDrawer, HWND hwnd);
```

PARAMETERS:

```
somSelf    - Pointer to the object on which the method
             is invoked.
ulDrawer   - LaunchPad or drawer being set. Values:
                 0
                 >0
hwnd       - Handle of frame window for drawer. Value
             of NULLHANDLE indicates that view is
             closed.
```

RETURNS:

```
TRUE    - Successful completion
FALSE   - Error occurred
```

METHOD OVERRIDE:

```
This method can be overridden to know when a drawer view
is opened.
```

RELATED METHODS:

wpSetError

This instance method identifies an error condition.

INCLUDE IDENTIFIER:

```
#define INCL_WINWORKPLACE
```

FUNCTION PROTOTYPE:

```
BOOL wpSetError(WPObject *somSelf, ULONG ulErrorId);
```

PARAMETERS:

```
somSelf    - Pointer to the object on which the
             method is invoked
ulErrorId  - Error identity
```

RETURNS:

```
TRUE   - Successful completion
FALSE  - Error occurred
```

REMARKS:

This method sets the last error on an object. The error identity is retrievable by issuing a call to wpQuery-Error.

METHOD USAGE:

This method can be called at any time to identify an error condition. This method is typically called prior to returning unsuccessfully from a method.

METHOD OVERRIDE:

This method is not usually overridden.

RELATED METHODS:

wpQueryError   Page 302

wpSetFileSizeInfo

This instance method sets the file size values in the instance data.

INCLUDE IDENTIFIER:

```
#define INCL_WINWORKPLACE
```

FUNCTION PROTOTYPE:

```
ULONG wpSetFileSizeInfo(WPFileSystem *somSelf,
                        ULONG cbFileSize,
                        ULONG cbEASize);
```

PARAMETERS:

```
somSelf      - Pointer to the object on which the
               method is invoked
cbFileSize   - Size of file
cbEASize     - Size of file's extended attributes
```

RETURNS:

```
0       - No error
Other   - Error occurred
```

METHOD OVERRIDE:

This method usually is not overridden.

RELATED METHODS:

wpQueryEASize   Page 301
wpQueryFileSize   Page 305

wpSetFldrAttr

This instance method changes the current view attributes of a folder.

INCLUDE IDENTIFIER:

```
#define INCL_WINWORKPLACE
```

FUNCTION PROTOTYPE:

```
BOOL wpSetFldrAttr(WPFolder *somSelf, ULONG ulAttr,
                   ULONG ulView);
```

PARAMETERS:

```
somSelf - Pointer to the object on which the method
          is invoked.
ulAttr  - Flag indicating object's attributes.
          These are CV_* attributes defined by
          container-control window. See CNRINFO
          structure for detailed description.
ulView  - Flag indicating object's open view.
          Values:
             OPEN_CONTENTS
             OPEN_DETAILS
             OPEN_TREE
```

RETURNS:

```
TRUE    - Successful completion
FALSE   - Error occurred
```

REMARKS:

The flags should be valid for the specified view. For example, CV_TREE should not be specified for details view.

METHOD USAGE:

This method can be called at any time to set the view attributes.

METHOD OVERRIDE:

This method is not usually overridden.

RELATED METHODS:

wpSetFldrDetailsClass

This instance method sets the class for which details in a folder are displayed.

INCLUDE IDENTIFIER:

```
#define INCL_WINWORKPLACE
```

FUNCTION PROTOTYPE:

```
BOOL wpSetFldrDetailsClass(WPFolder *somSelf,
                          M_WPObject *Class);
```

PARAMETERS:

```
somSelf - Pointer to the object on which the method
          is invoked
Class   - Pointer to the class object for which
          details are displayed
```

RETURNS:

```
TRUE    - Successful completion
FALSE   - Error occurred
```

REMARKS:

Because folders can contain objects of different classes that can have different details, it is often necessary for the user to specify which class of details is to be displayed. The value set by this method is not used until a details view of the folder is opened.

This method can be called to determine the class of details currently set. All column visibility states are reset by this method.

METHOD USAGE:

This method can be called at any time to set the current class of details to be displayed.

METHOD OVERRIDE:

This method is not usually overridden.

RELATED METHODS:

```
wpQueryFldrDetailsClass          Page 307
```

wpSetFldrFlags

This instance method changes the current flags of a folder.

INCLUDE IDENTIFIER:

```
#define INCL_WINWORKPLACE
```

FUNCTION PROTOTYPE:

```
BOOL wpSetFldrFlags(WPFolder *somSelf, ULONG ulFlags);
```

PARAMETERS:

```
somSelf  - Pointer to the object on which the method
           is invoked.
ulFlags  - Folder flags to be set. Values:
              FOI_POPULATEDWITHALL
              FOI_POPULATEDWITHFOLDERS
              FOI_WORKAREA
```

RETURNS:

```
TRUE   - Successful completion
FALSE  - Error occurred
```

METHOD USAGE:

This method can be called at any time to set a folder's flag.

METHOD OVERRIDE:

This method is not usually overridden.

RELATED METHODS:

wpSetFldrFont

This instance method changes the current font of a folder.

INCLUDE IDENTIFIER:

```
#define INCL_WINWORKPLACE
```

FUNCTION PROTOTYPE:

```
BOOL wpSetFldrFont(WPFolder *somSelf, PSZ pszFont,
                   ULONG ulView);
```

PARAMETERS:

```
somSelf  - Pointer to the object on which the method
           is invoked.
pszFont  - Pointer to buffer containing font name. If
           NULL, font presentation parameter is set
           back to default font. If pointer to
           NULL string passed, font presentation
           parameter is set to currently defined font.
ulView   - Flag indicating an object's open view.
           Values:
              OPEN_CONTENTS
              OPEN_DETAILS
              OPEN_TREE
```

RETURNS:

```
TRUE   - Successful completion
FALSE  - Error occurred
```

REMARKS:

The font name should be a valid presentation parameter string.

METHOD USAGE:

This method can be called at any time to change the current font for a view.

METHOD OVERRIDE:

This method is not usually overridden.

wpSetFldrSort

This instance method sets the sort attributes on the folder window and saves those values in the instance data.

Note: This method is valid only for folders in an icon view.

INCLUDE IDENTIFIER:

```
#define INCL_WINWORKPLACE
```

FUNCTION PROTOTYPE:

```
BOOL wpSetFldrSort(WPFolder *somSelf,
                   PVOID pSortRecord,
                   ULONG ulView, ULONG ulType);
```

PARAMETERS:

somSelf   - Pointer to the object on which the
                method is invoked.
pSortRecord   - Pointer to SORTFASTINFO structure
                containing sort record information. If
                this value is NULL, sort attributes
                are reset to default sort values.
ulView   - Flag indicating type of folder view.
                Values:
                    OPEN_CONTENTS
                    OPEN_DETAILS
                    OPEN_TREE
ulType   - Flag indicating folder type.

RETURNS:

TRUE   - Successful completion
FALSE   - Error occurred

REMARKS:

This method refreshes any open views of the folder that match *ulView* and *ulType* with selected sort attributes.

Note: This method is called for every open view of this object.

METHOD OVERRIDE:

This method should not be overridden.

RELATED METHODS:

wpSetFldrSortClass

This instance method sets the sort class for a specified folder.

INCLUDE IDENTIFIER:

```
#define INCL_WINWORKPLACE
```

FUNCTION PROTOTYPE:

```
BOOL wpSetFldrSortClass(WPFolder *somSelf,
                        M_WPObject *Class);
```

PARAMETERS:

```
somSelf - Pointer to the object on which the method
          is invoked
Class   - Pointer to the sort class object
```

RETURNS:

```
TRUE   - Successful completion
FALSE  - Error occurred
```

REMARKS:

The sort class determines which class details can be
used as candidates for the default or current sort field
for a given folder (displayed in the sort submenu on the
folder's context menu) as well as on the Sort Settings
page of the object. The default sort class for all
folders is WPFileSystem.

METHOD OVERRIDE:

This method usually is not overridden.

RELATED METHODS:

wpSetFloatOnTop

This instance method sets whether the LaunchPad is forced to float on top of all other windows.

INCLUDE IDENTIFIER:

```
#define INCL_WINWORKPLACE
```

FUNCTION PROTOTYPE:

```
VOID wpSetFloatOnTop(WPLaunchPad *somSelf,
                     BOOL fState);
```

PARAMETERS:

```
somSelf - Pointer to the object on which the method
          is invoked.
fState  - Flag indicating whether to force the
          LaunchPad to float on top of all windows.
          Values:
             TRUE
             FALSE
```

RETURNS:

None.

METHOD OVERRIDE:

This method can be overridden to force a particular value.

RELATED METHODS:

wpQueryFloatOnTop   Page 312
wpRefreshDrawer   Page 362

wpSetHideLaunchPadFrameCtls

This instance method hides the system menu and the title bar for
the LaunchPad.

INCLUDE IDENTIFIER:

```
#define INCL_WINWORKPLACE
```

FUNCTION PROTOTYPE:

```
VOID wpSetHideLaunchPadFrameCtls(WPLaunchPad *somSelf,
                                 BOOL fState);
```

PARAMETERS:

```
somSelf - Pointer to the object on which the method
          is invoked.
fState  - Flag indicating whether to hide frame
          controls. Values:
             TRUE
             FALSE
```

RETURNS:

None.

METHOD OVERRIDE:

This method can be overridden to force a particular
value.

RELATED METHODS:

```
wpQueryHideLaunchPadFrameCtls    Page 315
wpRefreshDrawer                  Page 362
```

wpSetIcon

This instance method sets the current icon of an object.

INCLUDE IDENTIFIER:

```
#define INCL_WINWORKPLACE
```

FUNCTION PROTOTYPE:

```
BOOL wpSetIcon(WPObject *somSelf,
               HPOINTER hptrNewIcon);
```

PARAMETERS:

```
somSelf      - Pointer to the object on which the
               method is invoked
hptrNewIcon  - Pointer to the object handle
```

RETURNS:

```
TRUE   - Successful completion
FALSE  - Error occurred
```

REMARKS:

If the OBJSTYLE_NOTDEFAULTICON style is currently set for the object, the object's icon is destroyed if the object is destroyed or made dormant.

METHOD USAGE:

This method can be called at any time to change the visible icon for this object. To permanently change the icon, wpSetIconData should be called.

METHOD OVERRIDE:

This method is not usually overridden.

RELATED METHODS:

wpSetIconData

This instance method permanently sets the current icon of an object.

INCLUDE IDENTIFIER:

```
#define INCL_WINWORKPLACE
```

FUNCTION PROTOTYPE:

```
BOOL wpSetIconData(WPObject *somSelf,
                   PICONINFO pIconInfo);
```

PARAMETERS:

```
somSelf    - Pointer to the object on which the
             method is invoked
pIconInfo  - Pointer to an ICONINFO structure
             containing an icon specification
```

RETURNS:

```
TRUE   - Successful completion
FALSE  - Error occurred
```

METHOD USAGE:

This method can be called at any time to permanently change the icon for this object. To temporarily change or refresh the icon for this object, wpSetIcon should be called.

METHOD OVERRIDE:

This method is not usually overridden.

RELATED METHODS:

wpSetIconHandle

This instance method sets the icon handle for a specified object.

INCLUDE IDENTIFIER:

```
#define INCL_WINWORKPLACE
```

FUNCTION PROTOTYPE:

```
BOOL wpSetIconHandle(WPObject *somSelf,
                     HPOINTER hptrNewIcon);
```

PARAMETERS:

```
somSelf       - Pointer to the object on which the
                method is invoked.
hptrNewIcon   - Pointer to icon handle to be set for
                given object.
```

RETURNS:

```
TRUE    - Successful completion
FALSE   - Error occurred
```

REMARKS:

This method does not alter the icon permanently. It is equivalent to WM_SETICON for frame window. To permanently set the icon, use wpSetIconData. If OB-JSTYLE_NODEFAULTICON is currently set for the object and the object is destroyed or made dormant, the object's icon is also destroyed. If the object is visible, refresh its appearance everywhere, including the title-bar icon.

METHOD USAGE:

This method can be called at any time.

METHOD OVERRIDE:

This method should never be overridden.

RELATED METHODS:

wpSetIconData   Page 442

wpSetLinkToObject

This instance method links the shadow object to the specified object.

INCLUDE IDENTIFIER:

```
#define INCL_WINWORKPLACE
```

FUNCTION PROTOTYPE:

```
BOOL wpSetLinkToObject(WPShadow *somSelf,
                       WPObject *FromObject);
```

PARAMETERS:

```
somSelf     - Pointer to the object on which the
              method is invoked
FromObject  - Pointer to object to be linked to
              shadow
```

RETURNS:

```
TRUE   - Successful completion
FALSE  - Error occurred
```

METHOD USAGE:

This method can be called at any time to link a shadow to an object.

METHOD OVERRIDE:

This method usually is not overridden.

wpSetMinWindow

This instance method sets the minimized window behavior of an object.

INCLUDE IDENTIFIER:

```
#define INCL_WINWORKPLACE
```

FUNCTION PROTOTYPE:

```
VOID wpSetMinWindow(WPObject *somSelf,
                ULONG ulMinWindow);
```

PARAMETERS:

```
somSelf      - Pointer to the object on which the
               method is invoked.
ulMinWindow  - Flag indicating minimized window
               behavior. Values:
                  MINWIN_DEFAULT
                  MINWIN_DESKTOP
                  MINWIN_HIDDEN
                  MINWIN_VIEWER
```

RETURNS:

None.

METHOD OVERRIDE:

This method usually is not overridden.

RELATED METHODS:

wpQueryMinWindow   Page 327

wpSetNetIdentity

This instance method sets the instance data containing the fully qualified network name of this network group.

INCLUDE IDENTIFIER:

```
#define INCL_WINWORKPLACE
```

FUNCTION PROTOTYPE:

```
BOOL wpSetNetIdentity(WPNetgrp *somSelf,
                      PSZ pszNetIdentity);
```

PARAMETERS:

```
somSelf   - Pointer to the object on which the method
            is invoked
```

RETURNS:

```
pszNetIdentity  - Fully qualified network name of
                  this network group
```

RETURNS:

```
TRUE    - Successful completion
FALSE   - Error occurred
```

METHOD OVERRIDE:

```
This method usually is not overridden.
```

RELATED METHODS:

446

wpSetNextIconPos

This instance method changes the next icon position of a folder.

INCLUDE IDENTIFIER:

```
#define INCL_WINWORKPLACE
```

FUNCTION PROTOTYPE:

```
BOOL wpSetNextIconPos(WPFolder *somSelf,
                      PPOINTL pptl);
```

PARAMETERS:

```
somSelf  - Pointer to the object on which the method
           is invoked
pptl     - Position within the folder
```

RETURNS:

```
TRUE   - Successful completion
FALSE  - Error occurred
```

REMARKS:

The next icon position usually is set during a drag and drop operation to ensure that the items dropped into a folder are located where the user wanted them.

METHOD USAGE:

This method can be called at any time to set the next icon position at which objects will be inserted in the folder. If this method is used, the previous next position should be queried and restored afterwards.

METHOD OVERRIDE:

This method is not usually overridden.

RELATED METHODS:

wpQueryNextIconPos   Page 331

wpSetObjectID

This instance method sets the object id assigned to this object. The instance data is set, but the .INI file is not modified.

INCLUDE IDENTIFIER:

```
#define INCL_WINWORKPLACE
```

FUNCTION PROTOTYPE:

```
BOOL wpSetObjectID(WPObject *somSelf,
                   PSZ pszObjectId);
```

PARAMETERS:

```
somSelf       - Pointer to the object on which the
                method is invoked.
pszObjectId   - String containing unique object id, for
                example, "PM_DESKTOP".
```

RETURNS:

```
TRUE    - Successful completion
FALSE   - Error occurred
```

REMARKS:

The install routine uses the object id to ensure that a given object is never re-installed, thereby avoiding duplication of objects.

The object id is always lost when the object is copied; therefore, only one object ever exists within a given object id.

RELATED METHODS:

wpQueryObjectID   Page 332

wpSetObjectListFromHObjects

This instance method adds a set of objects defined by a set of HOBJECTs to the LaunchPad or drawer.

INCLUDE IDENTIFIER:

```
#define INCL_WINWORKPLACE
```

FUNCTION PROTOTYPE:

```
BOOL wpSetObjectListFromHObjects(WPLaunchPad *somSelf,
                                 ULONG ulDrawer,
                                 ULONG ulNumObjects,
                                 HOBJECT *phobjects,
                                 ULONG ulAfter);
```

PARAMETERS:

somSelf	– Pointer to the object on which the method is invoked.

ulDrawer	– LaunchPad or drawer being set. Values:
	    0
	    >0

ulNumObjects	– Number of objects pointed to by *phobjects*.
phobjects	– Pointer to list of objects to be added

ulAfter	– Number of object after which new objects are inserted. Values:
	    ADD_OBJECT_FIRST
	    ADD_OBJECT_LAST
	    Other

RETURNS:

```
TRUE   - Successful completion
FALSE  - Error occurred
```

METHOD OVERRIDE:

This method can be overridden to know when objects are being added.

RELATED METHODS:

wpRefreshDrawer   Page 362

wpSetObjectListFromObjects

This instance method adds a set of objects defined by a set of objects to the LaunchPad or drawer.

INCLUDE IDENTIFIER:

```
#define INCL_WINWORKPLACE
```

FUNCTION PROTOTYPE:

```
BOOL wpSetObjectListFromObjects(WPLaunchPad *somSelf,
                                ULONG ulDrawer,
                                ULONG ulNumObjects,
                                WPObject *Objects,
                                ULONG ulAfter);
```

PARAMETERS:

```
somSelf        - Pointer to the object on which the
                 method is invoked.
ulDrawer       - LaunchPad or drawer being set. Values:
                    0
                    >0
ulNumObjects   - Number of objects pointed to by
                 Objects.
Objects        - Pointer to list of objects to be added
ulAfter        - Number of object after which new
                 objects are inserted. Values:
                    ADD_OBJECT_FIRST
                    ADD_OBJECT_LAST
                    Other
```

RETURNS:

```
TRUE   - Successful completion
FALSE  - Error occurred
```

METHOD OVERRIDE:

This method can be overridden to know when objects are being added.

RELATED METHODS:

wpRefreshDrawer   Page 362

wpSetObjectListFromStrings

This instance method adds a set of objects defined by a string list to the LaunchPad or drawers.

INCLUDE IDENTIFIER:

```
#define INCL_WINWORKPLACE
```

FUNCTION PROTOTYPE:

```
BOOL wpSetObjectListFromStrings(WPLaunchPad *somSelf,
                                ULONG ulDrawer,
                                PSZ pszSetup,
                                ULONG ulAfter);
```

PARAMETERS:

```
somSelf   - Pointer to object on which method invoked.
ulDrawer  - LaunchPad or drawers being set. Values:
               0
               >0
pszSetup  - Setup string that defines list of object
            ids or path and file names of objects to
            be added. Each entry in list is terminated
            by NULL character; last entry is ended by
            two successive NULL characters.
ulAfter   - Number of object after which new objects
            are inserted. Values:
               ADD_OBJECT_FIRST
               ADD_OBJECT_LAST
               Other
```

RETURNS:

```
TRUE   - Successful completion
FALSE  - Error occurred
```

METHOD OVERRIDE:

This method can be overridden to know when objects are being added.

RELATED METHODS:

wpRefreshDrawer   Page 362

wpSetObjectNetId

This instance method sets the network id of the shared-directory object to which this object is linked.

INCLUDE IDENTIFIER:

```
#define INCL_WINWORKPLACE
```

FUNCTION PROTOTYPE:

```
BOOL wpSetObjectNetId(WPNetLink *somSelf,
                      PSZ pszNetIdentity);
```

PARAMETERS:

```
somSelf         - Pointer to the object on which the
                  method is invoked.
pszNetIdentity - Pointer to network id string.
                  Network name is in following format:
                  "<NetworkId>\<ServerId>\<Share Name>"
```

RETURNS:

```
TRUE    - Successful completion
FALSE   - Error occurred
```

REMARKS:

The shared-directory object uses this id to make its network calls. The id is not stored in the object's data.

METHOD USAGE:

This method can be called any time to set a network id.

METHOD OVERRIDE:

This method usually is not overridden.

RELATED METHODS:

```
wpQueryNetIdentity              Page 329
wpQueryObjectNetId              Page 334
wpQuerySrvrIdentity             Page 355
```

wpSetPaletteInfo

This instance method sets palette information.

INCLUDE IDENTIFIER:

```
#define INCL_WINWORKPLACE
```

FUNCTION PROTOTYPE:

```
BOOL wpSetPaletteInfo(WPPalette *somSelf,
                      PPALINFO pPalInfo);
```

PARAMETERS:

```
somSelf   - Pointer to the object on which the method
            is invoked
pPalInfo  - Pointer to a PALINFO structure
```

RETURNS:

```
TRUE   - Successful completion
FALSE  - Error occurred
```

REMARKS:

The palette information can be retrieved by issuing a call to wpQueryPaletteInfo.

METHOD USAGE:

This method can be called at any time to set the palette information.

METHOD OVERRIDE:

This method is not usually overridden.

RELATED METHODS:

wpQueryPaletteInfo   Page 337

wpSetPowerConfirmation

This instance method enables or disables the confirmation message displayed when a Standby or Suspend request is made from the pop-up menu of the Power object.

INCLUDE IDENTIFIER:

```
#define INCL_WINWORKPLACE
```

FUNCTION PROTOTYPE:

```
BOOL wpSetPowerConfirmation(WPPower *somSelf,
                            BOOL fConfirm);
```

PARAMETERS:

```
somSelf  - Pointer to the object on which the method
           is invoked
fConfirm - Confirmation message. Values:
             TRUE  - Enabled
             FALSE - Disabled
```

RETURNS:

None.

RELATED METHODS:

wpSetPowerManagement

This instance method enables or disables the OS/2 Power Management support.

INCLUDE IDENTIFIER:

```
#define INCL_WINWORKPLACE
```

FUNCTION PROTOTYPE:

```
BOOL wpSetPowerManagement(WPPower *somSelf,
                          BOOL fPower);
```

PARAMETERS:

```
somSelf - Pointer to the object on which the method
          is invoked.
fPower  - Power-management indicator. Values:
              TRUE
              FALSE
```

RETURNS:

```
TRUE   - Successful
FALSE  - Unsuccessful
```

RELATED METHODS:

wpSetPrinterName

This instance method sets the name of the printer.

INCLUDE IDENTIFIER:

```
#define INCL_WINWORKPLACE
```

FUNCTION PROTOTYPE:

```
BOOL wpSetPrinterName(WPPrinter *somSelf,
                   PSZ pszPrinterName);
```

PARAMETERS:

```
somSelf          - Pointer to the object to set the
                   printer name
pszPrinterName   - Printer name to be set
```

RETURNS:

```
TRUE    - Successful completion
FALSE   - Error occurred
```

METHOD OVERRIDE:

```
This method is not usually overridden.
```

RELATED METHODS:

```
wpQueryPrinterName              Page 340
wpSetComputerName               Page 412
```

wpSetProgDetails

This WPProgram instance method changes the program details of
an object.

INCLUDE IDENTIFIER:

```
#define INCL_WINWORKPLACE
```

FUNCTION PROTOTYPE:

```
BOOL wpSetProgDetails(WPProgram *somSelf,
                      PPROGDETAILS pProgDetails);
```

PARAMETERS:

```
somSelf       - Pointer to the object on which the
                method is invoked
pProgDetails  - Pointer to the program details
```

RETURNS

```
TRUE   - Successful completion
FALSE  - Error occurred
```

METHOD USAGE:

```
This method can be called at any time to set the details
for this object.
```

METHOD OVERRIDE:

```
This method is not usually overridden.
```

RELATED METHODS:

```
wpQueryProgDetails              Page 342
```

wpSetProgDetails

This WPProgramFile instance method changes the program details of an object.

INCLUDE IDENTIFIER:

```
#define INCL_WINWORKPLACE
```

FUNCTION PROTOTYPE:

```
BOOL wpSetProgDetails(WPProgramFile *somSelf,
                      PPROGDETAILS pProgDetails);
```

PARAMETERS:

```
somSelf        - Pointer to the object on which the
                 method is invoked
pProgDetails   - Pointer to the program details
```

RETURNS:

```
TRUE    - Successful completion
FALSE   - Error occurred
```

METHOD USAGE:

```
This method can be called at any time to set the details
for this object.
```

METHOD OVERRIDE:

```
This method is not usually overridden.
```

RELATED METHODS:

```
wpQueryProgDetails              Page 342
```

wpSetProgIcon

This WPProgram instance method sets the visual icon for the
current program to the appropriate default or custom icon.

INCLUDE IDENTIFIER:

```
#define INCL_WINWORKPLACE
```

FUNCTION PROTOTYPE:

```
wpSetProgIcon(WPProgram *somSelf, PFEA2LIST pfeal);
```

PARAMETERS:

```
somSelf - Pointer to the object on which the method
          is invoked
pfeal   - Pointer to the list of FEA2 structures
          containing icon extended attributes (EAs)
```

RETURNS:

```
TRUE  - Successful completion
FALSE - Error occurred
```

METHOD USAGE:

This method can be called at any time.

METHOD OVERRIDE:

This method usually is not overridden.

RELATED METHODS:

```
wpRestoreState              Page 377
wpSetProgDetails            Page 457
```

wpSetProgIcon

This WPProgramFile instance method sets the visual icon for this program to the appropriate custom or default icon.

INCLUDE IDENTIFIER:

```
#define INCL_WINWORKPLACE
```

FUNCTION PROTOTYPE:

```
wpSetProgIcon(WPProgramFile *somSelf,
              PFEA2LIST pfeal);
```

PARAMETERS:

```
somSelf - Pointer to the object on which the method
          is invoked.
pfeal   - Pointer to the list of FEA2 structures
          containing icon extended attributes (EAs).
          Value of NULL indicates that icon EAs are
          not available.
```

RETURNS:

```
TRUE    - Successful completion
FALSE   - Error occurred
```

METHOD USAGE:

```
This method can be called at any time to set an icon for
a given program file.
```

METHOD OVERRIDE:

```
This method usually is not overridden.
```

RELATED METHODS:

wpSetProgramAssociations

This WPProgram instance method sets the program associations in the .INI file.

INCLUDE IDENTIFIER:

```
#define INCL_WINWORKPLACE
```

FUNCTION PROTOTYPE:

```
BOOL wpSetProgramAssociations(WPProgram *somSelf,
                             PSZ pszAssoc,
                             BOOL fFilter);
```

PARAMETERS:

```
somSelf   - Pointer to the object on which the method
            is invoked.
pszAssoc  - Pointer to string of data-file association
            types or filters, separated by commas. If
            fFilter is TRUE, pszAssoc should contain
            filters instead of types.
fFilter   - Filter flag. Values:
               TRUE
               FALSE
```

RETURNS:

```
TRUE    - Successful completion
FALSE   - Error occurred
```

METHOD USAGE:

```
This method can be called at any time.
```

METHOD OVERRIDE:

```
This method usually is not overridden.
```

RELATED METHODS:

```
wpQueryProgramAssociations      Page 344
```

wpSetProgramAssociations

This WPProgramFile instance method returns the program associations from the .INI file.

INCLUDE IDENTIFIER:

```
#define INCL_WINWORKPLACE
```

FUNCTION PROTOTYPE:

```
BOOL wpSetProgramAssociations(WPProgramFile *somSelf,
                             PSZ pszAssoc,
                             BOOL fFilter);
```

PARAMETERS:

```
somSelf    - Pointer to the object on which the method
             is invoked.
pszAssoc   - Pointer to string of data-file association
             types or filters, separated by commas. If
             fFilter is TRUE, pszAssoc should contain
             filters instead of types.
fFilter    - Filter flag. Values:
                 TRUE
                 FALSE
```

RETURNS:

```
TRUE    - Successful completion
FALSE   - Error occurred
```

METHOD USAGE:

This method can be called at any time.

METHOD OVERRIDE:

This method usually is not overridden.

RELATED METHODS:

```
wpQueryProgramAssociations        Page 345
```

wpSetQueueOptions

This instance method sets the queue options of the printer object.

INCLUDE IDENTIFIER:

```
#define INCL_WINWORKPLACE
```

FUNCTION PROTOTYPE:

```
BOOL wpSetQueueOptions(WPPrinter *somSelf,
                       ULONG ulOptions);
```

PARAMETERS:

```
somSelf    - Pointer to the object on which the
             method is invoked.
ulOptions  - Flag indicating queue option settings.
             The following flags can be ORed together:
               PO_APPDEFAULT
               PO_DIALOGBEFOREPRINT
               PO_PRINTERSPECIFIC
               PO_PRINTWHILESPOOLING
```

RETURNS:

```
TRUE   - Successful completion
FALSE  - Error occurred
```

METHOD USAGE:

```
This method can be called at any time.
```

METHOD OVERRIDE:

```
this method usually is not overridden.
```

RELATED METHODS:

```
wpQueryQueueOptions            Page 346
```

wpSetRealName

This instance method sets the physical name of a file-system object.

INCLUDE IDENTIFIER:

```
#define INCL_WINWORKPLACE
```

FUNCTION PROTOTYPE:

```
BOOL wpSetRealName(WPObject *somSelf,
                   PSZ pszFilename);
```

PARAMETERS:

```
somSelf      - Pointer to object where method invoked
pszFilename  - Pointer to a new filename; this file
               can not be fully qualified
```

RETURNS:

```
TRUE   - Successful completion
FALSE  - Error occurred
```

REMARKS:

Usually, the file-system object's real name and title are identical. When a title is set that the file system cannot handle, the real name is different; then the real name is set to a truncated title. When the real name and the title are different, the title is stored in the file's .LONGNAME extended attribute.

METHOD USAGE:

This method can be called at any time to set the physical name of a file-system object.

METHOD OVERRIDE:

This method is not usually overridden.

RELATED METHODS:

wpQueryRealName   Page 348

wpSetRefreshRate

This instance method sets the status-window update rate for the Power object when automatic refresh is enabled.

INCLUDE IDENTIFIER:

```
#define INCL_WINWORKPLACE
```

FUNCTION PROTOTYPE:

```
BOOL wpSetRefreshRate(WPPower *somSelf
                      ULONG ulRefreshRate);
```

PARAMETERS:

```
somSelf        - Pointer to the object on which the
                 method is invoked
ulRefreshRate  - Refresh rate value in minutes; range
                 is 1-30
```

RETURNS:

```
TRUE   - Successful completion
FALSE  - Error occurred; refresh rate is out of range
```

RELATED METHODS:

wpAddPowerPage	Page 125
wpAddPowerViewPage	Page 126
wpChangePowerState	Page 154
wpQueryAutoRefresh	Page 275
wpQueryPowerConfirmation	Page 338
wpQueryPowerManagement	Page 339
wpQueryRefreshRate	Page 350
wpSetAutoRefresh	Page 409
wpSetPowerConfirmation	Page 454
wpSetPowerManagement	Page 455

wpSetRemoteOptions

This instance method sets the job view options for a printer object.

INCLUDE IDENTIFIER:

```
#define INCL_WINWORKPLACE
```

FUNCTION PROTOTYPE:

```
BOOL wpSetRemoteOptions(WPPrinter *somSelf,
                        ULONG ulRefreshIntervals,
                        PULONG pflAllJobs);
```

PARAMETERS:

```
somSelf             - Pointer to the object on which
                      the method is invoked.
ulRefreshIntervals  - Time interval, in seconds, when
                      printer object is refreshed.
pflAllJobs          - Flag indicating which jobs to
                      display. Values:
                        TRUE
                        FALSE
```

RETURNS:

```
TRUE   - Successful completion
FALSE  - Error occurred
```

METHOD USAGE:

```
This method can be called at any time.
```

METHOD OVERRIDE:

```
This method usually is not overridden.
```

RELATED METHODS:

```
wpQueryRemoteOptions              Page 351
```

wpSetShadowTitle

This instance method sets the title on the shadow without affecting the title on the object it is shadowing.

INCLUDE IDENTIFIER:

```
#define INCL_WINWORKPLACE
```

FUNCTION PROTOTYPE:

```
BOOL wpSetShadowTitle(WPShadow *somSelf,
                      PSZ pszTitle);
```

PARAMETERS:

```
somSelf    - Pointer to the object on which the method
             is invoked
pszTitle   - Pointer to a title
```

RETURNS:

```
TRUE    - Successful completion
FALSE   - Error occurred
```

METHOD USAGE:

This method can be called at any time to set a title on a shadow object without affecting the title on the object it is shadowing.

METHOD OVERRIDE:

This method is not usually overridden.

RELATED METHODS:

wpSetTitle   Page 470

wpSetSortAttribAvailable

This instance method sets the availability of sort attributes for the current folder.

INCLUDE IDENTIFIER:

```
#define INCL_WINWORKPLACE
```

FUNCTION PROTOTYPE:

```
BOOL wpSetSortAttribAvailable(WPFolder *somSelf,
                             ULONG Index,
                             BOOL Available);
```

PARAMETERS:

```
somSelf     - Pointer to the object on which the
              method is invoked.
Index       - Column index for current details view.
Available   - Flag indicating whether to show or hide
              sort attributes. Values:
                 TRUE  - Show
                 FALSE - Hide
```

RETURNS:

```
TRUE    - Successful completion
FALSE   - Error occurred
```

METHOD OVERRIDE:

This method usually is not overridden.

RELATED METHODS:

wpIsSortAttribAvailable   Page 226

wpSetStyle

This instance method sets the current style of an object.

INCLUDE IDENTIFIER:

```
#define INCL_WINWORKPLACE
```

FUNCTION PROTOTYPE:

```
BOOL wpSetStyle(WPObject *somSelf, ULONG ulNewStyle);
```

PARAMETERS:

```
somSelf       - Pointer to object where method invoked
ulNewStyle    - Values:
                      OBJSTYLE_CUSTOMICON
                      OBJSTYLE_NOCOPY
                      OBJSTYLE_NODELETE
                      OBJSTYLE_NODRAG
                      OBJSTYLE_NODROPON
                      OBJSTYLE_NOLINK
                      OBJSTYLE_NOMOVE
                      OBJSTYLE_NOPRINT
                      OBJSTYLE_NORENAME
                      OBJSTYLE_NOSETTINGS
                      OBJSTYLE_NOTVISIBLE
                      OBJSTYLE_TEMPLATE
```

RETURNS:

```
TRUE    - Successful completion
FALSE   - Error occurred
```

METHOD USAGE:

This method can be called any time to change the style.

METHOD OVERRIDE:

This method is not usually overridden.

RELATED METHODS:

```
wpQueryStyle                    Page 356
wpclsQueryStyle                 Page 547
```

wpSetTitle

This instance method sets the current title of an object.

INCLUDE IDENTIFIER:

```
#define INCL_WINWORKPLACE
```

FUNCTION PROTOTYPE:

```
BOOL wpSetTitle(WPObject *somSelf, PSZ pszNewTitle);
```

PARAMETERS:

```
somSelf        - Pointer to the object on which the
                 method is invoked
pszNewTitle    - Pointer to a zero-terminated string
                 that contains the title of the object
```

RETURNS:

```
TRUE    - Successful completion
FALSE   - Error occurred
```

REMARKS:

Valid titles must be less than CCHMAXPATHCOMP characters
in length, currently defined as 256.

METHOD USAGE:

This method can be called at any time to set an object's
title.

METHOD OVERRIDE:

This method is not usually overridden.

RELATED METHODS:

```
wpQueryTitle                    Page 358
wpclsQueryTitle                 Page 549
```

wpSetTitleAndRenameFile

This instance method sets the current title of an object and renames the file to match the title.

INCLUDE IDENTIFIER:

```
#define INCL_WINWORKPLACE
```

FUNCTION PROTOTYPE:

```
BOOL wpSetTitleAndRenameFile(WPFileSystem *somSelf,
                             PSZ pszNewTitle,
                             ULONG fConfirmations);
```

PARAMETERS:

```
somSelf         - Pointer to the object on which the
                  method is invoked.
pszNewTitle     - Pointer to new title of object, a
                  zero-terminated string that contains
                  new title of object.
fConfirmations  - Confirmation flag. Values:
                    CONFIRM_RENAMEFILEWITHEXT
                    CONFIRM_KEEPASSOC
                    0
```

RETURNS:

```
TRUE    - Successful completion
FALSE   - Error occurred
```

REMARKS:

wpSetTitle is preferred for setting an object's title unless you want to override the confirmations (for example, if you want to rename a file and change its title without prompting the user).

METHOD USAGE:

This method can be called at any time.

METHOD OVERRIDE:

This method usually is not overridden.

RELATED METHODS:

wpConfirmKeepAssoc   Page 165
wpSetTitle   Page 470

wpSetType

This instance method changes the file type of an object.

INCLUDE IDENTIFIER:

```
#define INCL_WINWORKPLACE
```

FUNCTION PROTOTYPE:

```
BOOL wpSetType(WPFileSystem *somSelf, PSZ pszTypes);
```

PARAMETERS:

```
somSelf    - Pointer to the object on which the method
             is invoked
pszTypes   - Pointer to a buffer containing type to
             set; can contain a list of types
             delineated by a line-feed character
```

RETURNS:

```
TRUE    - Successful completion
FALSE   - Error occurred
```

REMARKS:

```
This method causes the file's .TYPE extended attribute
to be set.
```

METHOD USAGE:

```
This method can be called at any time to set the type
on the file object.
```

METHOD OVERRIDE:

```
This method is not usually overridden.
```

wpSetup

This instance method enables the newly created object to initialize itself.

INCLUDE IDENTIFIER:

```
#define INCL_WINWORKPLACE
```

FUNCTION PROTOTYPE:

```
BOOL wpSetup(WPObject *somSelf, PSZ pszSetupString);
```

PARAMETERS:

```
somSelf          - Pointer to the object on which the
                   method is invoked
pszSetupString   - Pointer to setup string
```

RETURNS:

```
TRUE    - Successful completion
FALSE   - Error occurred
```

REMARKS:

If this method returns FALSE, the creation of the object is terminated.

The pszSetupString parameter contains a series of "KEYNAME=value" pairs separated by semicolons that change the behavior of the object. Each object class defines the keynames and the parameter it expects to see immediately following the keyname.

All parameters have safe defaults; it is never required to pass parameters to an object. If a comma or semicolon is needed in the setup string, the escape character ^ can be used.

METHOD USAGE:

This method usually is called only by the system during the processing of wpclsNew, WinCreateObject, and WinSetObjectData.

METHOD OVERRIDE:

This method is overridden by classes that introduce their own keynames.

RELATED METHODS:

wpScanSetupString   Page 394
wpclsNew   Page 506

wpSetupCell

This instance method initializes a cell.

INCLUDE IDENTIFIER:

```
#define INCL_WINWORKPLACE
```

FUNCTION PROTOTYPE:

```
BOOL wpSetupCell(WPPalette *somSelf, PVOID pCellData,
                 ULONG ulcb, ULONG ulx, ULONG uly);
```

PARAMETERS:

```
somSelf     - Pointer to the object on which the
              method is invoked
pCellData   - Pointer to the data to be stored
ulcb        - Size of the data to be stored
ulx         - X-coordinate of the cell to be setup
uly         - Y-coordinate of the cell to be setup
```

RETURNS:

```
TRUE    - Successful completion
FALSE   - Error occurred
```

METHOD USAGE:

This method can be called at any time to initialize a cell.

METHOD OVERRIDE:

This method is not usually overridden.

wpSetupOnce

This instance method performs a one-time initialization of an object after the object has been created.

INCLUDE IDENTIFIER:

```
#define INCL_WINWORKPLACE
```

FUNCTION PROTOTYPE:

```
BOOL wpSetupOnce(WPObject *somSelf,
                PSZ pszSetupString);
```

PARAMETERS:

```
somSelf         - Pointer to the object on which the
                  method is invoked
pszSetupString  - Setup parameters for object
```

RETURNS:

```
TRUE    - Successful completion
FALSE   - Error occurred
```

REMARKS:

If wpSetupOnce returns FALSE, the creation of the object is terminated.

The *pszSetupString* contains a series of "KEYNAME=value" pairs, that change the behavior of the object. Each object class documents the keynames and parameter immediately following the keyname. All parameters have safe default; it is never required to pass parameters to an object.

METHOD USAGE:

This method should not be called when an object is awake. It is only called when it is created.

METHOD OVERRIDE:

This method can be overridden to do the one time initialization; however, the parent method must be called first.

RELATED METHODS:

wpSetup
Page 474

wpShowPalettePointer

This instance method displays the applicator pointer for the palette.

INCLUDE IDENTIFIER:

```
#define INCL_WINWORKPLACE
```

FUNCTION PROTOTYPE:

```
BOOL wpShowPalettePointer(WPPalette *somSelf);
```

PARAMETERS:

```
somSelf  - Pointer to the object on which the method
           is invoked
```

RETURNS:

None.

REMARKS:

To provide the user with a visual clue to the purpose of the palette window, the mouse cursor is always changed to the applicator symbol when it is within the bounds of an open palette-view window. For example, when the cursor is within the color-palette window, it displays a paintbrush.

This method should cause only the applicator to be displayed. When wpDragCell is invoked, the applicator *plus* the attribute should be shown, if possible. For example, the paint brush used in the color palette appears to have been dipped in the color that is being applied.

METHOD USAGE:

This method may be called at any time.

METHOD OVERRIDE:

All subclasses of WPPalette need to override this method to ensure that the cursor changes to an applicator while it is within the palette window.

RELATED METHODS:

wpDragCell   Page 188

wpStartJobAgain

This instance method starts printing a job object again.

INCLUDE IDENTIFIER:

```
#define INCL_WINWORKPLACE
```

FUNCTION PROTOTYPE:

```
BOOL wpStartJobAgain(WPJob *somSelf);
```

PARAMETERS:

```
somSelf  - Pointer to the object to be restarted
```

RETURNS:

```
TRUE    - Successful completion
FALSE   - Error occurred
```

METHOD OVERRIDE:

```
This method is not usually overridden.
```

wpSwitchTo

This instance method gives focus to the specified open view of an object.

INCLUDE IDENTIFIER:

```
#define INCL_WINWORKPLACE
```

FUNCTION PROTOTYPE:

```
BOOL wpSwitchTo(WPObject *somSelf, ULONG ulView);
```

PARAMETERS:

```
somSelf - Pointer to the object on which the method
          is invoked.
ulView  - Flag indicating open view to which focus is
          to be given. Values:
              OPEN_CONTENTS
              OPEN_DEFAULT
              OPEN_DETAILS
              OPEN_HELP
              OPEN_RUNNING
              OPEN_SETTINGS
              OPEN_TREE
              OPEN_USER
```

RETURNS:

```
TRUE   - Successful completion
FALSE  - Error occurred
```

REMARKS:

The focus is given to the specified open view of the object if it exists. This is done by scanning the in-use list.

METHOD USAGE:

This method can be called at any time to switch to an existing view of this object.

METHOD OVERRIDE:

```
This method is not usually overridden.
```

RELATED METHODS:

wpOpen   Page 248

wpUnInitData

This instance method frees the allocated resources of an object.

INCLUDE IDENTIFIER:

```
#define INCL_WINWORKPLACE
```

FUNCTION PROTOTYPE:

```
VOID wpUnInitData(WPObject *somSelf);
```

PARAMETERS:

```
somSelf  - Pointer to the object on which the method
           is invoked
```

RETURNS:

```
None.
```

REMARKS:

The parent method must be called after completing your own processing.

METHOD USAGE:

This method usually is called only by the system when the object is made dormant. This occurs when it is destroyed or when there are no open views and the object and folder containing the object are not open.

METHOD OVERRIDE:

This method is overridden to deallocate resources allocated during the processing of wpInitData.

RELATED METHODS:

wpInitData   Page 214

wpUnlockObject

This instance method decrements the lock count of an object.

INCLUDE IDENTIFIER:

```
#define INCL_WINWORKPLACE
```

FUNCTION PROTOTYPE:

```
BOOL wpUnlockObject(WPObject *somSelf);
```

PARAMETERS:

```
somSelf  - Pointer to object where method is invoked
```

RETURNS:

```
TRUE   - Successful completion
FALSE  - Error occurred
```

REMARKS:

This method unlocks the specified object, which auto-matically becomes dormant when it has no open views and the container it is in is no longer open (lock count=0).

METHOD USAGE:

This method can be called at any time to decrement the lock count of an object. It is used in conjunction with other methods that create new instances of objects. If these methods are called with the fLock flag set to TRUE, the new object is locked into the awake state until wpUnlockObject is called.

METHOD OVERRIDE:

This method is not usually overridden.

RELATED METHODS:

wpVerifyUpdateAccess

This instance method verifies the update access of the current file system.

INCLUDE IDENTIFIER:

```
#define INCL_WINWORKPLACE
```

FUNCTION PROTOTYPE:

```
ULONG wpVerifyUpdateAccess(WPFileSystem *somSelf);
```

PARAMETERS:

```
somSelf  - Pointer to the object on which the method
           is invoked
```

RETURNS:

```
DosOpen error return code. Values:

   ERROR_ACCESS_DENIED
   ERROR_CANNOT_MAKE
   ERROR_DEVICE_IN_USE
   ERROR_DISK_FULL
   ERROR_DRIVE_LOCKED
   ERROR_FILENAME_EXCED_RANGE
   ERROR_FILE_NOT_FOUND
   ERROR_INVALID_ACCESS
   ERROR_INVALID_PARAMETER
   ERROR_NOT_DOS_DISK
   ERROR_OPEN_FAILED
   ERROR_PATH_NOT_FOUND
   ERROR_PIPE_BUSY
   ERROR_SHARING_BUFFER_EXCEEDED
   ERROR_SHARING_VIOLATION
   ERROR_TOO_MANY_OPEN_FILES
   NO_ERROR
```

METHOD OVERRIDE:

```
This method usually is not overridden.
```

wpViewObject

This instance method opens a view, or surfaces an existing view, of an object.

INCLUDE IDENTIFIER:

```
#define INCL_WINWORKPLACE
```

FUNCTION PROTOTYPE:

```
HWND wpViewObject(WPObject *somSelf, HWND hwndCnr,
                  ULONG ulView, ULONG param);
```

PARAMETERS:

```
somSelf - Pointer to the object on which the method
          is invoked.
hwndCnr - Handle for the view to the container of the
          object.
ulView  - Flag indicating which object to view.
          Values:
              OPEN_CONTENTS
              OPEN_DEFAULT
              OPEN_DETAILS
              OPEN_HELP
              OPEN_PALETTE
              OPEN_RUNNING
              OPEN_SETTINGS
              OPEN_TREE
              OPEN_USER
param   - Optional parameter.
```

RETURNS:

```
Window handle of the view opened or resurfaced.
```

REMARKS:

```
Parameters are passed to wpOpen to open a view of this
object or to wpSwitchTo to surface an existing view,
depending on if the view already exists and if multiple
concurrent views are set for this object.
```

```
This method should be used instead of wpOpen.
```

METHOD USAGE:

This method can be called at any time to view an object.

METHOD OVERRIDE:

This method should not be overridden.

RELATED METHODS:

wpOpen   Page 248
wpQueryConcurrentView   Page 279
wpSwitchTo   Page 482

wpWaitForClose

This instance method pauses the application until the specified views are closed or the time-out value is reached.

INCLUDE IDENTIFIER:

```
#define INCL_WINWORKPLACE
```

FUNCTION PROTOTYPE:

```
ULONG wpWaitForClose(WPObject *somSelf,
                     LHANDLE lhView,
                     ULONG ulViews, ULONG ulTimeOut,
                     BOOL bAutoClose);
```

PARAMETERS:

somSelf   - Pointer to the object on which the method is invoked.

lhView   - Handle of view that must close before application can continue. If value of NULL is passed, this method waits for all views of specified type (*ulViews*) to close.

ulViews   - Type of views to wait for used only *lhView* is NULL.

ulTimeOut   - Time to wait for views to close.

bAutoClose - Flag indicating whether to automatically close. Parameter should not be used as standard method to close views. It exists only to handle possibility of timing hold where all specified views are closed and another thread (probably due to user input) opens another view of same type before wpWaitForClose returns. Values:
              TRUE
              FALSE

RETURNS:

Success   - Return value from WinWaitEventSem; the maximum amount of time the user allows the thread to be blocked. Values:
              0
              -1

REMARKS:

If a view must finish closing before processing is continued, this method can be called to act as event semaphore. This method can also be used to block the thread until an executable exists and is executed from a program object.

METHOD USAGE:

This method can be called at any time.

METHOD OVERRIDE:

This method usually is not overridden.

Chapter 4
Workplace Class Methods

This chapter contains an alphabetical listing of the Workplace class methods. These methods act on class data common to all instances of the class. *Metaclasses* define class methods and their properties.

wpclsCreateDefaultTemplates

This class method allows the specified class to create default template instances of its class.

INCLUDE IDENTIFIER:

```
#define INCL_WINWORKPLACE
```

FUNCTION PROTOTYPE:

```
ULONG wpclsCreateDefaultTemplates(M_WPObject *somSelf,
                                  WPFolder *Folder);
```

PARAMETERS:

```
somSelf - Pointer to the class object
Folder  - Pointer to the folder in which to create
          the templates
```

RETURNS:

```
Number of templates created.
```

METHOD USAGE:

This method usually is called only by the system when the class is registered. A class is registered by a call to WinRegisterObjectClass. When the system calls this method, *Folder* is a pointer to the Templates folder.

METHOD OVERRIDE:

This method should be overridden by classes that need to create default template instances of their class.

wpclsDecUsage

This class method decrements the class-usage count.

INCLUDE IDENTIFIER:

#define INCL_WINWORKPLACE

FUNCTION PROTOTYPE:

VOID wpclsDecUsage(M_WPObject *somSelf);

PARAMETERS:

somSelf - Pointer to the class object

RETURNS:

There is no return value for this method.

REMARKS:

The class usage count is used by the system to dynamically load and unload DLLs containing classes.

METHOD OVERRIDE:

This method is generally not overridden.

RELATED METHODS:

wpclsIncUsage   Page 500

wpclsFileSysExists

This instance method returns the object if the specified file or directory already exists in the given folder.

INCLUDE IDENTIFIER:

```
#define INCL_WINWORKPLACE
```

FUNCTION PROTOTYPE:

```
WPObject wpclsFileSysExists(M_WPFileSystem *somSelf,
                            SOMAny *Folder,
                            PSZ pszFilename,
                            ULONG attrFile);
```

PARAMETERS:

```
somSelf      - Pointer to the class object.
Folder       - Pointer to the folder in which to look
               for the file or directory specified in
               pszFilename
pszFilename  - Name of the file or directory
attrFile     - File-system attribute flag that
               indicates whether pszFilename is a file
               or directory
```

RETURNS:

```
WPObject * - Pointer to found file or directory object
NULL       - Object not found
```

METHOD USAGE:

This method can be called at any time.

METHOD OVERRIDE:

This method is generally not overridden.

wpclsFindObjectEnd

This class method ends the find operation started by a call to wpclsFindObjectFirst.

INCLUDE IDENTIFIER:

```
#define INCL_WINWORKPLACE
```

FUNCTION PROTOTYPE:

```
BOOL wpclsFindObjectEnd(M_WPObject *somSelf,
                        HFIND hFind);
```

PARAMETERS:

```
somSelf - Pointer to the class object
hFind   - Handle associated with a previous call to
          wpclsFindObjectFirst or wpclsFindObjectNext
```

RETURNS:

```
TRUE   - Successful completion
FALSE  - Error occurred
```

METHOD USAGE:

This method should be called to terminate a find operation that was started by a previous call to wpclsFindObjectFirst.

METHOD OVERRIDE:

This method is not usually overridden.

RELATED METHODS:

wpclsFindObjectFirst

This class method finds workplace objects.

INCLUDE IDENTIFIER:

```
#define INCL_WINWORKPLACE
```

FUNCTION PROTOTYPE:

```
BOOL wpclsFindObjectFirst(M_WPObject *somSelf,
                          PCLASS pClassList,
                          PHFIND phFind,
                          PSZ pszTitle,
                          WPFolder, *Folder,
                          BOOL fSubfolders,
                          PVOID pExtendedCriteria,
                          POBJECTS pBuffer,
                          PULONG pCount);
```

PARAMETERS:

somSelf	- Pointer to the class object.
pClassList	- Pointer to an array of class objects. The final element of this array should be NULL.
phFind	- Address of the handle associated with this method. This handle is used with subsequent calls to wpclsFindObjectNext and wpclsFindObjectEnd.
pszTitle	- Pointer to title specification for objects to be searched. This title may include the wildcard characters * and ?.
Folder	- Pointer to the folder in which to find objects. This pointer can be determined by issuing a call to wpclsQueryFolder.

fSubfolders	- Scope indicator. Values:
	    FALSE
	    TRUE

pExtendedCriteria	- Pointer to buffer that contains the class-specific extended search criteria.
pBuffer	- Pointer to buffer that contains an array of object pointers. The size of this buffer must be

large enough to hold the number
of requested entries specified
by pCount.

pCount   - Address of number of matching
                entries requested in pBuffer. On
                return, this field contains the
                number of entries in pBuffer.

RETURNS:

TRUE   - Successful completion.
FALSE   - Error occurred. FALSE can indicate:
            WPERR_BUFFER_OVERFLOW
            WPERR_OBJECT_NOT_FOUND

REMARKS:

This method returns object pointers (up to the number
requested in pCount) for as many objects that match the
specifications and that fit in pBuffer. On output,
pCount contains the actual number of object pointers
returned.

The wpclsFindObjectNext method uses the find object
handle associated with wpclsFindObjectFirst to continue
the search started by the wpclsFindObjectFirst request.

If wpclsFindObjectFirst returns FALSE, wpQueryError can
be called to retrieve the error code. The wpclsFindObjectEnd method should be called to terminate the find
operation.

METHOD USAGE:

This method can be called at any time to find objects.

METHOD OVERRIDE:

This method is not usually overridden.

RELATED METHODS:

wpclsFindObjectNext

This class method finds the next set of matching objects.

INCLUDE IDENTIFIER:

```
#define INCL_WINWORKPLACE
```

FUNCTION PROTOTYPE:

```
BOOL wpclsFindObjectNext(M_WPObject *somSelf,
                         HFIND hFind,
                         POBJECTS pBuffer,
                         PULONG pCount);
```

PARAMETERS:

somSelf - Pointer to the class object.
hFind   - Handle associated with previous call to
           wpclsFindObjectFirst or wpclsFindObject-
           Next.
pBuffer - Pointer to buffer that contains an
           array of object pointers. Size of this
           buffer must be large enough to hold
           number of requested entries specified by
           pCount.
pCount   - Address of number of matching entries
           requested in pBuffer. On return, this field
           contains number of entries in pBuffer.

RETURNS:

TRUE   - Successful completion.
FALSE - Error occurred. FALSE can indicate:
           WPERR_BUFFER_OVERFLOW
           WPERR_OBJECT_NOT_FOUND

REMARKS:

This method returns object pointers (up to the number
requested in pCount) for as many objects that match the
specifications and that fit in pBuffer. On output,
pCount contains the actual number of object pointers
returned.

wpclsFindObjectNext uses the find object handle associated with wpclsFindObjectFirst to continue the search started by the wpclsFindObjectFirst request.

If wpclsFindObjectNext returns FALSE, the wpQueryError method can be called to retrieve the error code.

The wpclsFindObjectEnd method should be called to terminate the find operation.

METHOD USAGE:

This method can be called at any time to find the next set of matching objects. This method should only be called after a previous call to wpclsFindObjectFirst returned an error of WPERR_BUFFER_OVERFLOW.

METHOD OVERRIDE:

This method is not usually overridden.

RELATED METHODS:

wpclsFindOneObject

This instance method finds an object matching a predefined set of properties.

INCLUDE IDENTIFIER:

```
#define INCL_WINWORKPLACE
```

FUNCTION PROTOTYPE:

```
WPObject *wpclsFindOneObject(M_WPObject *somSelf,
                             HWND hwndOwner,
                             PSZ pszFindParams);
```

PARAMETERS:

```
somSelf         - Pointer to the class object
hwndOwner       - Handle of owner window for dialogs
pszFindParams   - Setup string which defines
                  properties of object
```

RETURNS:

```
Pointer to the found object.
```

METHOD USAGE:

```
This method can be called at any time.
```

METHOD OVERRIDE:

```
This method should not be overridden.
```

RELATED METHODS:

wpclsIncUsage

This class method increments the class-usage count.

INCLUDE IDENTIFIER:

```
#define INCL_WINWORKPLACE
```

FUNCTION PROTOTYPE:

```
VOID wpclsIncUsage(M_WPObject *somSelf);
```

PARAMETERS:

```
somSelf  - Pointer to the class object
```

RETURNS:

```
None.
```

REMARKS:

```
The class-usage count is used by the system to dynami-
cally load and unload DLLs containing classes.
```

METHOD OVERRIDE:

```
This method should not be overridden.
```

RELATED METHODS:

```
wpclsDecUsage                    Page 492
```

wpclsInitData

This class method initializes the instance data of a class object.

INCLUDE IDENTIFIER:

```
#define INCL_WINWORKPLACE
```

FUNCTION PROTOTYPE:

```
VOID wpclsInitData(M_WPObject *somSelf);
```

PARAMETERS:

```
somSelf  - Pointer to the class object
```

RETURNS:

```
None.
```

REMARKS:

This method is called immediately after the class object is first awakened. When the class object is made dormant, calling wpclsUnInitData allows it to deallocate resources allocated during processing of wpclsInitData.

METHOD USAGE:

This method usually is called only by the system when the class object is awakened, which is when the first instance of this class is either awakened or newly created. It is made dormant again when the last instance of this class becomes dormant.

METHOD OVERRIDE:

Any class with metaclass-instance variables should override wpclsInitData so those variables are initially in a known state. This method must be passed to the parent class object before doing override processing.

RELATED METHODS:

wpclsUnInitData   Page 558

wpclsInsertMultipleObjects

This instance method inserts all specified objects into a specified
container and the in-use list.

INCLUDE IDENTIFIER:

```
#define INCL_WINWORKPLACE
```

FUNCTION PROTOTYPE:

```
wpclsInsertMultipleObjects(M_WPObject *somSelf,
                           HWND hwndCnr,
                           PPOINTL pptlIcon,
                           PVOID pObjectArray,
                           HWND pRecordParent,
                           ULONG NumRecords);
```

PARAMETERS:

somSelf	– Pointer to the class object
hwndCnr	– Handle to container window
pptlIcon	– Pointer to initial icon position for first icon inserted
pObjectArray	– Pointer to array of pointers to MINIRECORDCORE objects
pRecordParent	– Pointer to parent record for view
NumRecords	– Number of records in *pObjectArray* which need to be inserted; must be greater than 0

RETURNS:

TRUE	– Successful completion
FALSE	– Error occurred

REMARKS:

This method provides rapid insertion of many objects
into a container at once. wpCnrInsertObject performs the
same function as this method, but operates only on one
object at a time.

METHOD USAGE:

This method can be called at any time to add multiple
objects to a container.

METHOD OVERRIDE:

This method is generally not overridden.

RELATED METHODS:

wpclsMakeAwake

This class method allows the specified class to awaken an object.

INCLUDE IDENTIFIER:

```
#define INCL_WINWORKPLACE
```

FUNCTION PROTOTYPE:

```
WPObject *wpclsMakeAwake(M_WPObject *somSelf,
                         PSZ pszTitle,
                         ULONG ulStyle,
                         HPOINTER hptrIcon,
                         POBJDATA pObjData,
                         WPFolder *Folder,
                         ULONG ulUser);
```

PARAMETERS:

```
somSelf    - Pointer to the class object.
pszTitle   - Pointer to string containing title to
             set on object. If value is NULL, class
             default value will be used.
ulStyle    - Object style flags to set on object.
             If this value is NULL, current or
             default value is used. Predefined object
             style bits are as follows:
                OBJSTYLE_CUSTOMICON
                OBJSTYLE_NOCOPY
                OBJSTYLE_NODELETE
                OBJSTYLE_NODRAG
                OBJSTYLE_NODROPON
                OBJSTYLE_NOSETTINGS
                OBJSTYLE_NOLINK
                OBJSTYLE_NOMOVE
                OBJSTYLE_NOPRINT
                OBJSTYLE_NORENAME
                OBJSTYLE_NOTVISIBLE
                OBJSTYLE_TEMPLATE
hptrIcon   - Icon to set on object. If this value
             is NULL, class default value is used.
pObjData   - Pointer to object data. If this value
             is NULL, class default value is used.
Folder     - Pointer to folder object that contains
             new object. This pointer can be
             determined by calling wpclsQueryFolder.
```

```
ulUser      - Value defined by user and used by
              base storage class.
```

RETURNS:

```
NULL   - Error occurred
Other  - Pointer to the awakened object
```

REMARKS:

An object is made awake when it is created in an open
folder or when a folder containing the object is opened.
An object awakened by wpclsMakeAwake is automatically
locked. The wpUnlockObject method can be called to allow
the object to return to its dormant state.

METHOD USAGE:

This method usually is called only by base storage
classes to awaken an object from the dormant state.

METHOD OVERRIDE:

This method is not usually overridden.

RELATED METHODS:

```
wpclsNew                       Page 506
wpInitData                     Page 214
wpUnlockObject                 Page 485
```

wpclsNew

This class method makes a new instance of this class of object.

INCLUDE IDENTIFIER:

```
#define INCL_WINWORKPLACE
```

FUNCTION PROTOTYPE:

```
WPObject *wpclsNew(M_WPObject *somSelf, PSZ pszTitle,
                   PSZ pszSetupEnv,
                   WPFolder *Folder, BOOL fLock);
```

PARAMETERS:

somSelf   - Pointer to the class in which the new
               instance is to be created.
pszTitle   - Pointer to zero-terminated string
               that contains the initial title of
               the object as it is to appear when
               displayed on the user interface
               underneath an icon or on the title bar
               of an open object.
pszSetupEnv - Pointer to a zero-terminated string
               that contains the object-specific
               parameters of the new object. This
               string is extracted when wpSetup is
               called.
Folder   - Pointer to a folder object in which to
               place this new object. This pointer
               can be determined by issuing a call to
               wpclsQueryFolder.
fLock   - Lock object flag. If FALSE, the newly
               created object will be made dormant
               whenever the object and the folder
               containing the object are closed. If
               TRUE, the new flag remains awake until
               the caller issues wpUnlockObject.

RETURNS:

NULL   - Error occurred
wpclsNew - Pointer to the new object created

REMARKS:

This method is a modified version of somNew that takes arguments. These arguments provide a way to create a new object with a defined state.

METHOD USAGE:

This method can be called at any time to create a new workplace object. The created object is a persistent instance of the class specified by WPClass.

METHOD OVERRIDE:

This method can be overridden only in a metaclass.

RELATED METHODS:

wpclsObjectFromHandle

This instance method extracts the object pointer for an instance represented by the given handle.

INCLUDE IDENTIFIER:

```
#define INCL_WINWORKPLACE
```

FUNCTION PROTOTYPE:

```
WPObject *wpclsObjectFromHandle(M_WPObject *somSelf,
                                HOBJECT hObject);
```

PARAMETERS:

```
somSelf  - Pointer to the class object
hObject  - Persistent object handle
```

RETURNS:

```
pObject  - Pointer to object instance
```

REMARKS:

Each base class must store the relationship between the object handles and the folders they reside in.

METHOD USAGE:

This method can be called at any time to find the object pointer from a given handle.

METHOD OVERRIDE:

This method is generally not overridden.

wpclsQueryActiveDesktop

This instance method returns a pointer to the active WPDesktop object.

INCLUDE IDENTIFIER:

```
#define INCL_WINWORKPLACE
```

FUNCTION PROTOTYPE:

```
WPDesktop *wpclsQueryActiveDesktop
                        (M_WPDesktop *somSelf);
```

PARAMETERS:

```
somSelf  - Pointer to the class object
```

RETURNS:

```
WPDesktop  - Pointer to active Desktop object
```

REMARKS:

```
Multiple Desktop objects can be awake, but only one can
be active at a time.
```

METHOD USAGE:

```
This method can be called at any time.
```

METHOD OVERRIDE:

```
This method is generally not overridden.
```

RELATED METHODS:

```
wpclsQueryActiveDesktopHWND      Page 510
```

wpclsQueryActiveDesktopHWND

This instance method returns the handle of the active WPDesktop object.

INCLUDE IDENTIFIER:

```
#define INCL_WINWORKPLACE
```

FUNCTION PROTOTYPE:

```
HWND wpclsQueryActiveDesktopHWND
                          (M_WPDesktop *somSelf);
```

PARAMETERS:

```
somSelf   - Pointer to the class object
```

RETURNS:

```
hwndDesktop   - Handle of the active Desktop object's
                frame window
```

METHOD USAGE:

```
This method can be called at any time.
```

METHOD OVERRIDE:

```
This method is generally not overridden.
```

RELATED METHODS:

```
wpclsQueryActiveDesktop           Page 509
```

wpclsQueryAwakeObject

This instance method determines if the given object is awake.

INCLUDE IDENTIFIER:

```
#define INCL_WINWORKPLACE
```

FUNCTION PROTOTYPE:

```
WPObject wpclsQueryAwakeObject
                        (M_WPFileSystem *somSelf,
                         PSZ pszInputPath);
```

PARAMETERS:

```
somSelf        - Pointer to the class object.
pszInputPath   - Fully-qualified input path; must be a
                 valid path. The system does not call
                 the file system to determine if the
                 file exists.
```

RETURNS:

```
Object  - Awake object. Return value of NULL
          indicates that object is not already awake.
```

REMARKS:

This method requires that for an object to be awake, all path components prior to the object are also awake. If any path component is not found awake, then the routine assumes that the object for that passed file cannot be awake either.

METHOD USAGE:

This method can be called at any time.

METHOD OVERRIDE:

This method is generally not overridden.

RELATED METHODS:

wpclsMakeAwake   Page 504

wpclsQueryButtonAppearance

This class method returns the object pointer for a given object handle.

INCLUDE IDENTIFIER:

```
#define INCL_WINWORKPLACE
```

FUNCTION PROTOTYPE:

```
WPObject *wpclsQueryButtonAppearance
                          (M_WPObject *somSelf,
                           HOBJECT hObject);
```

PARAMETERS:

```
somSelf  - Pointer to the class object
hObject  - Handle to persistent object
```

RETURNS:

```
object   - Pointer to object instance. Return value of
           0 indicates that given object handle no
           longer exists.
```

METHOD USAGE:

```
This method can be called at any time to obtain a pointer
to the given object.
```

METHOD OVERRIDE:

```
This method is generally not overridden.
```

RELATED METHODS:

```
wpQueryButtonAppearance          Page 276
wpSetButtonAppearance            Page 410
```

wpclsQueryDefaultHelp

This class method specifies the default help panel for instances of
the class object.

INCLUDE IDENTIFIER:

```
#define INCL_WINWORKPLACE
```

FUNCTION PROTOTYPE:

```
ULONG wpclsQueryDefaultHelp(M_WPObject *somSelf,
                            PULONG pHelpPanelId,
                            PSZ pszHelpLibrary);
```

PARAMETERS:

```
somSelf          - Pointer to the class object.
pHelpPanelId     - Pointer to the help panel id.
pszHelpLibrary   - Pointer to the buffer in which to
                   place the name of help library.
                   This buffer should be at least the
                   length of CCHMAXPATH bytes.
```

RETURNS:

```
TRUE   - Successful completion
FALSE  - Error occurred
```

REMARKS:

This method is called during the default processing of
wpQueryDefaultHelp.

METHOD USAGE:

This method can be called at any time to determine the
default help panel for this object class.

METHOD OVERRIDE:

The default WPObject class does not process this method
other than to return FALSE.

RELATED METHODS:

wpclsQueryDefaultView

This class method specifies the default open view for an instance of the class object.

INCLUDE IDENTIFIER:

```
#define INCL_WINWORKPLACE
```

FUNCTION PROTOTYPE:

```
ULONG wpclsQueryDefaultView(M_WPObject *somSelf);
```

PARAMETERS:

```
somSelf  - Pointer to the class object
```

RETURNS:

```
OPEN_CONTENTS   - Open content view
OPEN_DEFAULT    - Open default view (double-click)
OPEN_DETAILS    - Open details view
OPEN_HELP       - Display Help panel
OPEN_RUNNING    - Execute object
OPEN_SETTINGS   - Open Settings notebook
OPEN_TREE       - Open tree view
OPEN_UNKNOWN    - Unknown view
OPEN_USER       - Class specific views have a greater
                  value than this
```

METHOD USAGE:

This method can be called at any time to query the default open view for instances of this class.

METHOD OVERRIDE:

All classes should override this method, so that new objects in their class will always have a sensible default view (divide objects typically have a default view of OPEN_SETTINGS). The default view is used for the conditional Open cascade menu and double_clicking on the object.

RELATED METHODS:

wpclsQueryDetails

This class method specifies the default details-view items for instances of the class object.

INCLUDE IDENTIFIER:

```
#define INCL_WINWORKPLACE
```

FUNCTION PROTOTYPE:

```
PCLASSDETAILS wpclsQueryDetails(M_WPObject *somSelf);
```

PARAMETERS:

```
somSelf  - Pointer to the class object
```

RETURNS:

```
NULL   - Error occurred
Other  - Pointer to details information
```

RELATED METHODS:

wpclsQueryDetailsInfo

This class method specifies the details to be used for instances of the class object.

INCLUDE IDENTIFIER:

```
#define INCL_WINWORKPLACE
```

FUNCTION PROTOTYPE:

```
ULONG wpclsQueryDetailsInfo(M_WPObject *somSelf,
                           PCLASSFIELDINFO
                           pClassFieldInfo,
                           PULONG pSize);
```

PARAMETERS:

```
somSelf           - Pointer to the class object
pClassFieldInfo   - Pointer to details information
pSize             - Total number of bytes of details
                    data; includes details added by
                    this class and ancestor classes
```

RETURNS:

The sum of the number of detail columns for the object. This sum includes details added by this class and ancestor classes.

REMARKS:

All objects that have information to display in details view must override this method.

METHOD USAGE:

This method usually is called only by the system.

METHOD OVERRIDE:

This method should be overridden by classes that introduce class-specific details to be displayed in details view. The parent method always must be called before appending the request information.

RELATED METHODS:

wpclsQueryDetails   Page 517
wpQueryDetailsData   Page 292

wpclsQueryEditString

This class method specifies the text to be used in the **Edit** push button of the open view of the palette object.

INCLUDE IDENTIFIER:

```
#define INCL_WINWORKPLACE
```

FUNCTION PROTOTYPE:

```
PSZ wpclsQueryEditString(M_WPPalette *somSelf);
```

PARAMETERS:

```
somSelf  - Pointer to the class object
```

RETURNS:

Pointer to the **Edit** push-button string.

METHOD USAGE:

This method can be called at any time to determine the text of the **Edit** push button.

METHOD OVERRIDE:

This method should be overridden to specify class-specific **Edit** push-button text. The parent method is not usually called.

wpclsQueryError

This class method queries the current error code held within a class object.

INCLUDE IDENTIFIER:

```
#define INCL_WINWORKPLACE
```

FUNCTION PROTOTYPE:

```
ULONG wpclsQueryError(M_WPObject *somSelf);
```

PARAMETERS:

```
somSelf  - Pointer to the class object
```

RETURNS:

The last error that occurred when using this class object.

REMARKS:

When an error occurs within a class method and that method subsequently fails, the calling procedure can retrieve the error code for that failed call by using wpclsQueryError.

The error code is always that of the *last method that failed*. A successful method does not modify the error code held with a class object. This function is analogous to the WinGetErrorInfo and the WinGetLastError functions used by Presentation Manager applications to diagnose the reason for the previous failing call to a PM function.

The system-provided class methods return error codes as defined in the header file PMERR.H.

METHOD USAGE:

This method should be called immediately after a class method has failed to diagnose why the failure occurred.

METHOD OVERRIDE:

Never override this class method.

RELATED METHODS:

wpclsSetError   Page 552

wpclsQueryExtendedCriteria

This class method specifies the extended criteria to be used on a
search for instances of a specified class.

INCLUDE IDENTIFIER:

```
#define INCL_WINWORKPLACE
```

FUNCTION PROTOTYPE:

```
BOOL wpclsQueryExtendedCriteria
                        (M_WPObject *somSelf,
                         PSZ Title,
                         ULONG ulSearchType,
                         PVOID ExtendedCriteria);
```

PARAMETERS:

```
somSelf          - Pointer to the class object.
Title            - Pointer to title specification for
                   objects to be search; can include
                   the wildcard characters * and ?.
ulSearchType     - Flag indicating type of search to
                   be performed. Values:
                      SEARCH_ALL_FOLDERS
                      SEARCH_THIS_FOLDER
                      SEARCH_THIS_TREE
ExtendedCriteria - Pointer to buffer that contains
                   class-specific extended search
                   criteria. This buffer can be
                   passed to wpDoesObjectMatch
                   method.
```

RETURNS:

```
TRUE   - Successful completion
FALSE  - Error occurred or user canceled search
```

REMARKS:

```
This method is called by the system during the processing
of the Find and folder Include facilities. It usually
prompts the user to select the extended criteria.
```

METHOD USAGE:

This method can be called at any time in order to determine the extended search criteria to be used for finding objects of this class.

METHOD OVERRIDE:

This method should be overridden by classes which introduce extended search criteria for use by the Find and folder Include facilities.

wpclsQueryFolder

This class method retrieves a pointer to a folder object that corresponds to a specified file-system location.

INCLUDE IDENTIFIER:

```
#define INCL_WINWORKPLACE
```

FUNCTION PROTOTYPE:

```
WPFolder *wpclsQueryFolder(M_WPObject *somSelf,
                           PSZ pszLocation,
                           BOOL fLock);
```

PARAMETERS:

```
somSelf       - Pointer to the class object.
pszLocation   - Folder location; the value can be in
                any of the following formats:
                * Predefined object ids of system
                  folders:
                     <WP_CONFIG>
                     <WP_DESKTOP>
                     <WP_DRIVES>
                     <WP_INFO>
                     <WP_NOWHERE>
                     <WP_START>
                     <WP_OS2SYS>
                     <WP_TEMPS>
                  * Real names specified as a fully
                    qualified path name
fLock         - Lock object flag. If FALSE, the newly
                created object is made dormant when
                the object and folder containing the
                object are closed. If TRUE, the new
                flag remains active until the caller
                caller issues wpUnlockObject.
```

RETURNS:

```
NULL    - Error occurred
Other   - Pointer to a folder object
```

REMARKS:

To obtain a real name from an object pointer, wpQueryRealName should be called.

METHOD USAGE:

This method can be called at any time to determine the
object pointer for a folder.

METHOD OVERRIDE:

This method is not usually overridden.

wpclsQueryIcon

This class method specifies the default icon to be used for instances of the class object.

INCLUDE IDENTIFIER:

```
#define INCL_WINWORKPLACE
```

FUNCTION PROTOTYPE:

```
HPOINTER wpclsQueryIcon(M_WPObject *somSelf);
```

PARAMETERS:

```
somSelf  - Pointer to the class object
```

RETURNS:

```
NULL    - Error occurred
Other   - Handle to an icon
```

REMARKS:

The class default icon can be loaded on wpclsInitData and freed on wpclsUnInitData.

METHOD USAGE:

This method can be called at any time to determine the default icon for instances of this class.

METHOD OVERRIDE:

This method is overridden to change the default icon for an instance of the class.

RELATED METHODS:

wpclsQueryIconData

This class method builds the class default icon for a specified class.

INCLUDE IDENTIFIER:

```
#define INCL_WINWORKPLACE
```

FUNCTION PROTOTYPE:

```
ULONG wpclsQueryIconData(M_WPObject *somSelf,
                         PICONINFO pIconInfo);
```

PARAMETERS:

```
somSelf    - Pointer to the class object.
pIconInfo  - Handle to the container control window.
             If NULLHANDLE, the size should still be
             returned correctly.
```

RETURNS:

```
The size of the buffer needed to accommodate the ICONINFO
buffer that is returned by this particular class object.
```

REMARKS:

```
If NULLHANDLE is passed for pIconInfo, the caller is
asking for the size of the ICONINFO buffer needed for
this class, usually for memory allocation purposes.
Otherwise, pIconInfo always can be assumed to be large
enough to accommodate the ICONINFO for this class.

The ICONINFO structure allows specification of the
default icon in 3 different ways:
```

- An icon filename
- A module name and resource identifier
- A block of binary data

```
However, only one mechanism need be supported any given
class. For example, a caller cannot request one of the
three formats by prefilling the ICONINFO structure.
```

METHOD USAGE:

This method may be called at any time. Typically, it would not be useful for another object class to make calls to this method.

METHOD OVERRIDE:

Workplace classes that wish to have a unique class default icon must override this method and fill out the appropriate fields within the ICONINFO structure. In addition, the correct size for the ICONINFO must always be returned.

RELATED METHODS:

wpQueryIcon	Page 316
wpQueryIconData	Page 317
wpSetIcon	Page 441
wpSetIconData	Page 442

wpclsQueryIconDataN

This class method builds the class default animation icon for a specified class.

INCLUDE IDENTIFIER:

```
#define INCL_WINWORKPLACE
```

FUNCTION PROTOTYPE:

```
wpclsQueryIconDataN(M_WPFolder *somSelf,
                    PICONINFO pIconInfo,
                    ULONG ulcbIconInfo,
                    ULONG ulIconIndex);
```

PARAMETERS:

```
somSelf        - Pointer to the class object
pIconInfo      - Pointer to icon information
ulchIconInfo   - Size of buffer needed to store
                 ICONINFO data returned by this class
                 object
ulIconIndex    - Animation icon index; value must be 1
```

REMARKS:

If NULLHANDLE is passed for the *pIconInfo* parameter, the caller is asking for the size of the ICONINFO buffer needed for this class usually for memory allocation purposes. Otherwise, the *pIconInfo* parameter can always be assumed to be large enough to accommodate the ICONINFO for this class.

The ICONINFO structure allows you to specify the default icon in three different ways:

- An icon filename
- A module name and resource identifier
- A block of binary data

However, only one mechanism needs to be supported for any given class. For example, a caller cannot request one of the three formats by prefilling the ICONINFO structure.

METHOD USAGE:

This method may be called at any time. Typically, it would not be useful for another object class to make calls to this method.

METHOD OVERRIDE:

Workplace classes that wish to have a unique class default animation icon must override this method and fill out the appropriate fields within the ICONINFO structure. In addition, the correct size for the ICONINFO must always be returned.

RELATED METHODS:

wpclsQueryIconN

This method specifies the default animation icon to be used for instances of the class object.

INCLUDE IDENTIFIER:

```
#define INCL_WINWORKPLACE
```

FUNCTION PROTOTYPE:

```
HPOINTER wpclsQueryIconN(M_WPFolder *somSelf,
                         ULONG ulIconIndex);
```

PARAMETERS:

```
somSelf      - Pointer to the class object
ulIconIndex  - Animation icon index; value must be 1
```

RETURNS:

```
hptr  - Handle to animation icon
NULL  - No animation icon
```

REMARKS:

This method is very similar to wpclsQueryIcon. The difference is that wpclsQueryIcon returns the handle for a normal object icon (the closed folder icon), while wpclsQueryIconN returns the handle for the animation icon (the open folder icon).

METHOD USAGE:

This method can be called at any time.

METHOD OVERRIDE:

This method is generally not overridden.

RELATED METHODS:

wpclsQueryInstanceFilter

This class method specifies file types for instances of the class object.

INCLUDE IDENTIFIER:

```
#define INCL_WINWORKPLACE
```

FUNCTION PROTOTYPE:

```
PSZ wpclsQueryInstanceFilter(M_WPFileSystem *somSelf);
```

PARAMETERS:

```
somSelf  - Pointer to the class object
```

RETURNS:

```
NULL   - Error occurred
Other  - Pointer to a string containing file-title
         filters, which can contain several filters
         separated by a comma
```

REMARKS:

The values returned by this class method should be restricted to class-specific filters. Returning a filter of *.* could effectively make the system unstable.

METHOD USAGE:

This method can be called at any time to see which file title filters are determining instances of this class.

METHOD OVERRIDE:

This method should be overridden to automatically designate file objects as instances of this class. The value returned by the override method replaces the current title-filter string used to designate instances. If the parent is called, it should be called first.

RELATED METHODS:

wpclsQueryInstanceType   Page 535

wpclsQueryInstanceType

This class method specifies file types of instances of the class object.

INCLUDE IDENTIFIER:

```
#define INCL_WINWORKPLACE
```

FUNCTION PROTOTYPE:

```
PSZ wpclsQueryInstanceType(M_WPFileSystem *somSelf);
```

PARAMETERS:

```
somSelf  - Pointer to the class object
```

RETURNS:

```
NULL    - Error occurred
Other   - Pointer to a string containing file types;
          can contain several file types separated by
          a comma
```

REMARKS:

Object classes should define their own special type strings.

METHOD USAGE:

This method can be called at any time to determine which file types are used to determine instances of this class.

METHOD OVERRIDE:

This method should be overridden to automatically designate file objects as instances of this class. The value returned by the override method replaces the current type string used to designate instances. If the parent method is called, it should be called first.

RELATED METHODS:

wpclsQueryInstanceFilter   Page 534

wpclsQueryObject

This class method returns the object pointer for a given persistent object handle.

INCLUDE IDENTIFIER:

```
#define INCL_WINWORKPLACE
```

FUNCTION PROTOTYPE:

```
WPObject *wpclsQueryObject(M_WPObject *somSelf,
                           HOBJECT hObject);
```

PARAMETERS:

```
somSelf  - Pointer to the class object
hObject  - Handle for a given object instance
```

RETURNS:

```
The pointer to the object that corresponds to the given
object handle or NULLHANDLE if that object no longer
exists.
```

REMARKS:

```
All workplace objects can be uniquely identified by a
persistent object handle within a specified machine.
After an object handle is obtained (with wpQueryHandle),
the handle can be used later even if the system was
powered off in the meantime, providing that the object
instance has not been destroyed.
```

```
This method is intended for use by objects that wish to
communicate with other objects using method calls. At
any point in time, an object can re-establish contact
with another object using this method.
```

```
The returned object is locked so that the called object
can access the returned pointer without the risk of the
object being made dormant. When the object pointer is
no longer needed, wpUnlockObject should be invoked to
permit the system to make that object dormant when all
other locks on it have been released.
```

METHOD USAGE:

This method can be called at any time.

METHOD OVERRIDE:

This method should not be overridden.

RELATED METHODS:

wpQueryHandle   Page 314

wpclsQueryObjectFromFrame

This instance method returns a pointer to the object associated with the specified frame window handle.

INCLUDE IDENTIFIER:

```
#define INCL_WINWORKPLACE
```

FUNCTION PROTOTYPE:

```
WPObject *wpclsQueryObjectFromFrame
                            (M_WPDesktop *somSelf,
                            HWND hwndFrame);
```

PARAMETERS:

```
somSelf     - Pointer to the class object
hwndFrame   - Handle to top-level frame window
```

RETURNS:

```
Object  - Pointer to object associated with hwndFrame
NULL    - Associated object could not be found or
          error occurred
```

REMARKS:

This method returns the object for which the handle is a view rather than the application implementing the view.

For example, if the *hwndFrame* of a folder's view is passed in, this method returns the folder object. If the *hwndFrame* of the system editor is passed in, this method returns the object which is currently being viewed by the editor. In this case, if an associated object cannot be found, the system editor program object is returned. For instance, if the system editor is launched from the command line and its *hwndFrame* is passed in, the editor program object is returned.

METHOD USAGE:

This method can be called at any time.

METHOD OVERRIDE:

This method should not be overridden.

RELATED METHODS:

wpContainsFolders   Page 168

wpclsQueryObjectFromPage

This class method returns the object pointer for a file or directory.

INCLUDE IDENTIFIER:

```
#define INCL_WINWORKPLACE
```

FUNCTION PROTOTYPE:

```
WPObject *wpclsQueryObjectFromPage
                        (M_WPFileSystem *somSelf,
                         PSZ pszFQPath);
```

PARAMETERS:

```
somSelf    - Pointer to the class object
pszFQPath  - String containing fully qualified path
             name or object id
```

RETURNS:

```
pObject  - Pointer to object that represents file or
           directory specified in pszFQPath.
```

REMARKS:

```
The object is initially locked, so there is no risk of
the object being made dormant before the object pointer
is obtained.
```

METHOD OVERRIDE:

```
This method is generally not overridden.
```

RELATED METHODS:

```
wpclsQueryObject                    Page 536
```

wpclsQueryOpenFolders

This class method enables a specified class to enumerate all open folders.

INCLUDE IDENTIFIER:

```
#define INCL_WINWORKPLACE
```

FUNCTION PROTOTYPE:

```
WPFolder *wpclsQueryOpenFolders(M_WPFolder *somSelf,
                                WPFolder *Folder,
                                ULONG ulOption,
                                BOOL fLock);
```

PARAMETERS:

```
somSelf    - Pointer to the class object.
Folder     - Pointer to a folder object; ignored
             unless QC_NEXT is specified in ulOption.
ulOption   - Flag indicating the folder to query.
             Values:
                QC_FIRST
                QC_LAST
                QC_NEXT
fLock      - Lock object flag. If FALSE, the newly
             created object is made dormant whenever
             the object and folder containing the
             object are closed. If TRUE, the new flag
             remains active until the caller issues
             wpUnlockObject.
```

RETURNS:

```
NULL       - Error occurred or QC_NEXT was requested
             on the last folder
FldrObject - Pointer to the specified folder object
```

METHOD USAGE:

```
This method can be called at any time to determine the
open folders.
```

METHOD OVERRIDE:

```
This method is not usually overridden.
```

wpclsQuerySearchInfo

This method enables a specified class to specify search information.

INCLUDE IDENTIFIER:

```
#define INCL_WINWORKPLACE
```

FUNCTION PROTOTYPE:

```
BOOL wpclsQuerySearchInfo(M_WPObject *somSelf,
                          PULONG ExtendedCriteria,
                          ULONG flReserved);
```

PARAMETERS:

somSelf	- Pointer to the class object
ExtendedCriteria	- Pointer to size in bytes of the extended search criteria, returned by wpclsQueryExtendedCriteria
flReserved	- Reserved value; must be NULL

RETURNS:

TRUE	- Successful completion
FALSE	- Error occurred

METHOD USAGE:

This method can be called at any time in order to determine the size of the extended search criteria buffer which is used for finding objects of this class.

METHOD OVERRIDE:

This method should be overridden by classes which override wpclsQueryExtendedCriteria.

wpclsQuerySettingsPageSize

This class method returns the default size of a settings page in dialog units for instances of this object class.

INCLUDE IDENTIFIER:

```
#define INCL_WINWORKPLACE
```

FUNCTION PROTOTYPE:

```
BOOL wpclsQuerySettingsPageSize(M_WPObject *somSelf,
                               PSIZEL pSizel);
```

PARAMETERS:

```
somSelf  - Pointer to the class object
pSizel   - Pointer to the size structure containing
           the cx and cy dimensions of the default
           settings page for this class
```

RETURNS:

```
TRUE   - Method-class call was successful
FALSE  - Method-class call was unsuccessful
```

REMARKS:

An object class that has abnormally shaped settings pages (for example, the pages may be very wide) can use this method to insure that when a Settings notebook is initially displayed for an instance of the object class, that notebook will be of a suitable size to view the whole settings page without clipping it.

The size specified by this method is used only the first time a Settings notebook is displayed. Thereafter the Settings notebook size and position is saved by the system on a per-object basis.

METHOD USAGE:

This function is callable, but unlikely to be useful.

METHOD OVERRIDE:

Object classes with unusual size requirements for their settings pages must override this class method and change the *cx* and *cy* values as necessary to accommodate their settings page sizes.

RELATED METHODS:

wpOpen   Page 248

wpclsQuerySetting

This instance returns the class object settings from the Settings notebook.

INCLUDE IDENTIFIER:

```
#define INCL_WINWORKPLACE
```

FUNCTION PROTOTYPE:

```
ULONG wpclsQuerySetting(M_WPAbstract *somSelf,
                        PSZ pszSetting, PVOID pValue,
                        ULONG ulValueLen);
```

PARAMETERS:

```
somSelf      - Pointer to the class object.
pszSetting   - Name of setting that is to be queried.
pValue       - Buffer in which settings values are
               returned. If NULL, only length of value
               of setting is returned.
ulValueLen   - Length of pValue.
```

RETURNS:

```
ulReturnedData  - Length of data returned in pValue
0               - Error occurred; no data is returned
                  in pValue
```

REMARKS:

This is a virtual method and must be overridden by a subclass. Each subclass documents the possible values for *pszSetting* and *pValue*. These settings and values are specific for each subclass. Note that all settings have safe defaults, so it is never necessary to pass unnecessary settings to an object.

For a list of settings and their associated values, see the individual classes.

METHOD USAGE:

This method should never be called. It is a virtual method and must be overridden by a subclass.

METHOD OVERRIDE:

This is a virtual method and must be overridden by a subclass.

RELATED METHODS:

wpclsSetSetting   Page 555

wpclsQueryStyle

This class method specifies the default object class style for instances of the class object.

INCLUDE IDENTIFIER:

#define INCL_WINWORKPLACE

FUNCTION PROTOTYPE:

ULONG wpclsQueryStyle(M_WPObject *somSelf);

PARAMETERS:

somSelf - Pointer to the class object

RETURNS:

Class Style	Do NOT Allow These Operations:
CLSSTYLE_DONTTEMPLATE	- Create template for object
CLSSTYLE_NEVERCOPY	- Copy of this object
CLSSTYLE_NEVERDELETE	- Delete of this object
CLSSTYLE_NEVERDRAG	- Drag of this object
CLSSTYLE_NEVERDROPON	- Drop on of this object
CLSSTYLE_NEVERLINK	- Create shadow of this object
CLSSTYLE_NEVERMOVE	- Move of this object
CLSSTYLE_NEVERPRINT	- Print of this object
CLSSTYLE_NEVERRENAME	- Renaming of this object
CLSSTYLE_NEVERSETTINGS-	Settings on this object
CLSSTYLE_NEVERVISIBLE -	Instances to be visible

REMARKS:

When an instance is initially created, it has the same object style (OBJSTYLE_*xxx*) flags as its class style (CLSSTYLE_*xxx*).

METHOD USAGE:

This method can be called at any time to determine the default style for instances of this class.

METHOD OVERRIDE:

This method should be overridden to modify the default object style for instances of this class.

RELATED METHODS:

wpQueryStyle   Page 356
wpSetStyle   Page 469

wpclsQueryTitle

This class method specifies the default title for instances of the class object.

INCLUDE IDENTIFIER:

```
#define INCL_WINWORKPLACE
```

FUNCTION PROTOTYPE:

```
PSZ wpclsQueryTitle(M_WPObject *somSelf);
```

PARAMETERS:

```
somSelf  - Pointer to the class object
```

RETURNS:

```
Pointer to default title for objects of this class.
```

REMARKS:

The title is used as the default for new instances; it also is used to describe the class in facilities such as Find, Include, Details, and Sort. The title can be loaded on wpclsInitData and freed on wpclsUnInitData.

METHOD USAGE:

This method can be called at any time to determine the default title for instances of this class.

METHOD OVERRIDE:

All classes should override this method so that new objects and their classes always have a sensible default title.

RELATED METHODS:

wpQueryTitle	Page 358
wpSetTitle	Page 470

wpclsRemoveObjects

This instance method removes all specified objects from a specified container and the in-use list.

INCLUDE IDENTIFIER:

```
#define INCL_WINWORKPLACE
```

FUNCTION PROTOTYPE:

```
BOOL wpclsRemoveObjects(M_WPObject *somSelf,
                        HWND hwndCnr,
                        PVOID *pRecordArray,
                        ULONG NumRecords,
                        BOOL RemoveAll);
```

PARAMETERS:

somSelf	-	Pointer to the class object.
hwndCnr	-	Handle to container object.
pRecordArray	-	Pointer to array of MINIRECORDCORE objects that are to be removed.
NumRecords	-	Number of records in *pRecordArray*.
RemoveAll	-	Flag indicating whether to remove all records. Values: TRUE FALSE

RETURNS:

TRUE	-	Successful completion
FALSE	-	Error occurred

REMARKS:

This method provides rapid removal of multiple objects from a container at one time. wpCnrRemoveObject performs the same function as this method, but it operates only on one object at a time.

METHOD USAGE:

This method can be called at any time to remove multiple objects from the container.

METHOD OVERRIDE:

This method is generally not overridden.

RELATED METHODS:

wpclsSetError

This class method sets the current error code within a class object.

INCLUDE IDENTIFIER:

```
#define INCL_WINWORKPLACE
```

FUNCTION PROTOTYPE:

```
BOOL wpclsSetError(M_WPObject *somSelf,
                   ULONG ulErrorId);
```

PARAMETERS:

```
somSelf    - Pointer to the class object
ulErrorId  - Error code
```

RETURNS:

```
TRUE   - Error was successfully stored
FALSE  - Error was not successfully stored
```

REMARKS:

This method can be used when writing class methods for workplace objects that return Boolean values. When a given class method fails, the class method can log its error code in the class object so that the caller can later retrieve it using wpclsQueryError. The function is analogous to WinSetErrorInfo, which is used by PM functions to log their error return codes.

METHOD USAGE:

This method should be called only by class methods when they do not execute successfully.

METHOD OVERRIDE:

Never override this class method.

RELATED METHODS:

wpclsQueryError   Page 521

wpclsSetIcon

This class method sets the icon handle for a given object.

INCLUDE IDENTIFIER:

```
#define INCL_WINWORKPLACE
```

FUNCTION PROTOTYPE:

```
BOOL wpclsSetIcon(M_WPObject *somSelf,
                  HPOINTER hptrNewIcon);
```

PARAMETERS:

```
somSelf       - Pointer to the class object
hptrNewIcon   - Icon handle to be set for object
```

RETURNS:

```
TRUE    - Successful completion
FALSE   - Error occurred
```

REMARKS:

This class default icon can be loaded using wpclsInit-
Data and freed using wpclsUnInitData.

METHOD USAGE:

This method can be called at any time to set the object's
default icon.

METHOD OVERRIDE:

This method is generally not overridden.

RELATED METHODS:

wpQueryIcon	Page 316
wpQueryIconData	Page 317
wpSetIcon	Page 441
wpSetIconData	Page 442
wpclsQueryIcon	Page 527
wpclsQueryIconData	Page 528

wpclsSetIconData

This class method sets the icon information for a given object.

INCLUDE IDENTIFIER:

```
#define INCL_WINWORKPLACE
```

FUNCTION PROTOTYPE:

```
BOOL wpclsSetIconData(M_WPObject *somSelf,
                      PICONINFO pIconInfo);
```

PARAMETERS:

```
somSelf    - Pointer to the class object
pIconInfo  - Pointer to icon information structure
```

RETURNS:

```
TRUE   - Successful completion
FALSE  - Error occurred
```

METHOD USAGE:

This method can be called at any time to set icon information.

METHOD OVERRIDE:

RELATED METHODS:

wpclsSetSetting

This instance sets the class object settings in the Settings notebook.

INCLUDE IDENTIFIER:

```
#define INCL_WINWORKPLACE
```

FUNCTION PROTOTYPE:

```
BOOL wpclsSetSetting(M_WPAbstract *somSelf,
                     PSZ pszSetting, PVOID pValue);
```

PARAMETERS:

```
somSelf      - Pointer to the class object
pszSetting   - Name of setting that is to be set
pValue       - Buffer which contains setting values
```

RETURNS:

```
TRUE   - Successful completion
FALSE  - Error occurred
```

REMARKS:

This is a virtual method and must be overridden by a subclass. Each object subclass documents the possible values for *pszSetting* and *pValue*. These settings and values are specific for each subclass. All settings have safe defaults; it is never necessary to pass unnecessary settings to an object.

For a list of settings and their associated values, see the individual classes.

METHOD USAGE:

This method should never be called.

METHOD OVERRIDE:

This method is a virtual method and must be overridden by a subclass.

RELATED METHODS:

wpclsSetSetting Page 555

wpclsSetSettingsPageSize

This class method returns the default Settings page size.

INCLUDE IDENTIFIER:

```
#define INCL_WINWORKPLACE
```

FUNCTION PROTOTYPE:

```
BOOL wpclsSetSettingsPageSize(M_WPObject *somSelf,
                             PSIZEL pSizel);
```

PARAMETERS:

```
somSelf - Pointer to the class object
pSizel  - Pointer to structure containing default
          width and height of Settings page
```

RETURNS:

```
TRUE    - Successful completion
FALSE   - Error occurred
```

METHOD OVERRIDE:

```
This method is generally not overridden.
```

wpclsUnInitData

This class method frees the allocated resources of the class object.

INCLUDE IDENTIFIER:

#define INCL_WINWORKPLACE

FUNCTION PROTOTYPE:

VOID wpclsUnInitData(M_WPObject *somSelf);

PARAMETERS:

somSelf - Pointer to the class object

RETURNS:

None.

METHOD USAGE:

This method usually is called only by the system when
the class object is made dormant. This occurs when the
last instance of this class is made dormant.

METHOD OVERRIDE:

Any class that overrides wpclsInitData to allocate
resource for its metaclass instance variables should
override this method to deallocate those resources. It
is essential to pass this method onto the parent class
object after performing override processing.

RELATED METHODS:

wpclsInitData   Page 501

Appendix A
Data Type Structures

All the data types used in this book that require a *typedef* structure are listed below in alphabetical order.

A

```
ACTIONS         typedef struct _ACTIONS {
                PSZ      pszTitle;
                ULONG    ulMenuId;
                } ACTIONS;
```

B

```
BOOL            typedef unsigned long BOOL;

BYTE            typedef unsigned char BYTE
```

C

```
CHAR            #define CHAR char

CELL            typedef struct _CELL {
                ULONG    cbData;
                } CELL;

CLASSFIELDINFO
                typedef struct _CLASSFIELDINFO {
                ULONG         cb;
                ULONG         flData;
                ULONG         flTitle;
                PVOID         pTitleData;
                ULONG         ulReserved;
                PVOID         pUserData;
                struct _CLASSFIELDINFO  *pNextFieldInfo;
                ULONG         cxWidth;
                ULONG         offFieldData;
                ULONG         ulLenFieldData;
                PFNOWNDRW     pfnOwnerDraw;
                ULONG         flCompare;
                PFNCOMPARE    pfnCompare;
                ULONG         DefaultComparison;
                ULONG         ulLenCompareValue;
                PVOID         pDefCompareValue;
                PVOID         pMinCompareValue;
                PVOID         pMaxCompareValue;
                PSZ           pszEditControlClass;
```

```
                PFNCOMPARE    pfnSort;
                PSZ           pNewComp;
                } CLASSFIELDINFO;

CNRDRAGINFO     typedef struct _CNRDRAGINFO {
                PDRAGINFO       pDragInfo;
                PRECORDCORE     pRecord;
                } CNRDRAGINFO;
```

D

```
DRAGITEM        typedef struct _DRAGITEM {
                HWND     hwndItem;
                ULONG    ulItemID;
                HSTR     hstrType;
                HSTR     hstrRMF;
                HSTR     hstrContainerName;
                HSTR     hstrSourceName;
                HSTR     hstrTargetName;
                SHORT    cxOffset;
                SHORT    cyOffset;
                USHORT   usControl;
                USHORT   usSupportedOps;
                } DRAGITEM;

DRAGTRANSFER typedef struct _DRAGTRANSFER {
                ULONG       cb;
                HWND        hwndClient;
                PDRAGITEM   pditem;
                HSTR        hstrSelectedRMF;
                HSTR        hstrRenderToName;
                ULONG       ulTargetInfo;
                USHORT      usOperation;
                USHORT      usReply;
                } DRAGTRANSFER;
```

F

```
FEA2            typedef struct _FEA2 {
                ULONG    oNextEntryOffset;
                BYTE     fEA;
                BYTE     cbName;
                USHORT   cbValue;
                CHAR     szName[1];
                ) FEA2;

FEA2LIST        typedef struct _FEA2LIST {
                ULONG   cbList;
                FEA2    list[1];
                ) FEA2LIST;
```

```
FDATE            typedef struct _FDATE {
                 USHORT    usday;
                 USHORT    usmonth;
                 USHORT    usyear;
                 ) FDATE:

FIXED            typedef LONG FIXED;

FILEFINDBUF4
                 typedef struct _FILEFINDBUF4 {
                 ULONG     uloNextEntryOffset;
                 FDATE     fdateCreation;
                 FTIME     ftimeCreation;
                 FDATE     ftimeLastAccess;
                 FTIME     ftimeLastAccess;
                 FDATE     ftimeLastWrite;
                 FTIME     ftimeLastWrite;
                 ULONG     ulcbFile;
                 ULONG     ulcbFileAlloc;
                 ULONG     ulattrFile;
                 ULONG     ulcbList;
                 UCHAR     uccchName;
                 CHAR      chachName[CCHMAXPATHCOMP];
                 } FILEFINDBUF4;

FTIME            typedef struct _FTIME {
                 USHORT    ustwosecs;
                 USHORT    usminutes;
                 USHORT    ushours;
                 } FTIME;
```

H

```
HBITMAP          typedef LHANDLE HBITMAP;

HELPTABLE        typedef struct _HELPTABLE {
                 USHORT    idAppWindow;
                 PSHORT    phsHelpSubTable;
                 USHORT    idExtPanel;
                 } HELPTABLE;

HFIND            typedef LHANDLE HFIND;

HINI             typedef LHANDLE HINI;

HMODULE          typedef LHANDLE HMODULE;

HOBJECT          typedef LHANDLE HOBJECT;

HPOINTER         typedef LHANDLE HPOINTER;

HPS              typedef LHANDLE HPS;

HWND             typedef LHANDLE HWND;
```

I

ICONINFO
```
typedef struct _INCONINFO {
ULONG      ulcb;
ULONG      fFormat;
PSZ        pszFileName;
HMODULE    hmod;
ULONG      ulresid;
ULONG      cbIconData;
PVOID      pIconData;
} ICONINFO;
```

L

LHANDLE
```
typedef ULONG *LHANDLE;
```

M

MINIRECORDCORE
```
typedef struct _MINIRECORDCORE {
ULONG             cb;
ULONG             flRecordSttr;
POINTL            ptlIcon;
PMINIRECORDCORE   pNextRecord;
PSZ               pszIcon;
HPOINTER          hptrIcon;
} MINIRECORDCORE;
```

MRESULT
```
typedef VOID FAR *MRESULT;
```

O

OBJDATA
```
typedef struct _OBJDATA {
WPSRCLASSBLOCK*   CurrentClass;
WPSRCLASSBLOCK*   First;
UCHAR             ucNextData;
USHORT            usLength;
} OBJDATA;
```

OBJECT
```
typedef WPObject *OBJECT;
```

P

PAGEINFO
```
typedef struct _PAGEINFO {
ULONG      ulch;
HWND       hwndPage;
PFNWP      ppfnwp;
ULONG      ulresid;
PVOID      pCreateParams;
USHORT     usdlgid;
USHORT     usPageStyleFlags;
USHORT     usPageInsertFlags;
USHORT     usReserved;
```

```
                PSZ        pszName;
                USHORT     idDefaultHelpPanel;
                USHORT     usReserved2;
                PSZ        pszHelpLibraryName;
                PUSHORT    pHelpSubtable;
                HMODULE    hmodHelpSubtable;
                ULONG      ulPageInsertId;
                } PAGEINFO

PALINFO         typedef struct _PALINFO {
                ULONG      ulxCellCount;
                ULONG      ulyCellCount;
                ULONG      ulxCursor;
                ULONG      ulyCursor;
                ULONG      ulxCellWidth;
                ULONG      ulyCellHeight;
                ULONG      ulxGap;
                ULONG      ulyGap;
                } PALINFO;

PBYTE           typedef BYTE *PBYTE;

PCELL           typedef CELL *PCELL;

PCLASSDETAILS
                typedef CLASSDETAILS *PCLASSDETAILS;

PFATTRS         typedef FATTRS *PFATTRS;

PHFIND          typedef HFIND *PHFIND;

PICONINFO       typedef ICONINFO *PICONINFO;

PMINIRECORDCORE
                typedef MINIRECORDCORE *PMINIRECORDCORE;

POINTL          typedef struct _POINTL {
                SHORT      x;
                SHORT      y;
                } POINTL;

PPAGEINFO       typedef PAGEINFO *PPAGEINFO;

PPOINTL         typedef POINTL *PPOINTL;

PPRINTDEST      typedef PRINTDEST *PPRINTDEST;

PPROGDETAILS
                typedef PROGDETAILS *PPROGDETAILS;

PRECORDINSERT
                typedef RECORDINSERT *PRECORDINSERT;

PRECTL          typedef RECTL *PRECTL;
```

```
PRINTDEST       typedef struct _PRINTDEST {
                ULONG           cb;
                LONG            lType;
                PSZ             pszToken;
                LONG            lCount;
                PDEVOPENDATA    pdopData;
                ULONG           fl;
                PSZ             pszPrinter;
                } PRINTDEST;

PSIZEL          typedef SIZEL *PSIZEL;

PSZ             typedef char *PSZ;

PULONG          typedef ULONG *PULONG;

PUSEITEM        typedef USEITEM *PUSEITEM;

PVOID           typedef VOID *PVOID;
```

R

```
RECTL           typedef struct_RECTL {
                LONG    xLeft;
                LONG    yBottom;
                LONG    xRight;
                LONG    yTop;
                } RECTL;
```

S

```
SIZEL           typedef struct _SIZEL {
                LONG    cx;
                LONG    cy;
                } SIZEL;
```

U

```
ULONG           typedef unsigned long ULONG;

USEITEM         typedef USEITEM *USEITEM;

USHORT          typedef unsigned short USHORT;
```

V

```
VIEWITEM
                typedef VIEWITEM *VIEWITEM;

VOID            #define VOID void
```

Appendix B
WIN Functions for WPS

This section contains an alphabetical list of the WIN functions that are available to the application for using and controlling Workplace Shell objects.

WinCopyObject

This function copies an object from its existing folder to a specified new destination.

INCLUDE IDENTIFIER:

#define INCL_WINWORKPLACE

FUNCTION PROTOTYPE:

```
HOBJECT WinCopyObject(HOBJECT hObjectofObject,
                      HOBJECT hObjectofDest,
                      ULONG ulFlags);
```

PARAMETERS:

```
hObjectofObject  - Handle of object being copied.
hObjectofDest    - Handle of folder into which
                   hObjectofObject is to be copied.
ulFlags          - Flags. Values:
                     COPY_FAILIFEXSTS
```

RETURNS:

```
hwndDlg     - Handle of newly created object
NULLHANDLE  - hObjectofDest is NULLHANDLE or object
              with same name as hObjectofObject
              exists in the destination folder
```

ERROR CODES:

```
0x1719   WPERR_INVALID_FLAGS
```

REMARKS:

Using HOBJECT for INI files or files in which an application uses a rename/save/delete sequence is not supported.

RELATED FUNCTIONS:

WinCreateObject   See Volume 1
WinDestroyObject
WinMoveObject
WinQueryObjectWindow
WinSaveObject

WinCreateShadow

This function creates a shadow of an object.

INCLUDE IDENTIFIER:

```
#define INCL_WINWORKPLACE
```

FUNCTION PROTOTYPE:

```
HOBJECT WinCreateShadow(HOBJECT hObjectofObject,
                        HOBJECT hObjectofDest,
                        ULONG ulReserved);
```

PARAMETERS:

```
hObjectofObject  - Handle of object being copied
hObjectofDest    - Handle of folder into which
                   hObjectofObject is to be copied
ulReserved       - Reserved value
```

RETURNS:

```
hwndDlg      - Handle of newly created object
NULLHANDLE   - hObjectofDest is NULLHANDLE or object
               with same name as hObjectofObject
               exists in the destination folder
```

REMARKS:

Using HOBJECT for INI files or files in which an application uses a rename/save/delete sequence is not supported.

RELATED FUNCTIONS:

```
WinCreateObject              See Volume 1
WinDestroyObject
WinMoveObject
WinQueryObjectWindow
WinSaveObject
```

WinCreateObject

This function is documented in Volume 1 - WIN Functions.

WinDeregisterObjectClass

This function is documented in Volume 1 - WIN Functions.

WinDestroyObject

This function is documented in Volume 1 - WIN Functions.

WinEnumObjectClasses

This function is documented in Volume 1 - WIN Functions.

WinFreeFileIcon

This function is documented in Volume 1 - WIN Functions.

WinIsSOMDDReady

This function returns the current state of the DSOM daemon started by the Workplace Shell process using WinRestartSOMDD.

INCLUDE IDENTIFIER:

```
#define INCL_WPCLASS
```

FUNCTION PROTOTYPE:

```
BOOL WinIsSOMDDReady();
```

PARAMETERS:

None.

RETURNS:

```
TRUE    - SOMDD has been started by Workplace Shell
          process
FALSE   - SOMDD has not been started by Workplace
          Shell process
```

REMARKS:

This function returns the state of the DSOM daemon started only by the Workplace Shell process using a call to WinRestartSOMDD. This does not include the status of the DSOM daemon if started by any other process.

Note: This function requires that the Workplace Shell is up and running.

RELATED FUNCTIONS:

```
WinIsWPDServerReady          See Volume 1
WinRestartSOMDD
WinRestartWPDServer
```

WinIsWPDServerReady

This function returns the current state of the Workplace Shell DSOM Server.

INCLUDE IDENTIFIER:

```
#define INCL_WPCLASS
```

FUNCTION PROTOTYPE:

```
BOOL WinIsWPDServerReady();
```

PARAMETERS:

None.

RETURNS:

```
TRUE   - Workplace Shell DSOM Server status
FALSE  - Workplace Shell DSOM Server is not ready
```

REMARKS:

This function returns the ready status of the Workplace Shell DSOM Server.

Note: This function requires that the Workplace Shell is up and running.

RELATED FUNCTIONS:

```
WinIsSOMDDReady                 See Volume 1
WinRestartSOMDD
WinRestartWPDServer
```

WinLoadFileIcon

This function is documented in Volume 1 - WIN Functions.

WinMoveObject

This function moves an object from its existing folder to a specified new destination.

INCLUDE IDENTIFIER:

```
#define INCL_WINWORKPLACE
```

FUNCTION PROTOTYPE:

```
HOBJECT WinMoveObject(HOBJECT hObjectofObject,
                      HOBJECT hObjectofDest,
                      ULONG ulFlags);
```

PARAMETERS:

```
hObjectofObject   - Handle of object being moved.
hObjectofDest     - Handle of folder into which
                    hObjectofObject is to be moved.
ulFlags           - Flags. Value:  MOVE_FAILIFEXSTS
```

RETURNS:

```
hwndDlg      - Handle of newly created object
NULLHANDLE   - hObjectofDest is NULLHANDLE or object
               with same name as hObjectofObject
               exists in the destination folder
```

ERROR CODES:

```
0x1719    WPERR_INVALID_FLAGS
```

REMARKS:

Using HOBJECT for INI files or files in which an application uses a rename/save/delete sequence is not supported.

RELATED FUNCTIONS:

```
WinCopyObject                  See Volume 1
WinCreateObject
WinDestroyObject
WinQueryObjectWindow
WinSaveObject
```

WinOpenObject

This function either opens a view of the given object or surfaces an existing view.

INCLUDE IDENTIFIER:

#define INCL_WINWORKPLACE

FUNCTION PROTOTYPE:

```
BOOL WinOpenObject(HOBJECT hObjectofObject,
                ULONG ulView, ULONG ulFlags);
```

PARAMETERS:

```
hObjectofObject   - Handle to Workplace Shell object
                    to be opened.
ulView            - View to open this object. Values:
                       OPEN_CONTENTS
                       OPEN_DEFAULT
                       OPEN_DETAILS
                       OPEN_SETTINGS
                       OPEN_TREE
ulFlags           - Flags. Values:
                       TRUE
                       FALSE
```

RETURNS:

```
TRUE    - Successful completion
FALSE   - Error occurred
```

REMARKS:

Using HOBJECT for INI files or files in which an application uses a rename/save/delete sequence is not supported.

RELATED FUNCTIONS:

```
WinCreateObject                 See Volume 1
WinDestroyObject
WinSaveObject
```

WinQueryActiveDesktop-
Pathname

This function returns the directory specification of the active desktop.

INCLUDE IDENTIFIER:

```
#define INCL_WINWORKPLACE
```

FUNCTION PROTOTYPE:

```
BOOL WinQueryActiveDesktopPathname(PSZ pszPathName,
                                   ULONG ulSize);
```

PARAMETERS:

```
pszPathName   - Memory allocated by caller in which
                directory specification is written
ulSize        - Number of bytes pointed to by
                pszPathName
```

RETURNS:

```
TRUE    - Successful completion
FALSE   - Error occurred
```

ERROR CODES:

```
0x1645    PMERR_INVALID_PARAMETER
```

REMARKS:

This function is used to find the directory specification of the current Desktop. The current Desktop is not
always \DESKTOP in the boot drive.

WinQueryObject

This function is documented in Volume 1 - WIN Functions.